REDISCOVERING LONE PINE

by

Andrew F. Popper

D1569028

First Edition

© 2009 Thomson Reuters
       610 Opperman Drive
       St. Paul, MN 55123
       1–800–313–9378

Requests for permission to make copies of any portion of this publication
must be submitted in writing to the publisher at the above address.

Printed in the United States of America

ISBN: 978–0–314–20698–5

Comments and Praise for
REDISCOVERING LONE PINE

"Andy Popper is that rare gem of the brilliant law professor who can also craft a compelling narrative. REDISCOVERING LONE PINE and its Discussion Guide are together a brilliant roadmap in which a stirring story charts a path to better legal thinking."

> *Thomas C. Goldstein, Partner, Akin Gump,*
> *Special Lecturer, Supreme Court Litigation,*
> *Stanford and Harvard Law Schools*

"Popper has put together a fast-paced, engrossing tale that illuminates the types of complex social dynamics that end up confronting lawyers. REDISCOVERING LONE PINE would be a good read if it were only a novel, but there is much more. The latter part of the book poses series of questions that confront the lawyers. The deeper factual development provides a more robust setting for wrestling with fundamentally hard questions than the relatively stark factual setting of appellate cases that are more traditionally used for instruction. This approach is not only deeper, it is far more fun!"

> *Philip J. Harter, Earl F. Nelson Professor of*
> *Law, University of Missouri School of Law,*
> *Columbia, Missouri*

"Andrew Popper's REDISCOVERING LONE PINE is more than a well-crafted, engaging legal thriller.

For those who have searched in vain for the perfect vehicle for teaching case theory and narrative, RE-DISCOVERING LONE PINE fills the void."

> *Rangeley Wallace, Author of NO DEFENSE (St. Martin's Press), Clinical Practitioner-in-Residence, American University, Washington College of Law, Washington, DC*

"Popper has delivered an engaging, quickly paced story that instructs while it entertains. Like his first novel, in addition to being an engrossing and well-written tale for anyone who loves a good mystery, REDISCOVERING LONE PINE and its accompanying Discussion Guide will be a boon for students, faculty, and virtually anyone interested in a captivating tale about law, lawyers, and friendship."

> *Donald R. Levy, Principal/CEO, The Rochelle Organization, Inc., Washington, DC*

"Popper proves he belongs among that small group of lawyers and legal academics who can write a novel that has appeal to a broad audience. His prose is accessible and evocative; this is a book you will want to read from start to finish in one sitting. I can't wait to read his next work."

> *Carl Monk, Dean and Distinguished Professor of Law and Former Executive Director, Association of American Law Schools, Washington, DC*

"REDISCOVERING LONE PINE is a wonderfully told story of mystery and adventure—both inside and outside of the courtroom, and a masterfully crafted work designed to explore deeply challenging issues of advocacy, legal ethics and professionalism. Popper tells a captivating story with interesting characters and vivid narration. At the story's end, via the Discussion Guide, Popper takes the reader on a second journey of discovery. In this instance it is to discover (or rediscover) many of the primary principles and skills needed to be an effective lawyer. All audiences will love it as a novel; all those in the lawyering profession will be stirred by its questions."

> *Kenneth Kandaras, Professor of Law and former Director of the Advocacy Program, John Marshall Law School, Chicago, Illinois*

"This is a fascinating and wonderfully readable account beautifully written by an eminent professor of law who is also a masterful novelist. This 'genre-busting' work of fiction illustrates in a lively and entertaining way the extent to which the law and imagination can reach new heights when given voice by a brilliant mind."

> *The Honorable Maria E. Villa, Albany, New York*

To Libby and Connie

[M]ake merry, and be glad; for this thy brother was dead, and is alive again; and was lost, and is found.

LUKE 15, VERSE 32

Contents

Part One

LONE PINE
1958–1959

– 1 –

Behind my house were twenty thousand acres of woods. This was my ocean of great trees and saplings, fast streams and small lakes, ancient stone walls and tiring hills. My friends and I knew worn paths and abandoned logging roads—and every now and then, on blistering summer afternoons, we jumped from mound to clump, crossing marshy fields, picking cattail called punk.

We spent more time in the woods than anywhere else, yet there were places we never saw. Jason Talbot knew the woods better than we did. We relied on his advice regarding unseen hazards and undue risks. He was twelve, two years older than Hannah, Mickey, and me, and never lied to us. "You won't see them at first, but they're there," he once said. "Snakes—so many snakes you can hardly stand without having one crawl up your dungarees."

On occasion my father threatened to sell our house and move south, closer to Albany—it would have been good for his small practice. And on occasion my mother seemed to agree. "We're too isolat-

1

ed," she would say, but we did not move. She was right in this sense: there were only nine houses on DeWitt Street, and, other than Hannah and Mickey, no other ten-year-olds for miles. The thought of moving, of leaving my woods, gave me nightmares.

We went to the woods to be hunters and soldiers, explorers and outlaws—and when the snow was right, we flew on sleds past elm and oak, rock piles and brush, bouncing over field lumps that sprout tall grasses.

—

Early one winter morning, Jason Talbot invited me—and just me—to go on a hike into those woods. Before that day, before the expedition that changed everything, there was a race.

– 2 –

December 1958

My runners hit coarse gray-black exposed pavement and I am out of control. I end up face-down halfway up the plow pile on the side of the road. I roll down to the street and there is Jason, stopped cold, standing on his sled. "Your hat?" he asks.

I nod. He slaps the snow off my hat, tosses it to me, turns downhill and is gone. No one in our town, Haydon, New York, population 1029, can sled standing—no one except Jason Talbot.

I flop on my sled, but without momentum, I barely make it to the bottom of DeWitt Street. I am dead last. "Who won?" I ask, looking at Jason. He always has the answers.

—

At dusk Mickey's father approaches, snow shovel in hand. "You want help?" I ask as Mickey is led away.

Mickey looks back helplessly and I hear Mr. Cabrera's voice: "A kind gesture, Master Harper, but all that is left is to shovel the front walk." Mickey and his family are from Cuba and while his father speaks with a slight accent, he has no difficulty understanding and turning down my offer.

When my mother speaks of Mr. Cabrera, she usually says he is "such a gentleman." I wonder if my father hears this as criticism.

"I better get home, too," Hannah says after Mickey leaves. "See you guys in the morning."

Jason turns to me. "You too?" he asks. I brush the snow off my dungarees and nod. We begin to walk up the hill toward my house. "Grant...." Jason stops in the middle of the street. "Think you could live on your own in the woods?"

"Now?" I ask.

"Summer in the woods is easy. You can make a lean-to, no sweat. Winter is harder."

"What would I eat?"

Jason hesitates. "The best thing would be if you knew a place that was stocked."

"I know. That would be the best." The truth is, I know no place that is stocked and am not one-hundred-percent sure what he means.

"I know a place." Jason leans toward me. "It takes six hours, maybe more. Right before you get there is a giant boulder ... and bushes and vines so thick you can hardly walk." I imagine branches snapping back at me, cutting my cheeks, and watch as Jason looks through the leafless trees. I squint, following his gaze and see nothing. "There is a huge pine, bigger than any tree you've ever seen, with no branches for the first twenty feet. On the ground there is nothing but pine needles, maybe a foot deep." He looks around making sure no one is spying on us.

I edge closer to Jason. "You ever been there?" I whisper.

"A few times." I neither move nor speak. "Thirty feet from the trunk is a wooden door dug into the base of the hill. That's the best part."

"Door to what?"

"I'll show you," he says. "You can't tell anyone."

"I won't say anything. I swear."

We are at my driveway. "See you tomorrow."

"Remember, don't tell anyone," he says as he walks up the hill toward his house.

"I swear," I say.

– 3 –

The next morning everything is frozen. It got up to the low-thirties yesterday but the temperature dropped twenty degrees overnight and turned the damp top level of snow into an inch of solid ice. Conditions like this happen once in a blue moon and while adults complain about the slick surface, the slippery crust means one thing for us: lightning-fast sledding in the woods.

Halfway up the street I see Mickey and Hannah walking away from Jason's house. "Hey, wait up." Running in boots is a struggle. My dungarees are already cold and stiff. "Where's Jason?" I can see my breath.

"Home," Mickey says. "No one answered the door."

"How do you know he's home if no one answered?"

"We heard them," Hannah says. "His father is yelling at everyone."

"Is he coming out later?"

Mickey tugs on his gloves. "I'm not going back to find out," he says.

"Maybe he can talk on the phone," I say. "This will be the greatest sledding ever."

We head down the hill and walk in the side door of my house. I take off my coat but leave on my new green hunting boots. Hannah and Mickey stand by the kitchen door.

"Who are you calling, Grant?" my mother asks.

"Jason." I listen to the rebounding clicks after each number. My mother catches my eye but says nothing more. The phone rings twice and Hack Talbot, Jason's father, answers.

"Who is this?" He hangs up before I have a chance to answer.

When we are in Jason's house and Mr. Talbot gets home, we leave. It is not just his moods that get us but his smell. Mickey has an uncle who drinks too much. He is one of my father's patients. Hack Talbot has the same smell as Mickey's uncle, except Mr. Talbot's drinking smell is mixed with toothpaste. Hannah says that makes it even more disgusting.

Mickey turns and looks out the kitchen door. "I wonder if the Talbots got their color TV?" he asks. "It was a present from Jason's grandfather." No one on DeWitt Street has a color TV.

"Connor Clarke," Hannah says.

"Who?" Mickey asks.

"The grandfather," Hannah says, exhaling loudly and shaking her head.

Mickey looks at me and shrugs his shoulders. I know exactly what he is thinking: why would we remember that name? However, he also knows there is no point arguing with Hannah.

We go back outside and head up DeWitt Street, walking up the canyon created by the snowplow. Sledding on the street would be good but nothing compared to the woods. We spend hours flying down and struggling up icy hills. When Hannah calls "last run," there is no argument. My legs ache and my pants are frozen well above my knees.

———

"I'm going to change my name when I'm eighteen," Hannah says as we head through the woods towards DeWitt Street.

"Hannah is a good name," Mickey says. "How'd you like to be called Miguel?"

"Not Hannah—Weiner—my last name. I'm tired of people making fun of my name."

"Weiner?" Mickey says. "Kids make fun of Grant's wiener when he gets ready for gym and you don't see him changing his name."

Other than my sister, Denise, and Valerie Talbot, Jason's older sister, Hannah is the only girl on DeWitt Street. Although she throws like a girl, throwing is the only girly thing about her. Hannah does not back down. She has hung out with Mickey and me since first grade and is fair game for Mickey's joke, even if it does involve a wiener.

——

I still hear Hannah and Mickey laughing as I pull open our kitchen door. Before my coat is off, my mother asks, "Did you see the police car?"

"No. We were in the woods."

"I saw it go up the street about an hour ago with its lights on," she says. "I hope it's not an accident." My father is the only doctor in our town and gets called after serious car accidents. Once, a snowplow came to our house and took my father to a farm where he helped with the birth of a calf. They called him because the veterinarian was out of town. The newspaper article about it is tacked to the bulletin board in our kitchen.

After dinner, the phone rings more than normal and Denise and I listen for clues. The police were at the Talbots' house at some point in the afternoon and no one in the neighborhood, despite all the frantic calling, has any idea why. By 9:30 I cannot stand it any longer. "What's going on?" I ask. "Is Jason hurt?"

"The police were at the Talbots' house for about an hour," my mother says. "Really, Grant, that's all I know."

—

I have a tiny bedroom on the second floor of our house with one window and a desk directly below the sill. It is there for me to do schoolwork, but tonight it is an ideal place to squat and stare at the stars. My mother loves the sky and I know Orion and Cassiopeia, Sirius and the North Star, the Pleiades, two Dippers, and the Crab. On nights like this, the stars reflect off the ice-covered snow and I can see deeply into the woods or straight to the center of the universe.

Standing next to the dictionary on the corner of my desk is a book of Greek myths, including the story of *Jason and the Golden Fleece*. It is impossible for me to hear that story and not think about Jason Talbot. I do not even try. To me, he is Jason, the brave Grecian sailor and warrior.

The Odyssey—read to me by my mom many times—is my favorite. Jason Talbot may rule the Argonauts, but there is only one Ulysses. The pictures in the book show Ulysses with his sword and shield. It seems wrong that he does not have a constellation or even a place in the part of the sky I watch. Some time ago, I decided that Orion and Ulysses were the same person. It only makes sense. Orion was his first name and Odysseus must be his last—and his friends called him Ulysses for short.

This is a conclusion I do not discuss with Hannah and Mickey . . . or anyone else.

My door opens before I have a chance to jump down from my desk. It is my father.

"What are you doing up there?" he asks.

"Looking at the stars," I say. "Thinking."

"About the police car—and the Talbots?" he asks. I turn back to Orion Odysseus, or, as I know him, Ulysses.

My father takes a few steps into the room. I wait for him to say everything is fine with the Talbots but he doesn't. "You are Jason's doctor. If he was hurt, you would tell me," I say.

He walks across the room and puts his hand on my shoulder. "What happens with my patients is very private." I have heard this speech before.

"Mickey and Hannah heard screaming at their house today. It isn't the first time," I say. I once saw Hack Talbot smack Jason so hard it left a handprint on his face. We were in their garage and Jason was using an electric drill purchased, he had just explained, by his Grandpop at Uniontown Hardware in Albany. Jason made us promise never to talk about things like this because it would only get him in more trouble—and I do not break promises.

My father rubs the back of my neck. "These things have a way of working themselves out." He takes his hand off my back and I hear his footsteps as he walks to the door. "Now get down off that desk or I'll tell your sister you are perched like a parakeet."

I check out Orion Ulysses Odysseus one last time, ease down to the floor, and crawl into bed.

– 4 –

I am up early, dressed, and in the dining room when my parents appear from their bedroom in the back of the house. We discuss plans for the day over breakfast. There is no new information about the police visit to the Talbots'. My father will drive to the Caulfield County Hospital twenty minutes away to make rounds and my mother will pay bills after doing some shopping in Haydon. The envelopes will sit, sealed, addressed and stamped, on the corner of her desk. On January 1, she will drop them off at the post office. My mother likes to stay ahead of the game.

My father is first to leave. I hear the crunch made by the chains on his tires as he backs down the driveway. "I'm going sledding." I walk toward the hallway closet.

"At 8:00 in the morning?" my mother asks. I look down, concentrating on zipping up my jacket. "Grant, don't you go bothering the Talbots this early. Let them have some peace." She examines the lining of my new green hunting boots. "They're still damp."

"I don't feel anything," I say. I know she wants me to wear the awful black rubber boots with metal clips—I would rather go barefoot on ice.

"Come in if you get wet."

The Talbots' house is all on one floor. The fireplace brick is tan, the long thin windows open with metal cranks, not the old-fashioned up and down type that gets stuck when it is humid. I climb over the plow pile dragging my sled, slide across the icy surface to the side of the house and wait by Jason's window. There is no yelling, no talking— nothing. I tap his window and wait again. When there is still no sound I knock harder. The bushes behind me rustle and I jump away from the house.

"Grant!" I nearly fall over backwards.

"I thought you were your dad," I say. I look back at the window. "Are your parents home?"

"They left with my Grandpop early this morning," Jason says. "They took Valerie to my aunt's house—she's going to stay there." He sucks in a gulp of air and his teeth chatter. He is not wearing a jacket. "Come in for a second."

I can see the kitchen from the front hall. There are newspapers on the floor, dirty dishes on the counter, and a huge wilting poinsettia on the table. There is no neat bulletin board on the wall with newspaper clippings, no calendar, no row of boots next to the radiator.

"Can you stay out all day?" Jason yells from his room.

"I have to ask first."

He returns from his room and looks approvingly at my boots. "They're real hunting boots. They keep the water out," I say.

He drops to the floor and starts lacing up his own boots—his are green shiny rubber, like mine, but have a double-thick black sole and leather laces. He opens the hallway closet and reaches for his coat. Our closet has church coats and an outside jacket for each of us. The Talbots' closet is three times the size of ours and is jammed full.

"I make sure my things are on one side, here, so I can find them." As he closes the door, I notice a knapsack on his back. "Let's go," he says.

"Where?"

He opens the front door. "Away from here."

We walk down DeWitt Street and stop at my house. I climb over the plow pile and put my sled in the garage. "I need to tell my mom where I'm going."

Denise is at the kitchen table still in her pajamas. "Where's Mom?" I ask.

"At the store," she says. "Why?"

"Tell her I'm going in the woods for a while with Jason."

"Is Valerie going?" she asks. Denise and Valerie Talbot are good friends.

"No way. Just him and me." I am out the door before she can ask another question.

We are close to the DeWitt Street dead end when Jason says: "We go in here." I watch as he climbs over the plow pile on the left side of the road. "You don't have to come." He lowers his voice. "This is a long way from any place you know—and really top-secret."

I stop. "Don't you want me to go with you?"

"Course I want you to come." Jason hesitates. "I could go alone, you know—no sweat."

"What about Hannah and Mickey?" I ask. "Should we get them before we go?"

"You swore not to tell anyone about this," Jason says.

"I didn't say a word," I say and start pulling myself up over the top of the plow pile, grabbing the icy chunks sticking out of the mound. "Are we going to that place you told me about?"

He takes a step toward the woods and stops as I come over the top of the plow pile. "Lone Pine," he says so quietly I can hardly hear him. "It's called Lone Pine."

– 5 –

Jason lengthens his stride and slides across the impossibly slick surface. As the glide slows, he pushes off with his back foot like speed skaters at the Caulfield County Hockey Rink, swinging his arms, his head turned upward. He slides toward a hickory, its trunk as wide as a baseball bat. He grabs the tree and sails around in a circle, once and then a second time, his feet flat to the ice, and when the spin brings him to a stop, I am next to him.

"My boots won't slide like yours," I say.

He looks down at my feet. "New boots have stick-um on the bottom. Mine are broken in." He lifts his right foot, grabbing his ankle and tilting the sole of his boot, just the way cowboys check a horse's hoof to see if the shoe is crooked. "Feel that," he says. The ridges on his boot are slightly worn and he is right—no stick-um.

We are in a more heavily forested area at the crest of a steep incline. Fallen branches stick through the icy surface of the hill. Jason sits down, holds the trunk of a tree to steady himself, then lets go and shoots down the hill on his rear-end. I start to slide down as well, but I do not have time to sit. I bend my knees and hold out my arms for balance. In seconds I will be flying past Jason, going like lightning, standing up, just like he does on a sled.

I fall almost immediately, crash through prickly bushes, just miss the upturned stump of a fallen tree, my fall ending at the bottom of the hill next to the base of a large gray beech, its smooth skin perfect for carving your name. I pull myself around the base of the trunk and see Jason lying on his back in an area where brown grasses stick through the ice, arms and legs spread wide, motionless.

I am up, running, slipping, down again, moving across the surface, out of control, grabbing at the branches that stick through the ice, and come to a stop near Jason. I yell his name and see that smile. His eyes open and he sits up. "A man's got to rest," he says.

We walk across the field that lies at the base of the hill and stop. A few steps in front of us, the land disappears. "It's a sinkhole—the flooding makes them. I usually jump down this one." We inch forward and I can see the drop-off is at least fifteen feet. "We can walk around it," he says. We make a wide arc around the sinkhole and are back in the woods.

Most of the year, when Hannah, Mickey, and I are in places like this we hear leaves crunch, sticks crack, and birds and buzzing insects everywhere. Sometimes we see grouse and quail, their take-off a storm of flapping. Less frequently, off in the distance, we see deer, rabbit, and even coyote. Now as Jason and I move across the ice-covered surface, it is dead silent.

We walk along the crest of a long ridge when, without warning, Jason holds out both arms, palms facing down. This means everyone stop. I freeze. Moving my head could produce noise, so I strain my eyeballs left and right but see nothing. "The coast is clear." Jason removes his knapsack from his back. "I brought Almond Joy—the inside is like a vegetable." I can see six or seven Almond Joy bars in his bag but he takes out one for him and one for me. "Rations," he says.

———

We walk another couple of hours, struggling up and sliding down slopes, across fields, and finally the stick-um leaves my boots. I am not as good as Jason, but I can make it without falling. "Are we close to Willis Creek?" I ask.

"Way past it," he says. "It was frozen over, remember?"

"Right," I say.

My legs ache and I have to go to the bathroom but all I say is: "How much longer?"

Jason points to his right. "Look at that," he says, ignoring my question. I see the remains of a brick chimney covered in ice and snow. As we get closer, I see what must have been the foundation of a house. Jason declares this place is called Stone House Corners and we continue.

Our walking is noisier than before and the snow creaks occasionally. Jason's cheeks are red and his forehead shines with sweat. Sometimes I think there is something wrong with me since I do not sweat much. Maybe I will sweat more when I am Jason's age.

"We don't have far to go," Jason says. We pick up the pace.

"I'm pretty cold," I say. I do not want Jason to see that my teeth are chattering. "Not too cold. Just kind of cold."

"Not me," Jason says. "See, you're pretty skinny and. . . ." Before Jason finishes his thought, he crashes through the surface. He pulls out his foot, slapping the snow from his pant leg and boot. The snow on his boot is wet, packing snow, the first we have seen since this journey began.

"This is swamp territory," Jason explains and falls through again. When he retrieves his foot, he lies flat on his back and pants like a dog. The ice groans and the whole surface moves. Jason jumps up and yells: "Run!"

The first time I fall through it feels like I have broken my leg. My momentum pushes the icy surface against my shin bone, near my knee. I pull out my foot and paw at the damp snow—some of it sticks to my dungarees just over the red stripe at the very top of my new hunting boots. In the next twenty minutes, we fall through every few steps. I have icy melting snow stuffed up my jacket and down my pants. I take off my soaking gloves and rub my wrinkled and slightly yellow hands.

"This is better," Jason says as we reenter woods and stand on more solid ice. "We should have gone around the swamp. There must be a way to get there without going through that." He looks at my feet. "Did water get in your boots?"

"A little," I say.

"Me, too," he says. He stops and looks through the trees. "We're close to the rock. Wait'll you see it."

I have seen lots of rocks in the woods, mostly in tall piles ... full of snakes. We have garter and ribbon snakes in my backyard, but down here there are black snakes. Jason says he has seen them eight feet long. I have seen some three or four feet. They are not poisonous but I could do without them. The rock piles are also home to copperheads, poisonous snakes that climb trees. I think I saw one once moving across the top of a fallen log. It was brown and about a foot and a half long. I did not see crisscross markings on its back but I was far away from it. Just thinking about snakes makes me nervous, but in the winter they are deep in the rock piles and I am safe until spring.

"What are you looking at?" I ask.

Jason points through the woods to a huge mound covered with snow. It sticks up higher than my house—I am sure of it—and blocks what remains of the sunlight.

"This is the right way," Jason says. "This is Cedar Dome Mountain—let's go!"

I had been shivering, but as we run toward the base of the mound, it stops. After a few minutes Jason says: "Here." Cedar Dome Mountain is cracked in several places. We enter a crevice so narrow that at points we have to slide sideways, our backs pressed against one side of the wall.

Deep in the Cedar Dome crevice, our path tilts upward—steeply. "We have to climb," Jason says. The incline is covered in solid ice and higher than the staircase to my bedroom. A tree sticks through at the top somehow growing in the rock. "That's the cedar," Jason says, looking up. He tries a few steps and slides back. "We need to size up the situation." After we stare at the icy incline for a minute—that is all it takes to size up a situation— he pulls a hatchet and knife from his knapsack. "We'll make steps." He whacks the ice, making an indentation large enough for his foot and hands me the knife to scrape clear the step.

We make four footholds and use the branches on the base cedar rock-tree to pull ourselves the last three or four feet. I wonder, but do not ask, just how the roots of this tree make their way into solid rock.

A few more sideways steps and we are out of the crevice and back in the woods. The trees thin and then the forest just stops . . . no trees or bushes or even brown grasses. "This is Muskrat Lake," Jason announces. As I start to walk on the smooth surface Jason grabs the hood of my jacket and I sail backwards.

"What if you fall through the crust and the ice below doesn't hold you?"

"I just figured it would," I say.

"Let's walk around the edge." The snow and ice crust is firm and there is little in our way. "A part of St. Clare Creek goes into Muskrat Lake. That creek runs from one end of the county to the other," Jason says. "You couldn't walk here in the spring—this is flood plain."

All of us have seen St. Clare Creek, a stream usually five or ten feet wide, become a quarter-mile wide and cover the lowest area of the woods after the snow melts. By late May, the flood recedes and leaves the area one big marsh perfect for pussy willow. Last spring we picked some and brought it back to sell. My mother bought a bunch for a quarter. Mickey's uncle gave us two dollars and then refused to take the pussy willow. Mickey told us he was soused.

The trees in the St. Clare Creek flood plain grow on unstable mounds. It is the only place in the entire woods where Jason says there are water moccasins. He saw one swallow a jackrabbit—a live one. He told us he saw the rabbit go in its mouth and jump around as it went down its gullet. I cannot imagine how large a water moccasin must be. My mother told me we are 500 miles north of any water moccasins. "She hasn't been in the deep woods," Jason says when I report my mother's theory. "I've seen them."

I realize we have been climbing when I turn and see the flat face of Muskrat Lake below us. When I turn back Jason has stopped.

"That's it," he says quietly. "That is Lone Pine."

We are victorious conquerors, valiant generals
who led legions in a brutal battle—Jason and the
Argonauts (at the moment, I am an important Argonaut Officer). We march toward a roaring fire,
deafening cheers, grateful families weeping with joy
as we stagger forward, then stand tall, taking the
last few steps to the center of the encampment. We
are at journey's end.

In a few minutes we stand alone underneath
Lone Pine. I look up the trunk rising twenty feet
before the first rung of giant lower branches. Jason
pokes at a whitish sap hole, the size and shape of
our Thanksgiving turkey platter, left after a limb
close to the ground broke off. On the far side of the
trunk and ten feet below us is a not yet fully frozen
section of what I think is St. Clare Creek, its deep
fast waters jet black.

– 6 –

Jason walks away from Lone Pine and St. Clare
Creek toward a steep slope, kneels, and begins to
chop with his hatchet at the icy snow near the base
of the hillside. As large clumps fall, I clear them
away until I touch the door, feel the wood, and
begin to understand.

We are on our knees, scraping around the surface of the door, creating a larger and larger hole.
"The hinges are on this side," Jason says. He chops
away more ice and snow until the door is clear. I
stand back as he grabs the handle.

"It's frozen shut. Use the knife and see if you
can pry it loose." I pick at the edge of the door.

"You've got to jam it between the door and the frame." He positions the tip of the knife along the edge and pounds the handle with his fist. "Like this."

"It might break if I do that," I say.

"So? My Grandpop gave me a new one for Christmas. You can keep this one." He hands me the knife. "It's yours."

I have never owned a hunting knife. Jason's knife—now mine—has a bone handle carved with light brown lines, and a gray steel blade. I am absolutely positive my parents will not let me keep it. I will need to hide it, maybe in the woods.

As I slash at the edges, Jason hammers at the door till it shakes. Jason grabs the handle ... and it opens. It is dark and cold inside the shelter, but the dirt floor is dry. Jason picks up a box of wooden stick matches from a shelf next to the door and lights a lantern.

Cans of food are stacked on a large shelf on one side of the shelter and on the other side, a wooden rack on which hangs a buck saw, an ax, and a bunch of chains with metal clamps on the end. This place is stocked. I am quite sure.

"Traps." He sets one on the floor, steps on a metal bar and carefully opens the jaws. "These are zeros and ones." He places a small hook over one end and then removes his foot. "Now it's set." He uses a wooden spoon to push down on a plate in the center of the trap and it jumps as it snaps shut. "This would take your finger right off."

He hangs the trap back on the wall. "Have you ever seen one of these before?"

"Sure," I say. "Lots of times."

"Baloney," he says—but he is smiling.

He sits on a cot covered with a green blanket and takes off his boots. I sit next to him undoing my laces. "This place was dug out of the hillside by hand," he says. "Once the hole was dug, they put planks on the walls and across the top, like a ceiling, so the dirt won't fall in on us."

"Who built it?" I ask.

"That is secret—and it doesn't matter anyway," Jason answers. "There are two rooms, this one and the fire-pit." He picks up the lantern and I follow him to the rear of the main chamber. There is a framed entrance about six feet across that opens into a second large room. A large pile of firewood is stacked in the corner. In the center of the room are a circle of stones and the charred remains of a fire. "There is a slat in the front door—you take it out when there is a fire. It lets in air."

He holds up the lantern and examines the ceiling. "That's the smoke vent. It sticks through the ground above us on the side of the hill."

"Will we get home before dark?"

"Maybe not—but I got it all figured out," he says. "I don't care if I'm late."

"Me neither," I say softly—and do not add I will be in serious trouble if I get home after dark.

Back in the main chamber, he flops on the cot, his hands behind his head. I do the same—right next to him but not touching—and we stare at the ceiling. "Valerie isn't coming home—not for a long time," he says. "It's better for her to be with our cousins. They're all girls, about the same age. Grandpop set it up."

I do not move my head. If we are going to talk about Valerie, about Jason's family, we should stare at the ceiling, not look at each other. "Your dad is going to let her move away?" I ask.

"He won't stop her," Jason says. "Anyway, if Grandpop says she will move, she will move. It was decided yesterday."

"Is that why the police came to your house?"

"How did you know the police were at my house?" Jason asks.

"Everybody knows. They came up the street with the lights on. I talked to my father about it last night but he wouldn't say anything."

"He isn't allowed to say anything. He's Valerie's doctor—mine too."

"So the police came because Valerie was moving?" I ask.

Jason is quiet for quite some time. "That's right. She's going to change schools and everything. The police need to sign papers so that can happen."

"Did my father need to sign any papers? I mean, so she can change schools?"

"Probably so," he says.

"Valerie really wants to do this?" I ask.

"You bet," Jason says quickly. "She couldn't wait to go. She told me she'd run away if she had to stay with Mom and Dad."

"Makes sense," I say.

"It doesn't make any sense," Jason says quietly. "None of it."

"None of what?" I ask.

"None of the stuff with Valerie," Jason says.

Valerie is fourteen, a year older than my sister. They talk on the phone for hours. She is a freshman in high school and my sister is in eighth grade. Last summer, Valerie had a boyfriend who rode a motorbike. Mickey, Hannah, and I saw him in the Talbots' backyard once and after he left, Jason told us about him. He was going to try out for the Haydon High School football team and could throw a pass longer than any of us, including Jason. We played touch football after Jason told us about the boyfriend—in the middle of the summer! Hannah is the only one of us who can throw a spiral, even though she throws like a girl.

Valerie was with the boyfriend more and more and then it stopped. We asked Jason if they broke up and he told us the boyfriend went to the Talbots' for dinner and got in an argument with Jason's father—a bad one. Valerie was crying, Jason said, and that was the last time the boy came around.

Valerie does not spend much time with us anymore, now that she is in high school. She has long hair, reddish-brown, and her smile looks the same as Jason's. "I bet she doesn't stay with her cousins long," I say.

"I'll bet she never comes home," Jason says.

I look at Jason for the first time in this discussion. "Never? Why?"

"Because . . . I just bet she never comes home," Jason says. "Listen, you can't say anything about this." He stands up. "I mean it. No one is supposed to know. You need to be like your father. You tell a doctor something, they go to jail if they tell someone else. For life."

I had no idea my father could go to jail if he talked about things his patients told him. "I won't say anything to anyone. Not even my parents."

"Let's get a fire going." Jason lights a second lantern and hangs it by the tool rack. "Ball up some of this old newspaper and put it in the pit, then take some of the kindling and stack it up on top of the paper like a Lincoln Log cabin. Once it catches, we can put on the bigger pieces. Whatever you do, don't light it yet." He begins to retie his boots.

"Are you going to light it?" I ask.

"The smoke vent is blocked. I'm going outside to knock the ice and snow away so we don't suffocate." He zips up his jacket. "It'll take a minute to climb up the slope because of the ice. I'll give a yell when it's clear—then you can light the fire."

Jason gives me the box of matches and opens the shelter door. "Keep this closed," he says. "You're never supposed to leave it open." I return to the fire-pit and begin the task of getting the fire ready. It is tricky to get my Lincoln Log cabin to balance on top of rolled-up paper balls, but after several minutes, I am satisfied. One match and we

will have a roaring fire. Our clothes will dry and we
will be ready to head back home.

– 7 –

I walk into the main chamber and look at the
cans on the shelf. There is a stack of oval-shaped
cans labeled "Sardines of Norway," a dozen cans of
soup, and two glass jars on which someone has
written "Hunter's Stew." I take the lantern and
walk around the room inspecting the walls. There
are a few cupboards with doors that look like shutters set into the wall, some with plates and aluminum forks and knives, while others have tools, an
oil can, and more lanterns. One cupboard is full of
books, mostly mystery novels like the ones my
father reads. I pick up the trap Jason showed me;
even with both hands, I cannot press together the
curved metal. I set it back on the ground and step
on it, just the way Jason did, and the jaws open.
When I release my foot, it snaps shut. This would
definitely take off a finger.

It will be hard to keep this a secret. Hannah
and Mickey would go nuts if they heard there are
real traps, a fire-pit, and Sardines of Norway hidden
away in the woods behind our homes, but I am
sworn to secrecy. I go to the door hoping to see
Jason, with whom I now share the greatest secret of
all time, and look through the air slot but all I see is
white ice and the thick trunk of Lone Pine.

I head back to the fire-pit to check my Lincoln
Log stack—this will burn up quickly. When Jason
does not come back inside, I walk through the main
room and open the shelter door. "Hey ... Ja-

son. . . ." No answer. I walk to the cot, put on my boots and jacket, and go back to the door. "Jason!" Nothing.

I close the door behind me and head out into the cold. I look up the hill but no one is there. "Jason!" I hear the water rush under the ice-covered parts of St. Clare Creek and nothing more. I see no tracks, no broken branches, no sign of Jason.

I try to walk up the mound but it is too slick and I end up on all fours, crawling, grabbing at branches, until I get to a place where there is a hole in the icy snow and see Jason's hatchet. This must be the smoke vent. I whack at the ground a few times, reach my hand down the opening and see the lantern light through the vent.

"I cleared the smoke vent." Nothing. Maybe he is getting firewood. The last thing we want to do is leave the shelter without firewood. I look up from the smoke vent opening and see something move— fast—way off in the distance—at least I think I do. I stand slowly, holding my arms out to help me balance on the icy slanted surface and stare at the area where something brown caught my eye. It could not be Jason. His jacket is red.

"Hey, Jason!" It is as loud as I can yell. The wind is louder than my voice but it does not matter. There is no answer and nothing moving off in the distance.

"Hey!" My voice is lost in a gust of wind.

I use my right hand to shield a sun that does not shine, turn in every direction, calling Jason's name but there is no reply, not even an echo. I take

a few steps toward the brown something that might
have been there and realize that everything not
white in this frozen forest is brown ... every tree
and branch, the grasses that stick through the
surface, the deer who are always there but never
close. If it was anything, it must have been a
whitetail deer, bounding to stay out of my line of
sight, but then I did not see any bobbing white tail.
I saw brown and it moved—fast.

I slide down the mound, go inside, and light the
fire. As the small dry pieces of wood burn, I sit
cross-legged, watch the flames, smell the kerosene
from the lantern, and follow the smoke upwards as
it crowds the hole at the top of the shelter. I
imagine the gray puffs emerging from a hole in the
middle of the icy mound and wonder if I am completely alone.

– 8 –

When my parents learn I went this far into the
woods without their permission, there will be consequences. I can hear my father talking about how
much he wants to trust me and how behavior like
this makes trust impossible. Even considering punishment and the bad feelings that go with it, I wish
my father was here right now. He would help me
stop shaking.

I wish Hannah and Mickey were with me so we
could talk. Hannah would have ideas. She always
does. "Grant," she would say, "Jason probably was
on top of the mound and saw a person—a person
wearing brown—off in the distance, someone in

trouble, and went to help out. Maybe there was no time to come back and get us." The thing is, Hannah and Mickey are not here. I have to figure this out alone.

I pick up a can of Sardines of Norway and find a key attached to the bottom. Maybe it unlocks a secret cupboard in the shelter. In truth, I have no idea why there is a key on the base of the sardine can—but I know this: I am in a large stocked shelter where someone could live for weeks and no one would know. It is a perfect hideout for gangsters, criminals who need to lay low until the police give up trying to find them. There is no place more hidden than Lone Pine.

I open the door of the shelter and inch outside. Ice falls from the area we chopped just above the door. I spin to see if someone is on the hill and fall backwards. If gangsters got Jason, they will come back and get me. I scramble to my feet, dive back into the shelter and close, but do not slam, the door. We did not think to be quiet as we approached Lone Pine. Even with the steady wind muffling sound, members of a gang could have heard us, maybe even watched from behind trees on top of the mound, keeping an eye on everything we did, waiting for one of us to come out alone.

I see a huge gloved hand covering Jason's mouth, a heavy arm locked across his chest, and Jason being dragged away by a gangster wearing a brown coat. He will fight, but even Jason is no match for a grown-up gangster.

I go to the fire-pit and push into a tight circle the few small pieces of wood still burning. I stick

Jason's knife between my belt and pants on my right side and his hatchet through my belt on the left. I blow out the lanterns and stand in the darkened shelter listening to the fire crackle in the pit.

I need to go—now— before they come back and get me.

I need to stay—Jason will come back and will have no idea where I am.

I need to get help. Jason might be hurt, lying in the snow, unable to make a sound.

I hear the wind, or maybe it is someone yelling, a voice off in the distance.

I take one step outside and run—as fast as anyone has ever run—a slippery sprint to the banks of Muskrat Lake, toward Cedar Dome Mountain, away from gangsters who will cover my mouth with their huge gloved hands as they drag me away.

I am well in the crevice before I stop. Maybe Jason is more than the gangster bargained for. Maybe he kicked one of them—hard—and then took off across the icy snow. No one can run like Jason. I see the gangster gasping, both hands on his gut, trying to take a breath, then straightening and running across the ice, knowing he will not catch Jason. I see his angry face as he holds a pistol with both hands, aiming carefully at Jason, and fires. I press against the icy wall and think about Jason falling, grasping his chest as blood comes through his jacket. Inside the shelter, covered with earth, a heavy layer of snow and ice, messing around with cans of Sardines of Norway, I did not hear the shot fired by the brown-cloaked gangster.

I am deep in the crevice, pushing sideways, bumping down the staircase we cut in the ice earlier, and then, finally, out on the far side of Cedar Dome Mountain. I scan the woods in front of me and strain my eyes to see all that is there. Without leaves to block my view I can see a long way, and I do not see gangsters, Jason, or any section of woods looking even slightly familiar. I know we entered the crevice directly behind me. We came out of the woods to get to this point, yet woods are everywhere. We made no tracks coming in and I have no idea how to get home.

—

It is getting dark and the constant wind makes my nose and eyes ache. I turn and shift my direction so the wind is at my back. Home could be anywhere. I pull my hood over my head and tie the drawstring under my chin. It is one foot in front of the other, sometimes a boot sliding sideways without my permission, calling Jason's name with every few deep breaths—but never a reply.

I see where the sun has set. I know this is west. I know this should help me find my way home—but I do not know how. If I could talk to Jason, we would make a map in the snow or scratch one on the ice and I would see where to go. We would make use of north, south, east, and west. After all, he is Jason of the Golden Fleece—and explorers know west. Now, on my own, west has no meaning.

The warmth I felt from the small fire in the shelter is gone—but I am a solitary explorer heading across the Arctic with stiff legs and frozen feet.

There is ice on the ends of the hair hanging outside
my hood, but I have no choice. I must keep going.

I find the two stars in the Big Dipper that point
to the North Star, but like the sun setting in the
west, this tells me nothing—yet it should. After all,
I am Orion Ulysses Odysseus, the hunter and clever
warrior, facing enemies and returning home. I have
a belt and sword, like the constellation Orion, and I
have the hatchet of Jason Talbot. I place my hand
on my jacket, pressing to feel the bone handle of the
knife and think of Ulysses approaching his home,
welcomed by his son, Telemachus, and his wife,
Penelope. When Jason comes home, there will be no
faithful dog, no loving family, only his awful father,
Hack, and his mother, Martha, with her nervous
face and quiet voice. His sister has moved out, an
action requiring my secretive father and our local
police, flashing lights and all.

I come to a hill and my first step does not hold.
I can try to reach from tree to tree and pull myself
up, but from where I stand the trees are separated
by too great a distance. I walk along the base of the
hill, hoping to find a place with a milder slope.
Walking forward and looking to my right, I do not
see the uprooted tree in my path and tumble head-
long into a tangled mound of dead limbs. Ice-covered branches pick at the skin on my face. I shut
my eyes tightly as the wood splinters and I finish
my fall.

I twist and sit, pushing away twigs that snap
and am flecked with pieces of cold, wet bark. I grab
and claw over branches and finally stand. I am
determined to keep my eyes forward and avoid risks
that are everywhere—and it is pitch dark.

– 9 –

The first flash of light through the trees drops me to my knees, hands stretched out, palms facing down, quieting ghosts behind me. It is gone in an instant but I am sure I have seen it. I know lightning and while I haven't seen the aurora borealis, I doubt this is it. I walk quickly in the direction of the light, calling as I slide and stumble. A second spray of light comes through the woods and is gone.

"Hey!" No reply.

Lights flash through the woods a third time. I am closer to them or they are closer to me. That light was brighter but darkness returns instantly. I cup my hands around my mouth but stop without making a sound. Somewhere in the woods people are looking for Jason and me—but why would they be flashing their lights and then turning them off? Maybe this is not a search party. Maybe this is the person who took Jason—a brown-coated gangster who has to eliminate witnesses. Whatever he did to Jason, he could do to me.

I have walked for hours since leaving Lone Pine and am lost—completely. For all I know, I have circled the icy forest floor and am approaching Lone Pine. The lights I see are a lookout. The gangster in the brown coat is waiting for me. I know what Hannah would say: "Quiet, Grant. Just watch." She says this when we see deer, always with the hope that a doe and fawn will be near. Deer families, however, are not my concern.

I am motionless when a bright light flashes by me, followed by another and another and then—

clear as a bell—a car horn. It does not take long to get to the edge of the road and realize I have been watching headlights flicker through the trees as cars round a corner on a real plowed road.

I climb to the top of the plow pile. It is taller than I, frozen solid and covered with sharp chunks of ice infected with dirt from the road's surface. Within a minute or two I see more lights in the distance. I slide down the plow pile and feel the chunks of coarse ice on my back. The road is covered with hard-packed snow and ice, just like DeWitt Street.

A car approaches and I hold out my right hand, thumb extended. At ten, I am not allowed to hitch-hike, but this is an emergency. If I can get a car to stop, the driver will tell me where I am, maybe even drive me home. My house will be warm and my parents angry at first since I have missed dinner, but I will tell them I got lost and a nice family picked me up along the road and drove me home. My hitchhike partners will wait in the car and speak briefly with my father. I will not hear them but they will be saying, "He's a good kid," and my father will nod. I will learn Jason is home. He arrived shortly before I did. He was also lost but made his way out of the woods. He and I make a pact: we will tell no one about how we journeyed to Lone Pine and how we got separated. He and I will have a secret for life.

I am certain the next car will pick me up, but what approaches is making far more noise than a car. I see a yellow flashing light above two bright headlights and the road shakes. The lights move toward me, the road vibrating, clumps of broken up snow and ice hard-pack flying through the air. It is a snowplow. Some of the ice hunks are landing on the plow pile on the side of the road making it even higher. Sparks fly from the bottom of the plow blade. It is too late to climb up the plow pile—the blade will get me as it comes by and I will be thrown back into the woods and left to die. Clumps of snow are flying as high as the cab where the driver sits. He will never see me.

My yelling is lost in the groaning and scraping of the plow and I am trapped between the canyon walls. I pull up my coat, reach down and grab the bone handle of Jason's knife. I wave it back and forth over the top of my head, screaming. My eyes are closed tight and the road shakes harder—and then the grinding noise changes. As the scraping stops, I open my eyes and am blinded by a spotlight from the top of the plow.

There is loud scratchy static and a moment later the door of the cab opens and large green boots, their tops covered by yellow plastic overalls, land on the running board. The driver is wearing a rubbery yellow jacket, unzipped in the front, and is pulling on a pair of mittens as he jumps onto the street.

"Put the knife down, kid, I'm not going to hurt you." I am still holding tight the bone handle of Jason's knife, although I let my hands rest on the top of my head and the blade now sticks up like the feather in the headdress in Hannah's Halloween costume.

"What's your name?" the driver asks.

My throat hurts and I am shaking.

"You Hack Talbot's kid?" I shake my head.

"You must be Dr. Harper's kid." I nod. "Your parents are worried about you." He hesitates. "You and your friend get separated in the woods?" I nod.

The driver yells to his partner who is still in the cab of the snowplow: "It's Dr. Harper's kid." I hear more loud static and squawking from the radio in the cab. The partner sticks his head out the window. "They want to know if he's okay."

The man kneeling in front of me turns to his partner in the truck. "He's scratched up and cold, but in one piece. They want us to take him home?"

"We're supposed to take him to the parking lot at the school down the street. A squad car is on its way. They'll take him home."

"Think you can get up into the cab of the truck?"

I want to say: "I have just walked from one end of the woods, all twenty thousand acres of it, to the other. I can climb over your truck if I have to," but instead I just nod.

The seat is wide and even with three of us there is room for two thermos bottles, a clipboard, a hat, several pairs of work gloves, and a newspaper. The thermos bottle has a picture of a smiling cowboy and his smiling wife, just like the thermos I use. As I pick it up, the driver says: "That's my son's. The glass on the inside of mine broke last week."

"It's like mine," I try to say but talking is hard.

We drive for a few minutes and pull into a parking lot. "This isn't my school," I say.

"There is the squad car." The driver brings the plow to a stop. I am transferred from the snowplow to the front seat of the police car. Before we are out of the lot, the officer picks up the handheld radio. "I have the Harper boy," he says.

"The mother is at the house with the Lieutenant. Take the kid straight home. The father is out with one of the search teams." These words pour out of the speaker on the dashboard of the police car.

My father does not share my love of the woods. He is neither a hunter nor hiker and now is walking over the same icy surface that carried me today. He will get scratched by branches and find it difficult to go down slopes and over mounds. "Can you call him on your radio and tell him I'm okay?" I ask.

"They'll take care of it," he says. The squad car goes slowly and the trip seems to take forever. As we pull up to my house, the policeman puts his hand on my shoulder. "Listen, your mom is going to be happy to see you and mad at you all at the same time. The best thing for you to do is to tell her you're sorry. I would save any long explanations for tomorrow. I've been through this before, and I can tell you, after a good night's sleep, the world looks very different."

"Is Jason home yet?" I ask.

"As far as we know, he hasn't popped out of the woods yet, but he will."

The front door is open and my mother is running toward us, Denise close behind. My mother hugs me as I get out of the squad car, right there in the driveway, and does not let go for a long time.

—

A man wearing a shirt and tie leans on our kitchen counter drinking coffee from one of our cups. There are several pieces of paper on the kitchen table, lined up, overlapping, the way cards look when my mother plays solitaire. She keeps the lines of cards neat, turning them always with a satisfying snap. These papers are written in my mother's handwriting and are covered with phone numbers and names and several star-shaped designs, the kind my mother makes when she speaks on the phone.

I take off my boots, jacket, and gloves and am introduced to Lieutenant Wallace Huntington of the Caulfield County Police Department, the stranger in my kitchen. We shake hands and I sit down at the kitchen table. My mother gives me a cup of hot tea mixed with lemon and honey, the same concoction I drink when I have a sore throat.

As I drink the tea, Lieutenant Wallace Huntington asks one question after the next, all having to do with finding Jason.

Did he say where he was going?

Did we agree to meet later in the day—but Jason never showed up?

In what part of the woods do I think Jason is lost? Hiding?

Did I know why Jason ran off?

If I were the Lieutenant, where would I look?

Why would Jason disappear and leave me alone?

After answering "I don't know" over and over again, my mother intercedes. "Let him thaw out, Lieutenant. Grant, finish your tea."

Lieutenant Huntington hands me a small notebook that looks like the one I use to write down my homework assignments. "Can you draw a map of where you were when you realized Jason had taken off?"

I stare at the little piece of paper and my mother turns to the Lieutenant. "Grant is ten years old and half-frozen."

He ignores my mother's comment and hands me a black ballpoint pen. "Start at your house and. . . ." The phone rings before he finishes his instructions and Denise gives the receiver to my mother. She listens for a long time and finally says, "No, Martha, he doesn't seem to know."

I can tell my mother is listening carefully. "Of course, everyone understands." She is quiet again for awhile. "If you need help, call us. I'll come up and we can talk."

She looks at Lieutenant Huntington. "Martha—Jason's mother?" She looks at Lieutenant Huntington for a glint of recognition but he sits motionless.

My mother sighs and continues. "Martha said Hack has had too much to drink. She was going to bring him down here—but. . . ." She stops. "He is quite drunk and in no shape to go in the woods and look for his own son."

The Lieutenant shakes his head. "I know Martha, and of course Hack—one hell of a guy—plays on our softball team." He smiles. "Quite the drinker." My mother is not smiling. She tilts her head and motions for the Lieutenant to come into the dining room where, outside of our hearing, she will tell the Lieutenant what both Denise and I know about Hack Talbot.

With my mother momentarily out of the room, Denise leaves her post by the phone and sits next to me. "Where did you go, Buddy?" She is the only one who calls me Buddy.

"We went into the woods."

"How did you get all the way over to Van Buren Elementary?" This is the first I have heard that the elementary school where the plow met the patrol car was Van Buren. Our school, Livingston Elementary, is a few miles from here. Van Buren is a long way away.

"That's just where I came out of the woods."

"You scared everyone, Grant. Why didn't you tell me this morning you were going to go that far away. I thought you were going sledding. When you didn't come home, all I could remember was that you said it was just Jason and you."

"I didn't know we were going as far as we did—did you call Hannah and Mickey?"

"The moment they found you," Denise says. "They wanted to go with Dad to look for you and Jason, but their parents wouldn't allow it. They were here for a long time. Mr. Cabrera took them home an hour ago—call them in the morning." I nod. "You should have told me you were going halfway to Gloversville before you left. You knew where you were going—you took off like a shot after you left the kitchen.''

"I did not." I lean close to her. "We ended up going to a place that's really secret and I swore not to say anything about it."

"About what?" Lieutenant Huntington asks as he and my mother come back into the room. They must have finished talking about Hack Talbot's drinking and neither is smiling. I look carefully at the Lieutenant, expecting to see a shoulder holster and pistol but there is none. "Van Buren is at least ten miles from here, Grant, maybe more. That's a long way to walk." This Lieutenant is impressed with how far I have gone. "Several groups are still out looking for Jason. Try and think, boy—if you can remember where the two of you got separated, it would help those men."

"We were in the woods, down by St. Clare Creek—at least I think it was St. Clare Creek—and Jason went up a hill—and then he left. I don't know where he went," I say.

"Maybe this will help," Lieutenant Huntington says. "Come over here a minute." I walk to the kitchen counter where he is standing. "This is a map of Haydon Township—here is St. Clare Creek." He runs his finger, with its fat square nail, along a blue line that goes from one end of the map to the other. "These are lakes—probably frozen solid—but if someone were to fall through the ice, it would be very serious."

"I think Grant knows what would happen if someone fell into icy water at this time of the year," my mother says.

Lieutenant Huntington raises his eyebrows and continues his explanation of the map. "This is your house." I place my index finger on the map at the spot identified by Lieutenant Huntington. "I want you to move your finger and show me where you and Jason walked today."

I stare at the map. "Where are the woods?"

Lieutenant Huntington sighs. "The green part is the woods, boy. This whole area—here." He points to an area behind my house. My finger has not left home just yet.

"Is this green area woods over here, too?" Using my other hand, I point to the opposite side of the map.

"That's Cason Apple Orchard," Lieutenant Huntington says. "The woods behind your house are right here." He points to a thick black line. "This is Park Drive. It's about a mile from where you came out of the woods." Lieutenant Huntington straightens up as if his back is hurting. My mother asks him if he wants more coffee. Some adults seem to need coffee the way cars need gas. "Yeah, sure—thanks." He pauses. "Look at the map, boy. It is impossible to get from the woods, from the area behind your house, to Van Buren Elementary, without crossing Park Drive. Do you remember doing that?"

My mother hands him the cup of coffee. He does not say thank you this time. Lieutenant Huntington puts down his cup. "We—the police—think it's possible one of Jason's friends, or more likely, someone in his family—met you today. Did that happen?"

"No." I take several deep breaths. "Who would meet us?"

"That's none of your affair," Lieutenant Huntington says. "You're sure?" I nod.

I look up at my mother. She turns from me and looks at the Lieutenant. "Grant is exhausted. We want to help but I need to get him in bed or he'll be sick by morning."

"I understand the situation quite well. The fact remains that your son is the last one to see Jason Talbot and has told us nothing about where he is or how we might find him." He makes a slurping sound as he sips his coffee and I see my mother raise her eyebrows. "Try again, boy—show me, using your finger, where you went with Jason."

I move my finger an inch or so into the woods and stop. "What's right here?"

"What do you mean?" Lieutenant Huntington asks.

"Is this near the Stone House Corners or Muskrat Lake?"

"Where?" Lieutenant Huntington leans down looking at the map. "There are no places with those names. Did the place you last saw Jason Talbot have a name?"

I stare at the Lieutenant and say nothing. "What about it, boy, did it have a name?"

"Lieutenant, the 'boy' is named Grant," my mother says abruptly.

"Did it have a name, Grant?" He stretches out the sound of my name—*Gerr—an—nnt* and that undoubtedly irritates my mother—but she says nothing.

"I don't know," I say.

"Of course you do, Grant—and I know you are going to tell me." Again, he stretches out the sound of my name and I see my mother shake her head.

"I can't say what it was called," I say.

"Can't or won't?" the Lieutenant asks.

"Can't and won't," I say. I have made a promise to Jason and I must keep it.

"Listen, boy," Lieutenant Huntington says quietly, "we have a duty to find the Talbot boy before he freezes to death—or before he takes off with whomever you met in the woods—if you were in the woods at all. Now is the time to tell me what happened. People can go to prison if they don't cooperate with...."

"Stop it, Lieutenant—now," my mother says.

"Don't interfere," Lieutenant Huntington snaps at my mother. "Look, kid, what happened today? Where is Jason Talbot?"

Before my mother can say anything, I say: "Nothing. I didn't do anything."

"Where were you when you did nothing? If you expect me to believe you, you better tell me—and I mean now."

I have no choice and say as quietly as I can: "What about Lone Pine? Have you ever heard of that?" As the words come out of my mouth, I need to go to the bathroom and am not sure I can hold it. "I got to go—now," I say and walk awkwardly to the bathroom and close the door. I can hear Lieutenant Huntington speaking with my mother but cannot make out what they are saying. I pee longer than I have ever peed before. I may be peeing more than anyone has ever peed in history.

"Look for yourself," Lieutenant Huntington says as I come back. "There is no Lone Pine in the woods behind your house—do you think you could find Lone Pine if we start walking back there tonight?"

"I'm not going to let him go back into the woods tonight, Lieutenant, you must know that." My mother's voice is firm.

"If Hack's boy is found dead tomorrow morning, and we didn't do everything possible to find him, there'll be hell to pay—and we'll have his death on our consciences the rest of our lives." Lieutenant Huntington raises his voice. "I want you to tell me about the last place you saw Jason—this Lone Pine."

"There is a huge tree ... and a hill." I leave out the part about the shelter dug into a mound—that is the most secret part. "Jason climbed on top of the hill to knock snow and ice off the smoke vent. When I came outside, he was gone." I can feel myself shivering, just like I shivered today in the woods—but I am not cold.

"Came out of what? What vent?" the Lieutenant asks, speaking loudly enough to be heard all over our house.

This is bad. I kept the secret all of about five seconds. "There is a cave—well, not really a cave—two big rooms—dug into the hill—with a door. The second room is a fire-pit. In the ceiling is a vent to let out the smoke. We were going to light a fire to warm up before heading home."

"Now we're getting somewhere," the Lieutenant says, more quietly this time. "You lied before, Grant." Once again he stretches out my name. "Don't let it happen again—sooner or later, I will trip you up, and you will end up in one hell of...."

"Stop talking to him like that—or leave," my mother says.

Lieutenant Huntington glares at her, takes a breath, and rubs his eyes. "Very well," he says. "Grant, tell me more about what happened."

"I was inside for a while, and when I came out, Jason was gone. I climbed up on top of the mound and called him—then I saw something brown. It moved—fast—at least I think it did. It might have been a gangster."

"A gangster?" Lieutenant Huntington says. "What makes you think that?"

"I just do. It was a long way from Lone Pine— but I saw something. Something brown—it might have been a deer—but what if it was a gangster and he got Jason?"

"You've been watching too much TV," my mother says. "Grant, honey, there aren't gangsters around here." Lieutenant Huntington looks at her. He is the cop—he knows about gangsters. I wait for him to straighten out my mother.

"This time, your mom is right. I don't think you and Jason ran into gangsters," Lieutenant Huntington says. "Gangsters—for Christ's sake," he says just loudly enough for us to hear. "Forget about the gangsters. Tell me what you did next."

"I got scared—and then I tried to walk home, but I must have gone in the wrong direction. I kept walking. . . ." My eyes spill tears and my mother is behind me, holding me.

My mother looks up at the Lieutenant. "This has gone on long enough."

Lieutenant Huntington sighs hard again. His sigh smells like the coffee he has been drinking all night. Finally he says, "I'll be by in the morning," and closes his little assignment pad.

Turning her back on Lieutenant Huntington, my mother looks at Denise. "Make sure he gets ready for bed," she says. My sister takes my hand. When I was little, Denise and I used to hold hands. That was a long time ago. As she pulls me toward the stairs, I see my mother give Lieutenant Huntington his jacket. This is known as "being shown the door" and I have seen my mother do it before. Every now and then a patient will come to our house, not during office hours, with nothing particularly wrong. My father will speak with the patient and not long after, my mother will come along and show him the door.

Once Lieutenant Huntington is gone, my mother walks into the kitchen, mutters something to herself, and starts writing on a paper slip on the table. Without looking up, she says: "Denise! Get going." My sister and I have gotten as far as the bottom of the stairs when my father opens the front door. His hair is frozen and his face reddish-blue. He does not remove his gloves, take off his coat, or even take off his boots which are caked with ice. He is across the room in a second, picks me up, and holds me.

The phone rings and Denise grabs it. "It's Mrs. Talbot again."

"Tell her I'll call back." My mother turns to walk upstairs with my father and me.

Denise puts her hand over the receiver. "She's crying," she says. My mother looks at my father, sighs, and takes the receiver from Denise.

—

My father sits on a stool in the hallway while I soak in a warm tub. He tells me about the search. "When we got beyond the stone wall, we spread out. We were about 50 yards apart and walked west." There it is again, directions based on the hands of the compass. "It was hard to stand up."

"Did you go to Lone Pine?"

He pauses. "I don't know where that is," he says.

—

I am finally warm. I see my father's back through the bathroom doorway. I have a bathrobe— I almost never use it but I do not want to be cold again so I put it on. My father continues to sit. He has not punished me nor talked about how he has lost his trust in me.

I walk out to the hallway. He is seated on a stool, his back against the wall, his mouth open, sound asleep.

I go downstairs and my mother is still on the phone with Martha Talbot. I hear her say: "Are you sure you don't need someone to look at that? Why don't you come down the street? It would be no problem for my husband to...." There is a long silence. "Of course, I won't say anything...." She hesitates. "I'm worried about you, Martha." Another long pause. "Passed out cold?" And then: "Maybe you should spend the night here."

She puts her hand over the receiver and whispers: "Go upstairs and get in bed. I'll be up in a minute."

"Dad's asleep in the hallway." I see her smile slightly for the first time today. Without speaking, she points and moves her mouth, shaping the words, "Go to bed."

I am halfway up the stairs when I hear: "Martha, I can send the police...." A pause. "If you say so—but if he wakes up and hits you again...." Another long pause. "If that happens, please, please call us—or better yet, call the police. Promise me, Martha."

I continue up the stairs and stop, standing next to my father. I shake his shoulder and he opens one eye. "I dozed off, there, Grant. You ready for bed?" I nod and he takes my hand and walks me into my room. I will not be squatting and looking at the stars tonight—I have seen enough of them for one day.

– 10 –

We have not yet started breakfast when the phone rings. My father answers, speaks quietly, and hangs up. "No word on Jason yet, Grant. They stayed out all night. It sounds like I have a couple of cases of frostbite to deal with. They're already at the hospital. I need to look in on them." He grabs his bag and is out the door. I hear his car start and the sound of his chains crunching through the hard pack on our driveway.

"I'm going to the Talbots' to see how Martha's doing," my mother says. I am surprised when I hear her car start. The Talbots' house is less than a five-minute walk.

Denise turns to me. "I think she is going to try to get Mrs. Talbot to come down here." Denise takes down the tin of coffee.

"You know how to make coffee?" I ask.

"I've seen Mom do it a million times." She reads the label on the side of the can and shakes her head. "This doesn't tell you anything. I don't want to set the house on fire."

I start to put on my jacket. "I'm going to get Hannah and Mickey."

"You're staying right here," she says. "Did you hear Mom say: 'If he hits you again, come down here'—or something like that?" I nod and she turns back to the coffee maker determined to unlock its secrets. "That's why the police went to their house."

"I don't think so—that was just paperwork. Valerie is going to live with her cousins and it had something to do with transferring schools."

"Is that what Jason told you?" I nod. "The police don't get involved when you change schools, Grant." She lowers her voice. "One night, I was talking to Valerie about her mom and the phone went dead. The next day she was still angry about it. Hack pulled the phone line in her room out of the wall. I heard her scream "get out" before the call just stopped."

As Denise puts away the gray steel coffee pot, unwilling to risk disaster, I call the Weiner's house and learn Hannah was up very late and will call me when she wakes up—not a moment sooner. "We are so thankful you got home safely, Grant," Mrs. Weiner says. "Now, let's pray Jason is found soon." She asks to speak with my mother and I tell her she is at the Talbots'. After a brief pause, Mrs. Weiner says she will also go see if she can be of assistance.

My next discussion is with Mickey's mother and I am told that he, too, is still asleep. "I know he will be at your door the moment he wakes up," Mrs. Cabrera says. "My husband is already out trying to find Jason. You young men must be more careful next time."

A Caulfield County Police Department car pulls into our driveway. We both go to the window and watch as Lieutenant Huntington walks up to our front door. As Denise lets him in, he looks in the direction of the coffee pot. He is going to be disappointed.

"Where are your folks?" he asks.

We tell him my father is at the hospital and my mother at the Talbots'. "We found nothing last night, Gerr-annt," he says. "There are about 50 men at the firehouse now and more on the way. We want to be in the woods as soon as possible. You need to come with me."

"I'll call the Talbots' house," Denise says. "Grant can't go unless my mother says it's okay." She dials and a moment later is speaking with my mother. There is a long silence and she says, "I will," and hangs up. She turns to Lieutenant Huntington: "My mother wants Grant to stay right here. She says she'll be home soon."

"We can't wait. Kid, put your winter clothes on . . . we're leaving."

I am lacing up my boots when my mother rushes into the house and grabs me. "I do not want my son spending the day in the woods. How can he possibly be of help? I am heartsick about Jason— but why take Grant? If anything, he'll slow you down. He's already told you he doesn't know how to get back to Lone Pine, wherever that is—how is this going to be helpful?"

"Ma'am, this is a police investigation at this point as well as a search. A twelve-year-old boy has been in the woods almost twenty-four hours. It's nine degrees outside this morning. We're going to do everything we can to find him and your son is the one who saw him last—that makes him a material witness—or a suspect."

I do not remember Lieutenant Huntington calling my mother "Ma'am" last night, but that does not seem to bother her. Calling me a suspect, however, is another matter. "What possible reason do you have to say such a thing? It's time to leave, Lieutenant."

"Sorry," he says, "it's not that simple. This is Hack's boy." The Lieutenant stops. "I told you— he's a friend of mine."

"I would think you'd look for any child who was lost, Lieutenant," my mother says.

"Damn right," he says. "And I doubt this boy got lost. You may not like it but children can—and do—hurt other children ... sometimes on purpose ... sometimes by mistake. I have a job to do. If Grant is not involved in any wrongdoing, he has nothing to worry about. All he has to do is cooper- ate—and frankly, Ma'am, you are interfering." My mother walks forward and is standing very close to Lieutenant Huntington. She speaks very slowly, using her quiet, angry voice. "He does not know where Jason is. Do you understand that? He is a ten-year-old boy, not a suspect."

"That's for me to decide, Ma'am," he says. He looks up at the ceiling. "We're getting nowhere. I need to speak with your husband, Ma'am." he says.

"I speak for my husband, Lieutenant. Grant stays here today."

"I'm going to use your phone." Lieutenant Huntington says. My mother is silent and Lieuten- ant Huntington goes to the corner of the kitchen. A moment later we all hear him say, clear as a bell: "Call the hospital and get hold of the kid's father." My mother is next to Lieutenant Huntington in a split second.

"I told you, I speak for my husband."

"And I told you this is a criminal investigation." My mother turns her back to Lieutenant Huntington and walks across the kitchen. It seems unlikely she will be making coffee for Lieutenant Huntington any time soon.

A few minutes later the phone rings and Denise grabs it. "It's Dad." She hands the receiver to my mother who listens briefly and then says, "Have you lost your mind? He'll freeze out there. They don't need him." She hangs up without saying goodbye. "I want him back before dark. I want him warm and well-cared for. I want someone with him every second—someone with a radio." Lieutenant Huntington nods.

"Can Mickey and Hannah go with us?" I ask. "They know the woods and I called them earlier...."

"You can see them when you get back—which I assume will be early this afternoon, well before sunset," my mother says. She turns to the Lieutenant. "He's going to have breakfast before he leaves."

"He can eat down at the firehouse with the men," Lieutenant Huntington says.

"Donuts and coffee are not a decent breakfast for a ten-year-old boy." My mother pulls a skillet out from the drawer underneath the stove and takes a carton of eggs out of the refrigerator.

"I'm sorry, Ma'am, but we just don't have time for this. A child's life is at stake. I'm sure you understand that."

There is a crash as my mother drops the frying pan on the top of the stove. She spins around and faces Lieutenant Huntington and whispers, "God help you if anything happens to my son."

– 11 –

We leave the diesel and coffee smells of the firehouse quickly, one of five different groups heading into the woods, and are dropped off just before the DeWitt Street dead end at the point where Jason and I entered the woods yesterday. "The kid is our bloodhound," Lieutenant Huntington says to the driver. "If he stays true to his route, we should come out just east of Van Buren Elementary."

Lieutenant Huntington is not properly dressed. Through the top of his jacket I can see his tie and the unbuttoned collar of his white shirt. His pants are thin and straight, not like my dungarees, and unless he is wearing long underwear, he will be cold. The cuffs of his pants are stuffed into the top of his black rubber boots—the kind with metal buckles. The palms of his gloves are leather but the rest of the glove is knitted. I have gloves like these and I hate them—they itch and get wet quickly.

The other searchers look like they are going hunting. Several wear red plaid jackets with floppy earmuffs. One carries a radio over his shoulder and others have backpacks. I hope they have brought more than Almond Joy.

As we climb over the plow pile I wonder if the ice surface will hold these men. "You lead the way, boy," Lieutenant Huntington says. Using my right foot, I push off from the plow pile and slide across the surface of the snow. I hear the footsteps of the team. Jason and I moved in silence across the flat ice cover, but this team makes noise. Their boots squeak as they penetrate slightly the surface and their pant legs make a soft rushing sound with each step. As I lean forward and begin to swing my arms back and forth like the speed skaters at the County Hockey Rink, I hear Lieutenant Huntington clear his throat. I expect him to tell me to slow down but instead he says: "Spread out. Make sure you can see the kid." The searchers move across the ice to my left and right and I continue to skate. I am the lead goose in a winter migration and we form a V as we head down the first hill.

Our formation ends abruptly as searchers begin to slip and fall on the slope. At the bottom of the hill, Lieutenant Huntington catches up with me. "Was it like this yesterday?" he asks.

"I fell a bunch of times. The downhills are the worst. Sometimes it's easier to sit on your behind and slide."

"Just keep going, kid," he says.

We walk across a field and back into the woods. Fifteen minutes later we begin our next hill. I stop at the crest and wait for Lieutenant Huntington and the others to catch up. When they are close by, I sit on my behind pulling my knees up to my chest and lean forward so that the soles of my feet press down on the ice. For the first part of the hill, I slow my slide by leaning forward using my boots as brakes. The hill gets steeper and I move faster. I push harder on my feet, barely steer clear of a hickory, control gone, and smash into a bush mound at full speed. I lie on my back and look at the network of thin branches that form the top of the leafless canopy of the woods. A moment later, I hear Lieutenant Huntington yell "Jesus Christ!" as he slides by me on his stomach.

I look from side to side. Fallen searchers are everywhere. Lieutenant Huntington swears some more—and loudly—then pulls himself up the hill towards me, bush by bush, branch by branch. He is out of breath and red-faced. He sits on the ice-covered mound that broke my fall, reaches in his jacket, and takes out a cigarette. The other searchers struggle across the hill and join us. "Is there a way to get to Lone Pine without going up and down so many hills?" he asks as he exhales smoke.

"I tried to tell you last night. I've only been to Lone Pine once—yesterday."

He unzips the top of his jacket slightly. "It's supposed to be a little warmer today. Maybe it will get easier as we go along." This is wishful thinking. If the sun gets stronger and it gets warmer, the searchers will crash through the ice surface. It is impossible to walk any distance if your feet crash through the surface with every step.

We continue in the V formation and walk in a flat part of the woods for almost an hour. Several times I stop, dropping to one knee, arms extended, palms facing the ground. Each time, I hear the squeaking sound of Lieutenant Huntington's flubbery boots as he forces himself forward.

The woods thin, opening to a field that slopes downward. I do not recognize the trees and the bushes and hope the sinkhole is just ahead. I keep walking, but at the far end of the field there is no sinkhole, only more woods.

Lieutenant Huntington calls out to the other searchers. It takes several minutes for our group to form. The men have reddish cheeks, tinged in blue. Lieutenant Huntington passes around a package of cigarettes and they all take one. A searcher takes a stack of aluminum cups and a thermos from a knapsack and pours coffee. This is the first time I have coffee and it is hot and bitter.

"How far are we from Lone Pine?" Lieutenant Huntington asks. He inhales deeply on his cigarette and I watch the smoke come out through his nose.

"I don't know," I say. "We got to Lone Pine sometime in the afternoon yesterday."

"We should get there soon, then," he says.

We haven't passed the sinkhole, crossed Willis Creek, come to Stone Cabin Corners—and I have no idea if we are on the same route Jason and I took yesterday.

Lieutenant Huntington pulls a round black disc from his pocket and opens it. "We've been heading due west since we entered the woods. If we turn slightly south and keep walking in a straight line, eventually we'll end up at the point where you hit the road last night."

It is another hour before we are out of the woods, in a field, and nothing looks familiar. At the end of the field is a long curving line of heavier bushes and trees and I know it is the edge of a stream. As we approach, I see places where the ice has not held and black icy water flows. "There is a bridge across Seneca Creek just south of here," one of the searchers says as he looks at a map.

"We were near St. Clare and Willis Creek yesterday," I say quietly. "But they were frozen over."

Lieutenant Huntington starts his third cigarette. It hangs from his mouth as he pulls out his compass and checks it again. "We're heading southwest," he says, not removing the cigarette from his mouth. It flops up and down with each word. "We should come to the footbridge in the next twenty minutes or so." Finally, he takes hold of the cigarette with his gloved hand—the leather palm is wet.

Lieutenant Huntington finishes his cigarette, walks to a mound clear of grasses and bush, and calls to one of the searchers. "Give me a hand." With help from the searcher, he manages to stand on the top of the ice-covered hump. The searcher hands him binoculars. He looks in every direction and has almost completed a full rotation before he loses his footing. The searcher holding him by his belt begins to slip as well and they crash to the ground. The ice surface gives way and they are both covered with snow. "Son of a bitch," the searcher says. After a few minutes of cursing, they are both back on their feet.

"See anything, Lieutenant?" one of the searchers asks.

"Woods, fields, and more woods," he says. "Which way, Grant?"

"I don't know," I say—and I really don't.

– 12 –

The bridge over Willis Creek—or St. Clare Creek—or Seneca Creek—who knows where we are—is nowhere to be found. "We're too far south," Lieutenant Huntington says, again checking his compass. "We need to cross soon or we'll end up out of the woods."

"Why don't we eat before going any farther," one of the searchers says. He does not wait for Lieutenant Huntington to agree. He takes off his backpack and removes a large brown bag. "They're all ham and cheese," he says. Lieutenant Huntington urges everyone to eat quickly so we can continue. I am still on the first half of my sandwich when Lieutenant Huntington finishes, but he lights another cigarette and passes the pack around. We drink more bitter coffee, now cold.

It is an hour later when one of the searchers yells, "I see a house ahead." Lieutenant Huntington swears a long connected series of curse words, some related to his mother, many of which I have never heard before. One of the searchers laughs and Lieutenant Huntington tells him to shut up. We are through the backyard and onto the street ten minutes later.

I sit on top of the plow pile and listen to a discussion between the searcher holding the radio and the man who dropped us off earlier this morning. Lieutenant Huntington has taken off his gloves and is warming his hands, blowing into them. The radio discussion ends. I hear Lieutenant Huntington say to another searcher: "What a goddamn sorry waste of time." In my opinion, he is right. Jason is lost somewhere—or trapped by gangsters—and the best I could do was waste the time of Lieutenant Huntington and a group of searchers.

Lieutenant Huntington sits next to me on the plow pile and says in a quiet angry voice, "This place, Lone Pine, why do you think you couldn't find it today . . . what in the name of Christ are you hiding?"

"It's hard to find—Jason told me it was the most secret place in the woods."

"It's so secret no one can find it," Lieutenant Huntington says. "We didn't come close and from what I've heard on the radio, no one has. Teams of men with dogs have walked through the woods, one the full length of Willis Creek and the other most of the way down St. Clare Creek. There is nothing resembling Lone Pine."

"Sometimes, people don't tell the truth when they're scared," the Lieutenant says, his voice more normal. "They even pretend they've seen or done things because they're afraid to tell the truth. Good people do this." His hand is on my shoulder. I smell cigarette smoke as he breathes. "No one has ever heard of Lone Pine. The one thing we know for sure is that your young friend is missing and you were the last person to be seen with him. Did you fight? You had a knife—I know that. How about it?"

"How about what?" I ask.

"How about telling me what really happened. As I see it, it's next to impossible to walk around in the woods because of the ice. For you to have walked ten or twelve miles yesterday ... that's pretty improbable. You see, the more we adults think about what you've said, the more it becomes necessary for us to ask you questions. Do you see what I'm saying?"

"I told you the truth," I say. "We went down to Lone Pine. It was slippery just like today. I was messing around in the shelter and Jason climbed up to the top of the mound, and then I didn't see him anymore." I look down. I do not want Lieutenant Huntington to see my eyes. I rub my gloves across my forehead like I am drying off sweat.

"You think about this, boy. I have dealt with children before—kids who did awful things. They never want to tell you at first—but in the end, they talk. And then they are in more trouble—lots more trouble. They get sent away, kid, to awful places—with no mother to protect them. Now, how about it?"

I cannot talk. I know I will cry if I do. He must know because after a while he says, "We'll talk more."

Not only do we talk more later but we talk for the rest of the week.

We talk every day and sometimes at night after dinner.

I talk to Mickey and Hannah for hours every day—when I am not being questioned by Lieutenant Huntington, Martha Talbot (my mother says she won't let Hack Talbot come within ten feet of me), or the police psychologist. When I talk to the psychologist, I cry and cry. He tells me not to feel bad because it is normal to cry. I do not know if he is here to make me feel better or to check and see if I am lying.

I know the police think I killed Jason.

I begin to wonder if I will go to jail.

I hear my father say that maybe we ought to hire a lawyer and my mother say her parents can pay for it if we need one.

—

Lieutenant Huntington stops by early in the morning. It is New Year's Eve and he tells my mother he will be glad when this year comes to an end.

"Tomorrow is just another day, Lieutenant." My mother is not big on this particular holiday. Her resistance has something to do with her view of the calendar. "These dates are a useful creation by pagans—they certainly do not represent any divine organization of time," she once said.

Lieutenant Huntington knows by this point that if he does not have a purpose with his visit, he will be shown the door. "I was speaking with Hack—since you won't let the boy talk to him directly, he wondered—did Grant bring anything home with him, other than the hatchet and knife he stole from the Talbot boy?"

"Grant didn't steal anything," my mother says sharply.

"We'll see about that ... anyway, it's a fair question. Did your son have anything that could confirm any part of his story?"

I look at Lieutenant Huntington and decide he has thought about this question before he knocked on the door. He hopes I will break down, confess that there is no Lone Pine, spill the beans—and if I had beans to spill, I would do just that. In what I consider a moment of great insight, I answer before my mother can respond. "My jacket smelled like smoke from the fire in the shelter."

Lieutenant Huntington turns to my mother. "Where is the boy's coat?"

"I washed it," she says angrily. "It was filthy."

"Did it smell?" he asks.

Under better circumstances, my mother probably would have said "his clothes always smell," but she does not. "I can't say I recall smelling smoke," she replies. "I guess it's possible—but it's clean now."

"That figures," Lieutenant Huntington says.

"If you knew the answer, why did you ask?" my mother responds.

Lieutenant Huntington takes out a cigarette and my mother gives him a look that requires no interpretation. He replaces the cigarette in the pack. "Mrs. Harper, your son is either confused, lying, or was set up. There is no Lone Pine in the woods behind your house—the military confirmed that—but there are reasons to understand why Jason Talbot would want to take off—his mother was overprotective and...."

"Is that what Hack told you?"

"What Hack said to me is confidential," the Lieutenant says.

As to the military, for Lieutenant Huntington and almost everyone one else involved, Lone Pine hasn't existed since the New York State National Guard entered the investigation. The evening after Jason vanished, Hannah saw them arrive in three Army trucks. She said the soldiers were sitting on wooden benches in the back of each. The weekend warriors, as my mother called them, were here for two days. They went into the woods behind my house and trudged from one end to the other—and found nothing.

"I don't know what Grant did, Mrs. Harper. Jason Talbot knew these woods—and a week of searching hasn't produced hide nor hair of him. I know, from everything I've learned from your neighbors, for whatever reason, Jason was fond of Grant—that means he wouldn't abandon him miles from nowhere. Maybe he fell ... or was pushed ... or worse." He looks me in the eye. "Children don't just disappear, boy. Jason—or what's left of him—is somewhere." He turns to my mother. "I'm convinced Grant knows where. Jason would not have left your kid—not in the middle of nowhere—not in weather like that ... and Grant,"—and this time he stretches out the sound of my name—"knows what happened."

My mother turns to me and says: "Do you?"

I shake my head.

"You call me when you decide to tell the truth—it will be better if you tell us before we find out on our own," Lieutenant Huntington says.

"Out, Lieutenant," my mother says, as she shows him the door.

—

In the last few days, Denise talks to me, sometimes twice a day. She gets angry at the people who ask questions and even tells my mother to leave me alone. Tonight, New Year's Eve, she and I will sleep downstairs in front of the fireplace. We lie in our sleeping bags and talk, even after my mother has turned out all the lights. "Will I have to go to jail?" I ask Denise. It is a question I will not raise with my parents. I am not sure they will tell me the truth. Denise will.

"Did you commit a crime?" she asks.

"I don't know. I couldn't find Jason."

"That's not a crime ... and it's not your fault," she says, and then, reading my mind, "Lieutenant Huntington is a jerk—but he's not the one who decides in the end—judges and juries do."

If Denise trusts this system, I should too—but I am not so sure.

We stay up until midnight and watch TV. It is the first time I see the ball drop in Times Square. I wake up the next morning. It is 1959 and Jason Talbot is gone.

– 13 –

March 1959

Since Jason's disappearance three months ago, when I think about the Talbot family, I think only about Jason. Until this morning.

"Hack Talbot had a heart attack in the middle of the night, Grant," my mother says as I walk into the kitchen. "Your father is with him at the hospital. We thought you'd want to know."

I am the son of a doctor and discussions of heart attacks are common. I know the term myocardial infarction and used it in school this year. Discussing a specific patient's case, however, is not something that happens often. "Did he die?" I ask.

"It's not good, Grant," she says. "Martha was visiting Valerie in Schenectady when it happened. She's at her sister's house more than she's home these days."

My sister walks into the kitchen and looks at me. "Did Mom tell you, Buddy?" she asks. I nod. "Serves him right," she says.

My mother stands up quickly. "Don't you talk like that. Hack Talbot could die."

Denise is defiant. "Valerie told me about her father."

My mother nods her head several times. "Did Valerie say Hack touched her?" She does not look at Denise as she asks the question.

"He hit her," Denise says. "And he beat the tar out of Jason."

I know Denise is telling the truth. If I wasn't sworn to secrecy, I would tell them how Mr. Talbot smacked Jason so hard that he left a handprint on his cheek—but I made a promise to Jason and a promise is a promise.

"Hack has a bad temper," my mother says. "But that's not what I was asking.... Grant, would you bring in the newspaper?" She turns to Denise but continues speaking to me. "Now, Grant."

I close the front door and stoop down on the porch and listen. "What I mean is whether he touched her private parts," she says to Denise.

My mother waits but Denise says nothing. "If you don't know, just say so," she says finally. "Grant, get away from the door."

I stoop even lower and hear Denise say: "I don't know ... Not for sure. Valerie said he was disgusting."

My mother breathes a deep sigh. "Valerie won't be going to the hospital. When I spoke to Martha, she said Valerie is still angry. It is really a terrible thing." There is a pause. "Get up Grant, come back in the house. Honestly!"

———

My mother, sister, and I are having breakfast Sunday morning when my father comes back from the hospital just before nine, his tie undone completely, hanging around his neck. The whites in the corners of his eyes are reddish-yellow and he walks to the coffee pot without speaking. "When did he go?" my mother asks.

My father fiddles with the sugar as he speaks. "Around 6:45. I thought he was going to make it. He was conscious around three but a second one hit, more damaging than the first, and after that, there was no hope."

I look carefully at Denise's eyes. Yesterday she wished for Hack Talbot's death. Now it has happened and I wait for, "serves him right," but it is not forthcoming. There is a watery film over her eyes and she dabs at them with a paper napkin.

"Where is Martha?" my mother asks. "I should be with her. I wish you would have called right away. These are our friends and I...."

My sister begins to speak before my mother has finished. "He got to die before he had to apologize to Valerie. She'll never hear him say he was sorry ... if he was." Her words are muffled by intermittent sniffling. "He owed her that—then he just died because he drank and smoked."

"We need to remember a father who cared for his family is gone," my mother says. "Whatever might have happened, the simple fact is that this is painful for the family ... and this is a family already suffering." My mother has taught Sunday school and on several occasions, given the lay sermon in the children's service. This is her sermon voice speaking. She instructs my father to take Denise and me to church. She will find Martha Talbot and comfort her.

—

Hack Talbot's funeral fills the pews, the temporary chairs set up at the end of each aisle, the balcony, and the church foyer. The front rows of pews are set aside for family before the service begins. It is barely enough. The Talbot family is huge. "There are Hack's brothers and sisters," my mother explains. "He comes from a large family." Hack's brothers talk audibly as they stand in the front of the church. At one point, they gather in a rough circle, are quiet for a moment, and then several laugh out loud.

"It's like a wedding," my father says quietly. "The Talbots on one side, the Clarkes on the other."

"Who are the Clarkes?" I ask.

"Martha's family," my father says. "It was good of them to come. They're here to help Martha and Valerie. There is no love lost between them and the Talbots."

"That's enough," my mother says. She continues to whisper like a golf announcer, keeping my father, sister, and me informed. "Those three are Martha's younger sisters," she muffles her voice with her hand. "Valerie has been living with Dolores—she has four kids and already has two grandchildren. Oh!" My mother inhales quickly and continues her whispering. "That's Martha's father, Connor Clarke. Martha's mother passed away some years ago—she was quite young."

"That's Jason's grandfather?" I ask. My mother nods.

Connor Clarke, Martha Talbot's father, has silver blond hair and a reddish face. He has a broad back and light blue eyes and looks like an angry Nordic god. His hair is longer than any of the men in either family. His hands are large and his wrists wide. Unlike some of the others, he does not shuffle up the aisle of the church, but instead strides purposefully. He looks at Hack Talbot's brothers and neither shakes a hand nor exchanges a word. Throughout the service, he stands, sits, and kneels without bending his back.

During prayer, his head stays straight and faces forward. There are only a few hymns during the first part of the funeral and I see Martha's father stand but his lips do not move.

Connor Clarke does not sing at this event.

The eulogy gives some details about Hack Talbot, praising him as a father, a community leader, a volunteer who spent a few seasons as a Little League coach, neglecting to mention that he swore at us all the time and once told me I was worthless. At one point, the minister refers to him as a person who probably had great wonder and curiosity about God and who, at the same time, was the life of the party. "How welcome he will be in the House of the Lord," the minister intones, "and how deeply he will be missed."

This is more than Denise can bear. She leans into my shoulder: "It's a major sin to lie in church."

My mother hushes her with a finger raised to her lips and hands her a Bible. "Read ... and be quiet."

Denise turns immediately to the Book of Revelations. You do not get to Revelations when you are ten years old in Sunday school, but I have heard that is where the action is.

Neither Martha, Valerie, nor anyone from the Clarke family plays a role in the funeral. I see Martha's shoulders shake just once. Valerie sits as straight as her grandfather. I know Denise wants to speak with Valerie, but there is no chance at the church.

We wait in our car in the parking lot for 45 minutes as the funeral director organizes the procession to the cemetery. Martha and Valerie do not emerge from the church until right before we leave. They are escorted by Connor Clarke to the front of the line and disappear in his limousine.

My mother points at a black sedan on the far side of the church parking lot. "Do you believe that?"

Denise and I both stare at the car. "It's Lieutenant Huntington," Denise says.

"He said Hack was a friend—you'd think he would have come inside," my father says.

"I don't think he wanted to confront Martha," my mother says. "She is angry—she has tried to get him to leave her and Valerie alone—but Lieutenant Huntington is pathologically persistent."

"Maybe Hack was pushing him," my father says.

"Unlikely," my mother says. "Apparently, he had a falling out with Hack a month ago. Martha told me that even Hack was getting tired of being pestered by the Lieutenant."

"You'd think he'd have better things to do with his time than take pictures at an event like this," Denise says.

"That man is not right." This is as close as my mother comes to calling someone crazy.

"Jason's disappearance has him at sixes and sevens," my father says.

This term throws both Denise and me. "Six and seven what?" she asks.

My father smiles. "It's an old phrase."

"That's an understatement," my mother says. "It's from Chaucer's *Troylus and Criseyde*—which puts it toward the latter part of the Fourteenth Century. I think it means confused ... at loose ends ... and Lieutenant Huntington is more than that. He is stark, raving ... obsessed.''

My father smiles. ''I have to admit, I kept wondering how they'd handle Jason's disappearance at the funeral. I guess the Lieutenant figured that he might learn something today based on who showed up.'' He hesitates slightly. ''Don't you think it was strange that Jason was not mentioned, even once?''

''I was wondering whether he would show up,'' Denise says. I spin on the back seat and look at my sister as if she has just grown horns. ''What are you looking at, Buddy?''

''Why would you expect him to show up?'' I say.

''I just thought he might,'' she says.

''Jason is a most resourceful boy,'' my mother says. ''I refuse to be pessimistic, particularly today.''

''You think he ran away after dragging Grant halfway across Caulfield County?'' my father asks.

''That's one of many possibilities,'' my mother says. Her voice sharpens slightly. ''But Hack's passing is enough to work on for one day.''

The third and final phase of the funeral takes place at the cemetery. The first event of the day, the reception and viewing at the funeral home, took place without Denise and me. ''It was an open casket event,'' my mother says as we pass hundreds of gravestones, following a long line of cars up a narrow road approaching an area where chairs are lined up in front of a mound of freshly excavated soil. ''When I die, I want you to promise my casket will be closed. This open casket business is just primitive."

"What did his face look like?" Denise asks. My mother shoots her a silencing look but she is not finished. "Did they have him smile?"

"Honestly, Denise," my mother says.

"Somber and at rest," my father says. He knows death—it goes with being a doctor—and his explanation ends the discussion.

The procession stops at the gravesite—just stops cold—right in the middle of a roadway not as wide as our driveway. As we get out, I wonder what will happen if other cars need to get by. I ask Denise and she ignores me.

There are only a few prayers said at the graveside. When the minister finishes, Martha stands, places a white rose on top of Hack Talbot's coffin, and leaves with Valerie and her sisters. They walk from the gravesite to the waiting limousine, led by Connor Clarke who enters on the passenger side and slams the door shut.

"Martha told me that she and Valerie are going to take a trip next month," my mother says. "I think they're going out of the country because she mentioned she had to check and make sure her passport was up to date."

"A long vacation would do both of them a world of good," my father says.

The moment the door is closed on Connor Clarke's black limousine, the Talbot family starts talking, shaking hands, and lighting cigarettes. One of the Talbots opens a small metal container—about the size of a bottle of maple syrup—and takes a long drink.

"That's Luther, Hack's oldest brother," my mother whispers in her golf announcer voice.

"You think he could wait until he got back to the house," my father says. "He is the spitting image of his brother."

"Hack Talbot probably would drink at his brother's funeral," Denise says.

"Really, Denise, I have quite had it," my mother says and heads toward Mr. and Mrs. Cabrera.

As I watch the Clarke limousine leave the cemetery, Hannah and Mickey find me. "This is the first funeral I've been to," Mickey says.

"I went to my grandmother's funeral," Hannah says. "There was a party at our house afterwards. I hated it."

"I remember," I say. "You came up to the baseball field still wearing your dress."

"When my grandmother died, everyone said it was a blessing. She had been sick a long time and was living in a home in New York City." Hannah looks at Mickey and then at me. "Do you remember my grandmother?" she asks.

"Kind of," I say. "She was really small, I remember that."

"I think there is a big difference between dying after you have been sick and just dropping dead," Hannah says. "We were getting ready for my grandmother's death for a long time. Every time we went to visit her, my mother would say, 'Don't complain.

She won't be around forever.' It's like she was dying for about six months and when it was over, she was completely gone. I don't feel that way about Mr. Talbot. I feel like if I turn around, he'll be standing there, smoking a cigarette, holding a drink, yelling at Jason and then joking with all his friends.'' Hannah folds her arms across her chest and shivers.

"My mother and Denise think Jason is still alive,'' I say. "I think that, too. I don't think of him as dying or dropping dead.''

"Did you think he might show up today?'' Hannah asks. Mickey and I both nod.

Driving home from the funeral, Denise asks: "What were your friends talking about, Buddy?''

"The difference between dropping dead and dying.''

"What?'' my mother asks.

"The difference between dropping dead and dying,'' I repeat, knowing this will not be the end of the discussion. Denise and I say 'drop dead' when we fight, usually before one of us gets sent upstairs. Of course we don't mean it, but it bothers my parents and they always make us take it back.

My mother turns slowly to the back seat. "What is the difference, Grant?'' she asks.

"Hannah says when someone drops dead, you keep thinking about them for a long time. It's like they haven't died in a way. That's different from someone who dies after being sick for a long time. Hannah's grandmother died a few years ago and she said as soon as she was dead, she was gone, pretty much."

"Whether expected or not, remember the person who is gone is in a better place," my mother says. "Some theologians see life on earth as a constant storm that waxes and wanes but never goes away. God's hand is always stretched out to pluck you from that storm. Sometimes, He plucks you when you least expect it, and other times you have been bounced around too long and with your last ounce of strength, you reach up and grab on and sail away." I am sure my mother's story is from a sermon she has heard. I am not sure I like the idea of God reaching down, constantly ready to grab you—unless it is an emergency.

"Do you think Jason was plucked up by God?" I ask. I imagine him sliding out of control down the hill by Lone Pine, crashing through the thin ice covering St. Clare Creek and getting swept by the current. Where the ice covers the stream, he is sucked under and cannot breathe. I see him coming up, gasping for breath, but the stream continues to push him and then the ice cover returns and he is pushed down again.

"If something has happened to Jason," my father says, "I have no doubt God plucked him up. If that's the case, by this time he has been reunited with his father."

Denise huffs loudly. "Can we stop talking about this? The whole point of what the minister was saying was to think about life, not death."

I barely hear Denise. I see Jason hurdling along, punching at the ice above him, unable to breathe. I blink my eyes hard. "Why would something happen to Jason and not me?" is all I can say.

"Grant, your sister is right. We should move on to more cheerful topics," my mother says.

My father drives with his right hand and rubs his temple with his left. "While we don't know what happened to Jason, we know what happened to you. Under the worst of circumstances, you walked alone for miles and miles. That takes courage. Give yourself a little credit, son. There aren't many boys your age who could have done that."

As my father speaks, I think of my favorite scene in *The Odyssey*. It is the scene I thought of the day Jason disappeared. Ulysses finally comes home after all of his adventures and is greeted first by his dog and then his son, Telemachus. In the version my mother reads, Telemachus hugs his "marvel of a father." Sometimes I think of my dad that way. I doubt seriously Jason Talbot thinks of his dad that way—and if they are reunited in heaven, I do not think their meeting will be like the reunion between Ulysses and Telemachus.

—

"Have you seen the grandfather before?" Hannah asks. We are in my backyard sitting in the folding aluminum chairs. Hannah adjusts her chair to a reclining position, but I leave the back rest straight so I can look into the woods. Mickey bounces a pink Spalding against the side of the garage, half-listening to the discussion.

"He owns that limousine—it's his car—it isn't like the ones the Talbots rented," Hannah says.

"Who owned what car?" I ask.

"Connor Clarke, the grandfather. Grant, are you listening to me?" I nod and continue to scan the woods for any sign of movement. It is not unusual to see deer passing along the back of our property line late in the afternoon except in hunting season, when they seem to disappear entirely. "Valerie and Jason like him. They call him Grandpop."

"Like who?" I ask.

"The grandfather," Hannah says, exasperated. "The big guy who looked like General Custer." She props herself up on her elbows. "My father told me that he's a millionaire. He bought houses for all of his kids, including the Talbots' house. He is going to pay for college for all of the grandchildren."

Although my gaze is not altered, Hannah has my attention. "Jason once told me his Grandpop had been a soldier and owns factories that make rifles for the government," I say.

"There was a big problem between the grandfather and Mr. Talbot," Hannah says. "The grandfather threw Mr. Talbot right out the front door one night and locked the door so he couldn't get back in. He slept in his car in their garage. The next day, I guess he apologized and Mrs. Talbot let him back in the house after the grandfather left—at least that's what my dad said. The two families, the Talbots and the Clarkes, hate each other. None of them cried," Hannah pauses. "Well, Mrs. Talbot did, but she is pretty emotional."

The ball Mickey has been throwing hits a root in our backyard and rolls past to me. I think about what it is like to pick up a grounder. "I'll be right back," I say. I return with my baseball glove and sit back down in the chair next to Hannah. I put the glove on my lap and scratch my initials in the thumb with my fingernail. The tan leather turns orange as I form the letters. Tiny leather fragments sit upright beneath my touch. This marking will not last. In a week or two, the leather will be perfectly smooth.

Mickey tosses me the pink Spalding and we switch places. As he settles into my chair, I throw the ball against the side of the garage over and over again. I usually catch it with my mitt on the first bounce. To test my ability to throw a curve, I snap my wrist as I throw the ball and it flies off to my left, hits the wall, and rolls to the edge of the woods near Hannah and Mickey. I run down to pick up the ball and freeze. In the leaves, no more than a foot from my hand, is a snake. I see its small eyes and thin fangs. Like me, it is motionless.

I reach down slowly to pick up the ball and the snake strikes. Its teeth find the thin skin between my thumb and my first finger. Hannah jumps and screams—it sounds like a lifeguard's whistle. Mickey takes off for my house.

"There it is!" Hannah hops along the edge of the woods and then does something I am positive neither Mickey nor any of my other friends could do. She leans over and grabs the snake just behind its head. It wriggles as she lifts it up and wraps itself around her arm. She holds it away from her, shrieks just once, and runs to the house.

—

My hand is scrubbed with soap and water and drenched in hydrogen peroxide. My mother wraps an Ace bandage between my wrist and my elbow, and my hand tingles. I lie on the couch, my arm on top of a stack of pillows, and shake. The poisons are in me. It is probably too late for anyone to suck them out. The things I fear most—and that includes snakes—are real.

The driveway is gravel and normally there is a heavy crunching sound when my father gets home. Instead, his car skids, the car door slams and he is in the house, bag in hand, at my side. He unties the Ace bandage and holds my hand up to the light. He makes a few pronouncements regarding the absence of swelling or redness and heads to the garage where Hannah has placed the snake in one of our garbage cans. "It's a garter snake," he says when he comes back in. "A pretty good-sized one." He looks at me. "It isn't poisonous."

"What about rabies?" my mother asks. Hannah and Mickey hang on every word.

My father turns and looks at her. "Very unlikely. We have the snake. We can keep an eye on it for the next few days. I'll give Davis a call." Davis Heck is the local veterinarian. Once, when he and my father were ushers in church on the same day, the minister commented it was finally safe in the church for both man and beast.

I hear my father on the phone and his voice is reassuring. There is even a soft laugh at the end of the discussion and I know, as he comes back into the living room, that things will be fine. He may not be a marvel of a father, like Ulysses, but he makes me safe. He has always made me safe.

The snake bite lasts longer than my scratched initials on my baseball glove, but by April Fool's Day, the two tiny dots are gone. My arms are just beginning to tan and spring has arrived.

– 14 –

April 1959

Four months without Jason has generated wild speculation about what might have happened. Everyone has a different theory. There is one matter on which every DeWitt Street parent is in agreement—the woods are out of bounds. Something about them is just too unsafe. Despite this absolute rule, Mickey, Hannah and I have decided to try and find Jason. I lost him—and they will help me find him.

We have a good plan but little time. By mid-April, St. Clare and Willis Creek flood, making walking impossible and the snakes take control of their domain. We have been planning this rescue— or disobedience, as my mother would say—for weeks. We do not spend much time talking about what will happen if we get caught. Instead, most of our discussion now involves snakes. I've been bitten once—Hannah and Mickey were there—and the woods are full of snakes.

The black snakes, lacking venom, are scary but nothing compared to the water moccasins and copperheads, and copperheads are not limited to the flooded fields. They wait in hiding throughout the woods. We anticipate this mortal threat and pose the problem to Mrs. Simeone, our teacher at Livingston Elementary. Her reassurance is limited. "They're more afraid of you than you are of them. Just don't disturb one, particularly a mama, near her nest. Snake mothers will attack to save their babies."

Unfortunately, Hannah notes as we leave Mrs. Simeone, copperheads do not post signs saying "Home Sweet Home—100 writhing poisonous babies inside."

We also explore the topic with my father. "Copperhead bites are not always fatal," he says as if this is good news. "If a person is bitten by a snake, the first thing to do is to get medical help. The victim should stay quiet and the area bitten should be elevated. If help is delayed, it may be necessary to extract the venom from the wound. Use a sharp clean knife, cut directly between the two points where the fangs went in and then suction the venom from the wound."

"We read about that," Mickey says. "What I don't get is how you keep from dying if you suck in the snake's poison." We turn to my father.

"This is the one time where I would encourage you to spit, not between your two front teeth, the way I see you doing, Grant, but mightily, expelling everything in your mouth."

"Won't some of the poison stick to your lips and the inside of your gums and your cheek and then slowly seep into your body and kill you?" Hannah asks.

"Unlikely," my father says. "Poison injected in the veins presents a greater risk than poison temporarily in one's mouth."

My father lets the information sink in and finally asks, "Have you seen snakes near the ball field or at the edge of the woods?" We shake our heads. "So why the concern? Are you doing a school project?" We shake our heads again. My father looks at me carefully and then glances at Mickey and Hannah. "Have you been playing in the woods?"

"No," I say. I knew I'd have to lie. I just didn't think I would have to lie before we started our search.

We leave my father and go to Hannah's garage where we have hidden our supplies. Hannah has found binoculars and I manage to take the map left at our house by Lieutenant Huntington. Mickey is supposed to find a knife—as I guessed, Jason's hunting knife was confiscated almost immediately. Once the garage door is closed, we take out our contraband and begin, once again, to talk about the night Jason disappeared. It is a familiar discussion and after a time, Mickey says: "What about the private detective the Talbots hired? Did he ever find anything?"

The Talbots' private detective visited us a number of times, asking me to make lines on a map with my finger, just as Lieutenant Huntington did. He made similar visits to everyone in the neighborhood. "I never figured the private detective would come up with much. He was a talker," I say, repeating my mother's critique, "and he wasn't very private. He's the one who spilled the beans about Mr. Talbot supposedly stealing money at work.''

"My dad says he was an embezzler,'' Mickey says. ''That's what you call someone who steals at work.'' He hesitates. ''Still, the detective was here a long time and tried to find Jason and Lone Pine—if he couldn't, why do you think we can?''

"Because Grant was there,'' Hannah says. ''That's all I need to know.''

—

Early on the first Saturday in April, we are ready. With Little League still a week away, my mother asks few questions before I leave. ''We want to see if we can play fifty innings,'' I say. The baseball marathon I describe explains the sandwiches and canteen. I leave with my mitt under my arm. After I am out the door, I go into the garage and place my mitt behind a snow shovel and then walk down the driveway.

The ground is partly frozen when we enter the woods, the surface a mix of puffy dirt and ice columns that crunch when you walk on them. We cross two undeveloped wooded lots with ''For Sale'' signs on each. New houses will be built here, my father has said, and the builder is asking $31,000 for each. My mother is convinced no one will pay such an outrageous price for a home on DeWitt Street.

This is a risky trip, but things have been hard since Jason disappeared. Hannah told us she has a diary where she writes down all the horrible accusations made by Lieutenant Huntington and that one day, he will be sorry he was not nicer to me and my family. Mickey and I both asked—pretty much at the same moment—if we could see her diary and both ended up with small black and blue marks on our arms. Hannah has a deadly knuckle punch.

We are well past the rear property line of the vacant lots and at long last back in the woods. Somewhere, an unknown number of miles away, there is Lone Pine, the shelter, and maybe even Jason.

It is easy going for the first hour. I try to follow the route I took with Lieutenant Huntington, down a series of small hills and across the fields, but it is spring and everything looks different. We emerge from a patch of dark woods and are in a field where the brown grasses have begun to green. About halfway across the field, Hannah climbs a grass mound and, using binoculars, surveys the terrain. "I see woods, no matter which direction I look. No ruins at Stone House Corners, no Cedar Dome Mountain ... no giant pine," she reports and steps down from the mound. "Look at the map with me."

As we kneel and study the map, Hannah opens the compass, by far the best piece of equipment we managed to squirrel away for this journey. It is not as nice as Lieutenant Huntington's—it looks like a cheap watch with a thin tin bottom, a scratched plastic face and a wobbly pointer that gets confused if we move the compass quickly. If we wait long enough, however, it settles down and points in one direction.

"This is where we came in," I say. "This is my house. These are the vacant lots. Hannah's house is here, and Mickey's is here. This way," I say, "is west." I have finally mastered my directions.

"How far have we gone?" asks Mickey.

"Maybe this far," I say putting my finger about two inches below the vacant lots.

"If Lone Pine is at the center of the map," Hannah says, "and we're here, then we should head this way."

The woods on the far side of the field are unpleasant. Bushes and branches are everywhere, many of them covered with vines. It is hard to find a place to walk without climbing over something. Everything about this place is damp. Mickey steps on a rock that sticks through the leaves and it flips over revealing dank earth that is home to gray-red worms and centipedes. We pick up the pace.

It is a long walk just to get out of the soggy woods and after a few steps, the earth turns soft—then slushy—then downright saturated and our sneakers are soaked even though they are high-tops. The ground sucks at our feet, letting go with a whoosh. There is standing water an inch or two deep in most places and large mounds made entirely of grasses that move when we try to stand on them. We splash forward, pants wet above the knees, run through the last few yards of swamp and are back in an elevated section of forest. "Is this where you and Jason went?" Mickey asks.

"I have no idea," I say. "At one point, Jason said we were in swamp territory—it went on for a long way. I can't tell if this is it."

"Does it look like this?"

"Quit asking," I say. "I'll tell you if I recognize anything."

The next section of woods is easier going. There are fewer bushes and branches in our way and at one point we find what appears to be a path. I expect it will take us through to the end of this section of woods but it stops unexpectedly at a pile of rocks about as tall as a snowplow.

"West is right over the top of the rock pile," Hannah says. "Maybe the path picks up on the other side." We begin a wide arc around the pile stepping over rocks the size of basketballs when Mickey screams: "Snake!"

"Where?" Hannah shrieks, standing on her tip-toes.

Mickey yells again and falls to the ground.

We are at his side and watch as he pulls up his pant leg exposing a single ugly red mark in the center of his hairless shin. "Oh—ow—shit, shit. Shit!" Mickey covers the red spot and grits his teeth.

"What did it look like, Mick," Hannah asks. She has already put her hands around Mickey's calf and is squeezing hard. Hannah is all business. She holds the leg, just like my father instructed, and looks carefully at Mickey. She knows what to do.

"I didn't see it," Mickey says. "I just felt it. Bang."

Hannah leans forward. "Let me look." She leans forward. "I just see one red mark, not two."

I am on my knees, my face no more than six inches from Mickey's leg. "There is a red spot—and a dark red point in the middle." One of us has to suck the poison. I am the one who lost Jason—it should be me. As soon as I suck the bite, I will get help. This time, I will get it right. I will not let down my friend.

"Don't touch it," Mickey says. "It will release more poison."

"You need to lie still," Hannah says. She has not released her hands.

"How am I going to get to a doctor?" Mickey says. "How can you get to a doctor and lie still at the same time?" This was a question my father's lecture never answered.

I stare at the red mark which is growing larger by the minute. "Did you see the snake before it bit you?"

"I saw the leaves move," Mickey says pointing at where I am sitting, "then I felt this bite." He sits up. "It could still be here."

"It was right here? Where I am?" I start to stand and the leaves next to me move. Hannah jumps and Mickey pushes himself backwards. The movement stops. "You've got to get up," I whisper. "It's still here."

"I'm not supposed to move," Mickey whispers.

"There should be two holes," Hannah says.

"Maybe one fang got through his dungarees and the other one didn't," I say.

Mickey looks at me and then at Hannah. He picks up a handful of leaves and small sticks and throws it at the area where we saw the snake move and nothing happens. Quickly, Hannah and I pelt the area with sticks, leaves, and dirt. Despite our relentless bombardment, there is no movement. I grab a large stick and start to push the leaves right where the snake has been lying, motionless. All I find is a long, curved branch just below the surface. "I'll bet you stepped on this," I say.

"The stick didn't bite me, doofus," Mickey says. He unrolls his dungarees and we discover in the soggy fold of his pants a large, dead wasp.

– 15 –

At the far side of the rock pile, we reconnect with the path and follow it until we hit a flooded field. We are close to Willis Creek—or St. Clare—maybe. Clumps of pussy willow blossom on cluster islands and a weeping willow grows on a ridge in the middle of the flood plain. If there are water moccasins in our woods, this is where they will be. We walk along the edge of the field. It goes without saying that this is an impassable barrier—and stop at a maple tree, its pointy leaves and sticky winged seeds already formed.

"I want to see where we are," Hannah says. "I'm going up. Help me." Mickey clasps his hands together like a stirrup and hoists Hannah, who puts her sneaker on top of my head to push upward. Between the three of us, she makes it to the first section of branches. She pauses as she stands on the branch and pants—tree climbing is hard work. She pulls herself to the second tier of branches, again stopping to get her breath before she moves on.

When she is twenty feet off the ground, Mickey yells: "Use the binoculars."

Hannah takes them in one hand, hugs the trunk of the tree with the other, and curls her body around the tree so she can look west. Mickey waits only a second before he yells: "See anything?"

"Swamp." Hannah continues to look. "Trees on the other side."

"Look down that way," Mickey says, pointing south. Hannah twists back, continuing to hold the tree with one arm.

"All I see are the trees," Hannah says. "I'm coming down. There is nothing but woods."

—

"Was it easy to see the shelter once you found Lone Pine?" Mickey asks after Hannah is back on the ground.

"No way," I say. "It's dug in the side of the hill. You could walk right by the door and never know it was there, unless you knew where to look. I wasn't going to tell anyone about it and now I've told just about everyone." Mickey opens his canteen. Hannah and I do the same. "Do you believe me?" I ask.

"Of course," Hannah says.

Hannah and I look at Mickey. Finally, Mickey says: "Are you telling the truth?"

"I swear to God," I say.

"If you and Jason hadn't found Lone Pine and made the fire, you would have frozen to death,"

Hannah says. "It was one of those things. That's what I think."

"What things?" Mickey asks.

Hannah smiles at Mickey. "You're teasing me," she says.

We finish what's left of our sandwiches and Hannah turns to me. "Let's go home, Grant."

"It'll be a long time before the fields are dry. Promise you'll go back with me?" They both nod.

We make no effort to backtrack on the path that runs through the woods, unwilling to risk another attack by wasps or worse. As we emerge from the woods, what lies ahead is a completely dry field with grasses that seem like wheat. The next minute we are running and I hear Hannah laugh as she pulls ahead of Mickey and me.

Running takes away the stiffness and we walk through the next section of woods, stretching our legs, expanding the length of our steps. An hour later we arrive at the base of a steep incline. As I look up it, the image comes to mind of Lieutenant Huntington sliding by on his stomach. We start to climb and are halfway up the hill when it hits me: I've never been here before. "I was at places like this the day after Jason disappeared—but not his place."

Hannah looks at the compass and checks her watch. "We'll be home before five," she says.

—

My mother asks how our baseball game went the minute I walk into the house. "It was pretty good," I say.

"Your sister went to find you about an hour ago. She went up to the field and you weren't there."

"We were probably looking for a ball," I say. "Mickey hit some really long ones."

My mother looks at me and raises her eyebrows. "I think your sister would have seen you if you were at the far end of the field." I say nothing. "Where were you, Grant?"

That did not take long. "We were just walking around," I answer. I've already taken off my sneakers and socks.

"How'd you get your feet wet?" my mother asks. "The field is bone dry."

Confession comes slowly and I await the consequences, but none are announced.

By May, I surrender my dungarees and put on shorts after school. Wild horses could not get me to wear shorts to school, no matter how hot it gets.

– 16 –

August 1959

Nine months and still no explanation for Jason's disappearance.

Mickey and I walk up DeWitt Street, trying to stay off the fresh tar and pebbles deposited by a Caulfield County road crew. The spattered weeds on the side of the road whip my ankles, leaving streaks. I have black stains on the bottom and sides of my sneakers. Were Hannah here, the soles of her feet would be black—she goes barefoot more than any kid I know.

Mickey nudges a tar bubble with a stick. "It has to be 200 degrees out here," he says, his voice melting in with the buzz of overheated insects. "Hannah's family picked a good week to be away. I asked my dad if we were going on vacation this year since it was so hot. He told me that this was like a spring day in Havana."

"Do you remember Cuba?" I ask. "Was it really this hot?"

"I remember a small canal that was not far from our house," Mickey says. "At night, we would take folding chairs and a picnic supper and watch the barges." He picks up a tar-coated pebble and throws it across the road. "Sometimes I think I remember Cuba, but other times I'm not sure whether it's a real memory or a story I heard about the way things were when I was little."

"You can always tell the difference between something you remember and a story someone has told you," I say. "Either you remember it or you don't."

"Not always," Mickey says. "You don't remember everything that happened the day you went in the woods with Jason."

"I know the difference between things that happened and things people said," I say. "It's too hot to talk about that, anyway."

We pass Hannah's house, a white Cape Cod with green shutters and a basketball hoop over the garage door. Hannah and her family have driven to Keene Valley, where they will stay in a small bungalow on Lake Porter. With the exception of the Talbots, none of the families on DeWitt Street can afford fancy vacations, and a few days adjacent to a freezing mountain lake is considered a luxury. A month after Jason disappeared, my mother started talking about the need to get away this summer. For reasons not shared with me, no vacation plans were made and, like Mickey, I am stuck here next to bubbling tar.

Mickey and I play flies-up for hours and any thought I had about the absence of the ability to sweat is gone. By three in the afternoon, we are caked in sweat and dust—and every part of me itches.

Mickey cuts across his front lawn retreating to the shelter of his cool basement. I am halfway down the street when Martha Talbot flies by in her big black sedan spraying me with tarry pebbles, leaving slick jet-black skid marks in the road in front of the Talbots' house. As Denise would say, Martha "peeled out" . . . and left the front door of her home wide open.

I stop and listen after each step toward their door, standing on the stairs a long time before I walk into the entranceway. I look down the hallway into the kitchen—and it is neat. The hallway closet, jammed full nine months ago, contains just a few coats. I walk back outside and close their front door. Mrs. Talbot would not want to come home and have squirrels running around her kitchen—that can happen if you leave the door open.

The Talbots' garage holds three cars and all three doors are in the up position. I recognize the array of hand and power tools on the bench at the rear of the garage. These belonged to the late Mr. Talbot and were not to be used by Jason—yet when we built forts or tree platforms, Jason always had a hammer, a saw, and pockets full of nails, secured without consent. Always, we were sworn to secrecy.

Instead of its usual place on the floor, Jason's bicycle hangs from a hook on the garage wall, the kick-stand tucked under the chain. As I reach up to touch the tires—they look flat—the back door of the garage blasts open. I am smothered in arms before I can turn, my face rammed into the folds of a sweaty stomach. I suck in air through my nose and smell the whiskey and the toothpaste.

I kick, grab a handful of pants, twist, but my head is locked, the hands iron. I get one foot on the wall, just below Jason's bike, but as I push, I am lifted in the air by my head. I am biting, trying to scream, trying to breathe—and then slammed to the floor of the garage. My scream does not exist as iron hands drag me across the garage and through the back door.

"Keep your mouth shut or I'll break your neck." The whiskey smell is stronger than the toothpaste. His knee is in the center of my spine and his hand on the back of my head pushes my face in the dirt. "Don't say anything till I tell you and don't move your head."

The knee in my back makes crying impossible. "You just walk into someone else's house?" the voice says.

I try to say the words, "I'm sorry," but cannot speak.

I move my head trying to get my mouth away from the grass and sticks. "Keep your face down and stop that goddamned crying." The knee on my back moves lower, more on my behind, an arm presses my chest and neck. "You tell me what happened to Jason or so help me God you'll never go home."

"I . . . we. . . ." I have to stop crying but can't.

"Is he dead?"

I try to move my shoulders but the forearm keeps me from gesturing. "Don't know," I manage to say.

"Who took him?"

"No one," I say.

"Don't you lie to me, you little shit. You tell me—what happened to that boy?"

"I don't know. He left . . . I never saw him again."

His fist is on the back of my head, his fingers pull my hair and scalp so that my eyes close. "I'm going to give you one last chance and then so help me God. . . ."

"I don't know. . . ."

A truck goes up DeWitt Street but does not stop. A second car passes, more pressure is on the back of my head—my nose is full of dirt. "You say one word, and I'll find you again," he says. "You stay right here. Don't move, not your head, not your legs, not your hands, nothing. Count to 500 before you move one muscle. I'm watching.''

I feel the knee come off of my back and the hand move from the back of my head. ''One word about today, one mention of this to anyone and I'll pick off your parents like tin cans on a split rail fence—BANG! You understand what I'm saying?''

I nod my head and I feel the hand again. ''I told you not to move. Just answer, you understand what I'm saying?''

''I understand,'' my words a shaky whisper.

''Like tin cans on a split rail fence—WHAM! Not one word. Now start counting so I can hear you.''

''One ... two ... three....''

''That's good—I'll be watching—you keep counting.''

I am at eight when I hear the back door of the garage close. I peel my face from the ground, turn and look through the window of that door. I see the back of his head—a crew cut, a sweaty neck. I am on my knees watching as he walks quickly, not quite a run, down the driveway. He wears loafers, no socks, khaki pants and a white tee shirt and moves in a way that I recognize: it is just like Hack Talbot.

I am at sixty-three when I hear a car start off in the distance and one-hundred-and-six when I hear it drive up the street, but I do not move. I start a new count, this time to sixty, and then stand. I brush away dirt and grasses from my clothes and face. There is no breeze to cool me, yet I am shaking, like I have been walking barefoot on the ice—and it must be 200 degrees.

I am in a wild run, arms and legs pumping, down the street, through the kitchen door and into the bathroom. There is not much there when I throw up but it burns my throat. I keep the water running so no one will hear. I use soap and water to clean my face and arms. I can leave no trace. Hack Talbot can shoot tin cans on a split rail fence—he has a rifle—and he can kill anyone.

Hack Talbot is also buried in the cemetery, nailed inside a coffin. My father pronounced him dead in the hospital and both my parents saw him at the viewing. Yet Hack Talbot and I made a deal—as long as I do not talk about this, as long as I make sure that no one ever learns he is alive, my parents will be safe.

—

I close the door to my room and turn on the small electric fan, more for noise than the heat. I stand so that the wind will blow on my face and say quietly: "Nothing happened. Nothing happened. Nothing happened. Nothing happened."

– 17 –

October 1959

Lieutenant Huntington is at our front door, subpoena in hand. A grand jury is being convened, he explains, and I will finally have to answer questions under oath about Jason's disappearance. Although my name is on the front of the legal document he holds, the Lieutenant understands he must deal with my mother. "You have no choice in the matter, Mrs. Harper. The District Attorney made this decision and we will enforce the subpoena if Grant does not appear."

"You know perfectly well Grant did everything he could to help find Jason. Having him appear in front of a grand jury and answer the same questions he's been asked for months is pointless," she says.

"The District Attorney believes he can get a more complete picture of the situation using the power of the grand jury. I'd guess you are uncomfortable with these proceedings—but that's your problem," the Lieutenant says.

"Uncomfortable?" My mother's voice is clear and angry. "Dragging Grant—and Valerie and Martha Talbot—in front of a grand jury? For what? No one is hiding anything, Lieutenant."

"When this began last December, Jason's file was labeled a 'lost child' file. A few weeks later, it was changed to read: 'disappeared under suspicious circumstances.' Some of your neighbors suspect an abduction or a kidnapping by his own father—but Hack's death caused that label to be removed from the file, and Jason became a missing person. This summer, his file was tagged a suspected homicide. It's the job of the state to investigate homicides. If Jason were your son, I think you would understand."

"Really, Lieutenant, did Martha Talbot greet the subpoena with pleasure?" My mother stops to catch her breath.

"That is none of your affair," the Lieutenant says. "I'm just delivering the subpoena."

The "don't murder the messenger" defense does not play well with my mother. "You are the one changing these labels on Jason's file, Lieutenant. You have an unsolved disappearance on your hands and you know darn well that Grant has done everything humanly possible to find Jason." She turns to me as she continues to blister Lieutenant Huntington. "Disobeying our very clear rules, Grant, Hannah, and Mickey have gone into the woods over and over again trying to find Jason. They have not been punished—as yet—because we understand that they're confused and as desperate as we are to come to some kind of understanding about Jason's disappearance. The problem is, Lieutenant, they, like everyone else, are at a loss."

This is not a moment to deny the obvious. I am better off keeping quiet and listening to Lieutenant Huntington battle with my mother. She will protect me and not put herself in jeopardy. She does not know that I broke into the Talbots' house in August and got caught, that the person who caught me was so angry that he said he would shoot her and my father like tin cans on a split rail fence—so she cannot bring up the topic with Lieutenant Huntington. All I have to do is stay with my plan—nothing happened—and everyone will be fine. So long as this investigation is all about Jason, I can do whatever I am asked and no one will be hurt.

"I've been back into those goddamned woods a dozen different times," Lieutenant Huntington says. "It's part of the reason the grand jury is being convened. The woods we searched cover an area roughly five by six miles, or thirty square miles. I can't say with confidence we covered all of it, and I realize that there are things that might have happened that would keep us from finding Jason, but at this point I am sure of one thing: we have ruled out coincidence—accidents—innocent events. Whatever happened to that boy was the result of intention. Either he left . . . or was killed."

The comment silences my mother. Finally she says, "Just what do you hope to accomplish in some stuffy courtroom miles from here? Do you think my son will suddenly remember something? Be honest for once—you know that won't happen. There is nothing more for him to recall. This, Lieutenant, is about you—and I guess the District Attorney—you are looking for someone to blame—and disgusting as it sounds, you are focused on a ten-year-old child who has done nothing but help you."

Lieutenant Huntington manages to get the door open wide enough to hand the subpoena to my mother. "Gerr-annt," he says, stretching my name out, "you won't have to go to school the day you give your testimony."

I look at my mother and it is clear that if I smile at this news, I will pay a price.

—

At the recommendation of Mickey's father, Juan Cabrera, a man my parents respect greatly, we hire Edwin Barkman, a prominent Albany lawyer. Just how Mickey's father makes these connections is known to my mother and father but not to me. I know Mr. Cabrera commutes to the capital nearly every day—and that's about it.

When my grandmother (who, as I understand it, is paying Mr. Barkman) raises some doubt about the referral, my father says: "Juan Cabrera knows the legal system inside and out. If he says Edwin Barkman is the right man, I believe him."

Attorney Edwin Barkman has dinner with us a few days after Lieutenant Huntington's visit. My mother believes that there is little to be gained by going to his office, particularly since I would have to miss more school. He tells us that it is most unusual to question children before a grand jury but that it happens from time to time and that I should be truthful in my responses.

"Will we be able to stay with Grant during the grand jury proceedings?" my mother asks Mr. Barkman.

"As a general rule, no one is permitted in the grand jury room other than the grand jurors, the prosecutor and the witness. We can wait in the hallway and if Grant wants to speak with us, he can ask to do so and they'll excuse him."

My mother sets down her fork. "You can't have a lawyer present in a grand jury proceeding?" she asks.

"So says the United States Supreme Court."

"This is just outrageous," my mother says. "Grant is going to be alone, facing the District Attorney, stared at by people he doesn't know, answering questions about Jason's disappearance?" She turns to my father. "We have to do something about this."

My father shakes his head. "Grant has nothing to hide. So long as he tells the truth, he will be fine." He looks at me: "I promise—nothing will happen to you." I notice Edwin Barkman raise his eyebrows as my father continues. "You know you can trust me—I give you my word."

My father's reassurance stays with me throughout the rest of the meal. I know he can protect me from the grand jury. I have no doubt about that. Whether I will be smart enough to stay quiet—stay with my plan of silence—and protect him from being picked off like a tin can on a split rail fence is a different question.

Before Mr. Barkman leaves, he asks if I have any questions. We have already gone over how long this will take and what questions I am likely to be asked.

"Will they ask me about anything else?" I ask.

"You mean other than Jason?" Mr. Barkman asks.

"Anything about this summer?"

"You mean whether you and your friends disobeyed your parents and went looking for Jason?" my mother asks. I nod.

"This grand jury has a mission, Grant. They're going to try to understand what happened to Jason. I doubt they will be interested in much beyond that." Edwin Barkman shakes my hand. "This too will pass," he says.

"Can Hannah and Mickey get out of school and come with me?" I ask.

"I don't think their parents would allow that," our lawyer says.

"I'll ask them, Grant," my mother says.

———

Unlike the preparation provided by Edwin Barkman, which does not put me all that much at ease, the grand jury game Hannah invents is a success. The day before I have to appear, we make our own grand jury room in Mickey's basement, based on the lawyer's description of what I will find in the Caulfield County Courthouse. Hannah is the prosecutor, Mickey the grand juror, and I am the witness. Hannah asks me to put my hand on a stack of *Classics Illustrated*, promise not to lie, and we begin.

After questions about the route we took to get to Lone Pine, none of which I can answer, Hannah asks: "Was it snowing when Jason got lost?"

"No, but it was cold and windy. I remember I thought it might snow."

This answer prompts Hannah to say: "Ah ha!" and begin to pace.

"Ask something," Mickey says, his interest in the game waning.

"I'm about to," Hannah snaps. She turns to me: "How long were you inside the shelter—after Jason left or got lost or...."

"I don't know. I think maybe ten minutes," I say.

"Why did you wait so long to look for Jason?" Mickey asks.

"I'm the prosecutor," Hannah says indignantly. "I'm the one who asks the questions." She turns to me. "What did you do in the shelter before you left to look for Jason?"

"I set up the firewood the way he asked and then looked around inside the shelter. Remember those cans of sardines I told you about?"

"You said there was some kind of stew," Mickey says before Hannah can get out her next question.

"Hunter's stew," I reply. Hannah ignores both of us.

"Did Jason tell you he was running away?" she asks, after a long silence. When I shake my head, she asks: "What did he say when he left the shelter?"

"I can't remember, Hannah."

"You are supposed to call me 'sir,' " Hannah says. As she paces back and forth, Mickey mumbles that she is imitating a TV lawyer. She shoots him a withering glance and he is silent. "I want to know about the thing that moved in the woods. What was it?"

"Something brown," I say. "I don't know what it was."

"A deer?"

"I don't know," I say.

"If it wasn't a deer, did you see what it was?" she asks.

"No. I started to walk to where I thought it was, but decided it wasn't there anymore so I turned around and stayed close to Lone Pine for awhile."

"Why didn't you chase it?" Mickey asks.

"Mickey, I'm the prosecutor!" Hannah says angrily.

"It was probably a deer," I say.

While Hannah asks me about deer for several minutes, focused particularly on fawn that have white spots when they are babies, Mickey starts to whistle "Take Me Out to the Ball Game," and I can tell our grand jury is about to come to an end.

"I wish I could be there with you," Hannah says as we head upstairs. "I would love to see a grand jury."

—

I get home from Mickey's and our front door is wide open. We keep our door unlocked but closed at all times. This is a family rule Denise and I observe faithfully, although I have wondered what it would be like to have squirrels in the kitchen—the apparent dreaded consequence of leaving the door wide open. I know my father is at the hospital and Denise and my mother are in Haydon buying groceries. I go upstairs and the door to my room is closed. It was open when I left this morning.

"Mom?" No answer. "Dad?" No answer.

I open the door and there, on the window sill by my desk, are two tin cans, each shot straight through, leaving sharp metal sticking out on one side where the bullet went on its way, barely slowed by the solid metal sides of the can.

I have no time to cry—these must be hidden.
The secret meeting with Hack Talbot has to be
protected. I open the lid of an almost full garbage
can in the garage, pull out several paper bags of
kitchen trash, put the dead tin cans in the bottom,
return the bags to make sure the cans are covered,
and run to Hannah's house.

"Grant, come in. Hannah is in the kitchen—do
you want something cold to drink?" Mrs. Weiner
asks as I stand at the door. I nod and go inside and
find Hannah.

"Want to play the grand jury game some
more?" she asks as I walk in. I cannot talk—it is
like being out of breath, but I am not winded. I am
shaking and all my insides are vibrating.

"Here, Grant," Mrs. Weiner says as she hands
me a glass of Kool Aid. "Drink something. You look
so hot."

After a few sips, I give it a try. "I...."

The crying starts and Mrs. Weiner sits next to
me. "You poor child. So much has happened. This
grand jury will be over before you know it."

Even if I could get a breath, even if I could stop
this stupid crying, I would not tell her what is really
on my mind. I will not tell anybody. Ever.

—

I understand the questions from Hannah much
more easily than the questions asked by the real
District Attorney before the grand jury—but neither he nor Hannah ask about the day I broke into
the Talbots'—and I am grateful and relieved.

Despite all of the fears of my parents, appearing before the grand jury turns out to be no different than being questioned by Lieutenant Huntington. I'm asked to tell the story of our hike to Lone Pine, Jason's disappearance, and my rescue by the plow driver. After I finish the entire tale, the District Attorney tells me he has just a few more questions.

"Grant, I want you to think for a moment if there is anything about that day that you have not discussed, particularly something that would suggest Jason planned on running away—or perhaps meeting up with someone else after he left Lone Pine."

I give the same answer that I gave to Lieutenant Huntington months ago: "Jason said he wanted to get away from his house before we left, but he never said he would run away. If he was going to run away, why did he bring me with him?"

"That's a good question, Grant."

As the District Attorney shakes his head sympathetically, it hits me. "Jason had Almond Joy candy bars in his backpack. We ate two of them, but there were at least four more in the pack. He told me they were like vegetables on the inside. We each ate one and then he said that we had to ration them for the rest of our trip."

"You said earlier that there was food in the shelter at Lone Pine. Do you know if Jason took any of the food before he went outside to clear the smoke vent?" the District Attorney asks.

"I don't think he did. I don't think he took his backpack with him."

"Do you remember seeing his backpack as you walked around looking for Jason before you headed home?" he asks.

"I don't remember, sir," I say. "I think it was still on the ground, near the door, but I'm not sure."

"But you're sure that there were several candy bars in the pack?" he says.

"Positive," I say. "Almond Joy."

The District Attorney closes a large notebook that sits on the table in front of him. "Grant, thank you for being so helpful. It sounds to me like Jason might have been thinking about running away. That would explain why he took some extra food with him. Why he brought you along, why he left in such a hurry is something we may never know."

"Am I going to have to come back here again?" I ask.

"That depends on what we hear from some of the other witnesses, but at this point I would guess that this investigation is going to come to a close."

—

My parents, Hannah, Mickey, and Edwin Barkman greet me as I walk into the corridor leaving the District Attorney and the grand jury behind me.

"You ask better questions than the District Attorney," I say to Hannah.

Hannah smiles. "I'm going to be a lawyer when I grow up," she says.

"You'll be a force to be reckoned with, Hannah," my father says.

We sit on a bench near the door of the grand jury room and I try to remember the questions I was asked and the answers I gave. "In the end, the only thing they seemed to be interested in was the Almond Joy candy bars in Jason's backpack."

"Well, I guess that makes all this worthwhile." Apparently this is a man's joke because Mr. Barkman and my father laugh and my mother looks disgusted.

"The District Attorney says this is probably the end of the investigation," I say.

"That would be a blessing," my mother says.

– 18 –

November 1959

It is six weeks short of a year since Jason disappeared and Valerie Talbot is home for the first time since her father died. Denise helps her carry suitcases from the house to the car and brings home the news that a "For Sale" sign is in the Talbots' front yard. Within the month the large house with its color television and once overflowing closets is sold. A moving van takes up almost the entire driveway and is there for a full day. All the worldly goods of the Talbots are boxed, labeled, and then disappear inside the truck.

No more tin cans are left in my room and there is no sign of the ghost of Hack Talbot—anywhere. I am on the front porch when the van rolls down DeWitt Street headed, as my father would say, for parts unknown. Much as Jason simply vanished at Lone Pine, the Talbots are gone.

Part Two

IN SCHOOL

—

Five Years Later
March 1964
– 19 –

Mickey is the only high school sophomore to make the varsity baseball team. During the one week tryout, we do not speculate about this possibility. Mickey and I have always been on the same team and now we will be in separate practices, and, depending on the schedule, coming home at different times.

Along with Hannah, we have walked home together on DeWitt Street for ten years, heading to and from the bus stop. Last year, during baseball season, Mickey and I started walking all the way from school to our homes, a 45 minute trek, the last two miles adjacent to the woods. This change in our normal patterns required Hannah to walk home with Denise, activating a deeper friendship between them—and initiating an exchange of gossip about Mickey and me, none of which Hannah will share.

There is one long stretch of DeWitt Street on which no houses have been built. When Hannah, Mickey and I pass this area, we search for squirrel, deer, rabbit, and an occasional hawk. For the next few months, there will be times when I will make this walk alone.

On these long afternoon walks, whether alone or with Hannah and Mickey, I am never far from the thought that something happened in those woods five years ago that I cannot explain. Somehow, Jason disappeared and Lone Pine itself became invisible.

—

On a warm Friday in mid-April, the varsity team has an away game and the JV a home game. I leave school an hour before the varsity bus will return. It is after five when I come to the long uninhabited section of DeWitt Street adjacent to the woods. A dump truck rumbles by and I step off the road into the weeds as it approaches, walk a few feet into the woods, and stop. At first, there is just the sound of rustling leaves. After a few minutes, the birds and squirrels that froze as I entered their world relax. In this moment of silence, I am part of the forest.

—

"How was the game?" my mother asks as I walk through the door.

"We lost," I say.

"I'm sorry." She is smart enough not to say, "I'm sure you did fine." I appreciate her restraint.

"I was thinking about Jason this afternoon," I say.

"Do you want to talk about it?" my mother asks. "You haven't mentioned him in a while." When I do not reply, my mother fills in the silence. "That reminds me, I got a letter from Martha the other day. She sounded happy. She visited Valerie in Colorado—they had a great time together." Valerie is in college, but she and Denise still talk on the phone every now and then. My mother sits down next to me. "I'd be happy to pick you up after practice—it's no fun walking all that way alone."

"I like walking," I say. "It helps me think about things."

"I have no doubt," my mother says. "I finish up at the clerk's office around 4:30. It would be easy for me to come and get you."

—

Three years ago, my mother started working at the office of the county clerk. She worked for a real estate title company before marrying my father and, as he tells it, the government was lucky to find her. Her job has meant extra income and I am less worried about the cost of college—and after that, law school.

There is no question about my career plans—like Hannah, I intend to become an attorney-at-law. While Hannah laid claim to the legal profession the day of the grand jury hearing, the thought entered my mind months earlier during the New Year's Eve campout with my sister. That night, Denise told me I should not worry—the legal system will protect me. I held on to that assurance throughout the year. I also realized that without competent lawyers—like Mr. Barkman—the system will not work.

———

"I really don't need a ride home," I say to my mother. "I'll let you know if I change my mind."

"The problem is your mind," my mother says. I hear concern in her voice. "You dwell on things. With the exception of Mickey and Hannah, I don't have a sense that you talk to very many people and I'm concerned about it."

"I talk to a lot of people at school. I just don't tell you about it."

———

I have not let my mother in on my private life, particularly when it comes to girls. It is not that I am uninterested—I had a girlfriend for a few months, Patty Heck, the veterinarian's daughter. That romance ended mutually last month and I do not think either of us was heartbroken. Patty was interested in making sure her grades were high enough to get into UCLA, apparently based on her never-ending war with her parents about whom Patty said: "Three thousand miles of separation is barely enough." She talked about school, who was dating whom, upcoming parties—and while I share those interests, my thoughts are more often about baseball—both major league and our high school teams—and the woods. Patty said more than once that the woods are for kids—I will not miss her much.

While we no longer build forts or pretend we are frontier explorers, Hannah, Mickey, and I still spend time in the woods. There are those occasional Friday and Saturday evenings when we head down one of our familiar paths to a place where large smooth rocks form seats—each of us has a favorite—and drink a couple of cans of beer, a modest infraction—but we are safe in the woods.

Countless times our forays into the woods have turned into unsuccessful Lone Pine expeditions. We have gone in the dead of winter, in early March when all comes alive, on sweltering summer days, in late fall when the ground is hard, visibility perfect, trees leafless, snakes safely in their rocky dens, and even then, we have not seen Muskrat Lake, Stone House Corners, Cedar Dome Mountain, Lone Pine, or the shelter.

As far as I know, I am not delusional—I did not imagine Lone Pine any more than I imagined being attacked in the Talbots' home, yet I acknowledge the complete absurdity of the situation.

For those who do not know DeWitt Street—or the sprawling township of Haydon located in northern Caulfield County—it might be hard to understand a woods so dense and sprawling could exist in New York State. It must be even harder to understand that within these woods there is a place that cannot be found.

—

"This is what I mean, Grant," my mother says. "You've been sitting there for a couple of minutes. We're in the middle of a discussion. Where are you?"

"Just thinking about a few things," I say.

"You believe if you think about Jason long enough, you're going to figure it out," my mother says. "You're a smart young man, Grant, but trying to figure out Jason's disappearance on your own is not going to work. The mind is an inaccurate echo chamber. Ideas race around up there and get contorted. Sometimes the insights you get from thinking about something are distortions disguised as genius."

I can already see the sign in front of our church advertising my mother's next sermon: "The Mind Is an Inaccurate Echo Chamber—Unless You Ask God," preaching today, Lay Minister Harper.

"What am I supposed to do to help me understand all of this?" I ask. My mother knows this is a rhetorical question and waits patiently. "I've tried to retrace my steps and I can't do it. It just isn't possible that a whole section of a woods vanished. What am I supposed to think?"

—

The baseball season is over and Mickey, Hannah and I are reunited. We decide we will not take the afternoon school bus ever again. The daily walk home will keep us in shape—until one of us has access to a car on a regular basis. Each of us has a driver's license but none of us can lay claim to a car.

We have school for the first three weeks of June and the walk home is hot.

"I'm glad we won't be cutting lawns anymore," Mickey says. Mickey and I had a modest lawn mowing business for the last few years. This summer, we have real summer jobs. Hannah is going to work at Blake's Pharmacy and Mickey and I will work construction. A contractor who purchased several vacant lots down the street started construction just before Memorial Day. As soon as school is out, Mickey and I will be working with the carpenters on the site. We have been told it will be hard work, but they pay $1.50 an hour—more money than ever before. Hannah will make exactly the same wage. Mickey thinks she is being overpaid because the druggist has a crush on her and was stupid enough to tell her his theory—he now has a black and blue mark on his arm where she knuckle-punched him.

"If we save our pay all summer, we should have enough to buy a car before school starts," Mickey says. He drops down on one knee, opens his composition book, and begins to multiply $1.50 an hour times eight hours, times five days a week, times nine weeks, times three people.

"It's over $1600," he says softly. Mickey calculates further. "If we take out ten percent for taxes, it's still over $1400. We can really buy a car."

We have a brief and excited discussion about the kind of car that will work best for us, but it ends because none of us knows much about the price of cars.

I disclose our plan to my family at dinner that night. My sister, who will be leaving for college in September, finds the plan hysterical. Between laughs, she says, "You'll never save that much money. Not only that, no one is going to let two goofy guys and a tomboy buy a car." She looks at my father. "Tell him."

"I want to hear more," my father says and Denise's mouth drops open. "Seriously, it's good to have a goal. It will help them save money."

Denise is incredulous. "You told me I had to save the money I made over the summer for college. You aren't serious about letting him buy a car, are you?"

"All I said was that I wanted to hear more about it." he says.

Denise turns to my mother, seeking help, but to no avail. "If he teams up with Hannah and Mickey, they might have enough." She gives my father a nod—this means she is on my side. "There is something quite special about you three," she says, now focusing on me. "I think this is a fine idea."

"We're going to do this," I say. Denise frowns. "I might even let you use it sometimes when you're home from college."

Construction work turns out to be hot, exhausting, dirty, and boring. Rather than the hammering and sawing we expect, we stack concrete blocks, rush wheelbarrows full of wet cement to pour footings, pull and stack lumber from trucks, load worksite debris into large trucks, and carry around heavy sheets of drywall.

By the last week in July, we break a thousand dollars. I nail the bank deposit receipt to the wall in our garage. The car we like best is the Mustang, a new model made by Ford, but it would cost us $2400, more than we can pay. My father has taken us to several different used car lots but is skeptical. "You're buying someone else's headache," he says.

We talk about little else but cars and by the third week of August we have $1350 in the bank. Mickey's parents invite Hannah's parents and mine to their home to discuss what will happen next, but the evening does not start well. There are questions of title and insurance followed by discussions of rules that will apply, assuming we ever get a car. Mickey's parents are of the opinion that the car should never be driven after dark. My parents add insult to injury by suggesting we should not be driving the car on interstate highways or parkways. "The traffic zips by at 60 or 70 miles an hour— that's no place for these kids," my mother says.

While the hamburgers are being grilled, Lou Wade, my father's insurance agent arrives. It is clear Mr. Wade has been briefed in advance. "Three teenage drivers and a used car is going to be a costly mix. It will probably be in the neighborhood of three to four hundred dollars a year, depending on their driving records—maybe more." He pauses. "Are your parents going to pay for gas and up-keep?" he asks.

"It's their car," Mickey's mother says. "They will have to cover all the costs."

Lou whistles softly. "Are you kids going to work during the school year?"

We look at each other and finally Hannah says: "If we need to."

"You'll need to," Lou says. "You're talking about a used car that's going to eat up gas and oil and is going to have regular maintenance costs."

"We've worked all summer for this," Hannah says. "If we need to work during the school year, we will. I can work evenings at Blake's Pharmacy," Hannah says. If this happens, Hannah will have almost no spare time; she plans to go out for track this spring—the first girl's track team in the area—and we have no doubt she will make it. She is still faster than both Mickey and me. Mickey and I agree to find part-time work as well, prompting Mr. Cabrera to state that such activities cannot come at the cost of grades. "They still must get their homework done—this car can't stand in the way of their futures," he announces.

Mr. Cabrera's remark is reinforced by a pronouncement from my mother that becomes a family rule for each of us: "No 'B's, no keys," she says. It is a clear standard—each of us must maintain at least a "B" average to drive.

A week before Labor Day, we purchase a 1958 Studebaker Lark for $800. We have enough money in the bank to keep the car gassed and to pay our insurance until next summer. On the first day of school we ride in luxury, windows open, radio blasting. We park at the far end of the lot, in the area marked "For Students." At the end of the school day, our car is surrounded by half the junior class and we enjoy their awe.

—

If there is any question regarding the ties that bind us, the car resolves it. We are sixteen, own and share one Studebaker Lark—and the arrangement works. One way or another, till the bitter end, if there is a bitter end, there will always be Hannah, Mickey, and me. I do not know whether Hannah and Mickey understand this, but it does not matter—to me it is clear as a bell.

—

A week after Labor Day my father and sister head north to the University of Vermont where she will begin college. My mother and I stand in the driveway and wave as they head up DeWitt Street. The moment the car is out of sight, my mother turns away and starts walking to the house. "I need to get dinner," she says. Her voice has an uncharacteristic shakiness and I know: her defenses have evaporated—she will miss Denise terribly.

"Come on. I'll take you for a ride in the Studebaker, Mom."

She stops midway to the door. "I can't go without my purse," she says without turning. "I'll be back in a moment."

I have the car every third day—today it is mine. I leave the engine running and open the door for my mother. She steps in gingerly. "Where are you taking me?" she asks.

"For a ride," I say. I turn on the radio and open the windows.

The wind blows her hair back and she closes her eyes. "I'm glad you have this car," she says quietly. "The things you work hard to get are the ones you appreciate most."

—

And Another Five Years Later

– 20 –

December 1969

Four weeks from now will be the eleventh anniversary of Jason's disappearance. Not much has changed in our neighborhood since I drove my mother up DeWitt Street and around the north end of the woods in the newly acquired Studebaker Lark, giving her the time and fresh air she needed. The Lark gave Hannah, Mickey, and me the mobility and freedom we needed before it came to an abrupt end.

The Studebaker dropped dead suddenly during the summer of our freshman year in college and, consistent with Hannah's theory on death, it lives prominently in my memory. The hard-working engine threw a rod with such force that it protruded through the block a full two inches. The mechanic who serviced the car declared this a first and took pictures. All that remains of the Studebaker are three framed copies of a picture of Mickey, Hannah, and me in front of the car the day we graduated from high school.

Notwithstanding the Studebaker's demise, our lives are affected by the mobility a car provides.

Mickey and Hannah became car owners by happenstance. Mickey's car, his uncle's Ford Fairlane, came through inheritance. Like Hack Talbot, Mickey's uncle's death came as a consequence of the accumulated effects of alcohol and tobacco and was no surprise. The inheritance, however, caught the Cabrera family off guard. The Ford—and a few thousand dollars in U.S. Savings Bonds—was left to Mickey and the rest went to the Catholic Church. Mickey's father calls it acquired repentance and says it was the one thing his brother did while intoxicated that makes sense. Mickey drives the Ford everywhere—including college. It is better than "found money" he says.

Hannah's car, an ancient Chevy, is a gift from Dr. Blake, the druggist in Haydon in whose pharmacy Hannah has worked part-time since her junior year in high school. The car, which Hannah used for years to deliver prescriptions, runs surprisingly well—and its survival is important to both of us.

Hannah and I attend the State University of New York at Albany and commute each day to save money. It is under an hour and we alternate: when one drives, the other studies, a good arrangement for both of us—despite the fact that we are labeled townies by the kids in sororities and fraternities.

Our commuting schedule is complicated since Hannah continues to work at Blake's Pharmacy in Haydon—she is paying her own tuition—and I have clerical job at Barkman and David in Albany, the firm that represented me during the grand jury proceeding that took place after Jason disappeared. Edwin Barkman now sees himself as my mentor and speaks with me occasionally about the legal profession. I am more sure than ever about my career—assuming I can get into law school when the time comes.

—

Hannah and I drive home from school in the Chevy the day before Thanksgiving. It has been in front of her house since then with a flat tire. It will not be driven tonight under any circumstance.

Although the Thanksgiving holiday is over, we won't go back to college just yet. "Are you sure they all know?" my mother asks when Monday morning rolls around and Hannah and I are not on our way back to Albany.

"Mickey left each of his professors a note," I say. Mickey goes to Fordham University and lives with three other students in a cramped apartment in the Bronx. "His roommates promised to make sure they knew he would be back in class in a few days."

"Grant, I meant you and Hannah. It's not like either of you to miss class."

"Hannah and I met with the Dean of Students last week. We're not the only ones staying home for this. The dean promised to tell our professors that we would be back after the lottery. We agreed to keep up with the readings although we'll miss class."

"When are you going back?" my mother asks.

"The morning after the lottery—we wanted to stay together, in Haydon." I know my mother understands. Tomorrow, December 1, 1969, is the United States Selective Service lottery. Mickey and I were born in 1948, are college seniors, and will lose our 2–S student draft deferments when we graduate this spring. Sometime in May, we will become eligible to be drafted. "When I told Hannah that this will decide whether we get drafted, she said: 'Don't turn this into a men's club thing.' "

"Are you ever going to ask her out?" This is an idle question, asked every so often by one of my parents, usually intended to change the subject.

"And ruin our friendship?"

"Whatever happened to Lisa—I thought she was quite nice."

—

My mother has been quietly concerned about the absence of a long-term female relationship in my life and was quite taken by my most recent girlfriend, Lisa Montgomery, a psych major at school.

Lisa, with her tight faded jeans and affirming smile, has perfected the art of active listening. When I speak, she nods—never losing eye contact— as if consuming every word and idea I utter. I experience her attention as affection. She lives off-campus in a duplex, and the first time I spend the night there she plays piano for an hour before we make dinner.

Hannah and I talk constantly—and when I tell her about the piano playing, she laughs till her eyes water. "She has your number."

"She took a risk—I admire that," I say.

"Grant, she was seducing you," Hannah says.

"She was just playing the piano," I reply.

"Like she just listens to you, fascinated, without interrupting, for hours on end as you natter on about growing up in Caulfield County and your theories about the decline of the Democratic Party?"

"She's interested in the same things that interest me."

"Right," Hannah says. "Tell her you plan to stay single at least until the end of law school, if that is still how you feel, and see how fast she runs—I dare you."

"You're on," I say.

—

Lisa says little as I explain my plans to limit my commitments until I am on my own, but when I ask her to come to Haydon for the weekend, an argument ensues. After an unpleasant hour Lisa says: "I can't go to Haydon."

"Do you have plans?" I ask, knowing she does not.

"I'm sorry, Grant. It isn't other plans. It's you. We've been seeing each other for three months— and it's been fun—but you have barriers...." Lisa's language tells me that she needs a break from her upper-level psychology courses at school and I stay silent as she continues her diagnosis. "There is a fully scripted drama taking place somewhere in your head, and I'm not even listed in the program. I'd hoped for more from you but you keep me at a distance. Spending another weekend in Haydon—much as I like your parents—isn't going to change that."

I imagine Lisa has been leading to this all afternoon but when she says it out loud, it stuns me. "I'm fond of you—isn't that clear?" I say.

" 'Fond' isn't what I was looking for," Lisa says. "What do you want me to tell you about Jason Talbot—or Lone Pine, for that matter? Would you like me to play back for you the woodland adventures you and your little girlfriend Hannah have taken over the years—or your theories about a family you haven't seen in more than a decade? You need to grow up and move on—you're stuck in the past, Grant. When we started going out, I thought your fixation with this loss was just a part of your past, but I was wrong."

"Why didn't you tell me it bothered you?" I ask.

"I did," she replies. "In my own way. I gave you all the space you needed to let me know what was on your mind and it boils down to Jason Talbot and your barely subconscious lusting for Hannah."

"You make it sound like I was a project for your clinical psychology course—and I do not lust, subconsciously or otherwise, for Hannah," I say.

"You're a good guy Grant Harper—but I can't compete with obsession. Frankly, I can't tell if it's Hannah or your guilt—or your confusion—about losing a friend when you were ten, but I can tell you that something keeps you at a distance, and before this gets any more difficult, I want to end it."

—

"I'm sorry, Grant," my mother says as I finish explaining why she will not be seeing much of Lisa in the future. "She seemed like such a nice girl."

"She was—is—but it just didn't work out. Anyway, it would be wrong to make too many plans at this point until I know what will happen with the draft lottery."

My mother looks away. "I can't believe this is really going to happen. Wouldn't you be better off in the National Guard? You won't have to go overseas if you are in the Guard."

"Unless my unit gets activated. The Guard is a six year commitment—if I'm drafted, it's just two years."

"I pray that doesn't happen," she says.

It is an all-too-frequent event in Haydon—drafting recent high school and college graduates—and it shakes the otherwise deeply conservative vision that dominates our local politics. My town in Upstate New York is patriotic and predominantly Republican—but over the years, the war in Southeast Asia has taken a toll on many from Caulfield County, including two from Haydon. By a small majority, those who can vote in our town still support our long-time congressman, a vocal advocate for the war, but death and injury of local boys can change perspectives and our town celebrates and honors those lost while debate rages quietly. Public voices talk of a memorial in front of Town Hall. Privately, there is no uniform view of the war, the draft, or even the memorial.

—

We decide to watch the lottery from Mickey's basement. "My father says this is a confusing time," Mickey says as we settle into his old couch and open the first three beers. "I'm not confused about this. We are at war—I wish we weren't, but that's just the way it is."

"When my father talks about World War II, he describes feeling a kind of urgency and obligation—how boys fifteen and sixteen years old lied about their age so they could join up," I say. "Our friends, even here in Haydon, talk about how they'll lie to get out of having to go and fight."

Hannah pours her beer into a glass. "We haven't been attacked—how is this a war?" Mickey and I listen. "You watch the news. Thousands of guys have died over there and there is no end to it. If you have a chance to stay home, promise me you won't be heroes." Mickey and I both nod and concentrate on our beers.

For Mickey, Hannah, and me, the Vietnam War, the peace movement in our colleges, even the patriotic events in Haydon—particularly the Fourth of July Parade—all seem intended for someone else. Up to this point, life presented options that did not require the possibility of ultimate sacrifice. Tonight, somewhere in Washington, a government official will draw dates and numbers out of large drums. These will be birth dates—and they will be matched with numbers. The lower the number matched with your birth date, the more likely it is you will end up drafted, in the army, in Vietnam, at war.

A reporter drones on about the fairness of the method to be used in the lottery. It is random selection, he says. "Random?" Mickey says. "No shit. A lottery is the definition of random." We are into our second six-pack when the drawing begins and close to drunk when it ends. I am number 219. Mickey is 21.

"Will they get to 219?" Hannah asks. She does not state the obvious. Mickey will be drafted.

"The guy at Caulfield County Regional Draft Board told my dad that 195 and below may have to report. That's me," Mickey says.

Hannah's eyes well up and she leaves the room, her hand over her mouth, but she is tough and a few minutes later is back, matching us curse for curse, beer for beer.

At 4:00 a.m. Mickey heads for the bathroom and when he returns ten minutes later he has shaved off most of his long black hair, leaving Hannah and me speechless. He chugs what's left of his beer, salutes us, flops back onto the couch, and slowly passes out. By 4:30, I am likewise drunk and very aware of the random nature of both divine providence and the lottery.

Hannah has her eyes closed, Mickey's head in her lap. I am not sure she is awake until she responds. "I'm cutting it all off," she says without opening her eyes. "Hair...."

"Lots of men—Mick—me too—just broken-hearted," I say, my slurring getting worse by the moment. Hannah comes to life, reaches across the couch and whacks me on the arm—she has not lost her knuckle punch.

"You and me, Grant Harper...." Hannah pauses, thinking through the alcohol mist. "We'll write Mickey ... every single week."

"I agree," I say.

"We'll pray with Cabrera ... family—at the Catholic...."

"Agree," I say.

"You ... Methodist ... I'm Jewish ... but ... does God care?" she says. "If he cared, Mickey's number ... 365." There is a long pause and Hannah seems close to the end of the evening.

"Catholic Church ... theological." I murmur.

Hannah laughs without opening her eyes. "The–o–logical ... spell it," she says.

"T-h-e-o...." Hannah is still laughing as I give up. "We don't go near protests ... if Mickey goes ... Vietnam."

"Good," Hannah whispers.

"To Miguel Cabrera."

"Mic...." Hannah mumbles as her lights go from dim to dark.

—

We eat breakfast at noon in Mickey's kitchen.

"Miguel, you have little cuts all over your head," his mother says. "Did you shave with the lawn clippers?" She runs her hand over the top of his head.

"No. Don't touch my head," Mickey says. "Please."

"Hannah, how about some eggs?" Mrs. Cabrera says.

I am quite sure the smell of eggs—perhaps even the thought of eggs—will send Hannah back to the bathroom. "No, thanks, Mrs. Cabrera. I'm not hungry," Hannah says.

"Young Mr. Harper . . . you have dried shaving cream in your ear," Mr. Cabrera says to me as he comes into the kitchen. "What went on last night beyond the fact that my son saw fit to cut off his hair?"

"Last night was the lottery, Dad," Mickey says.

"I know," Mr. Cabrera says. "I know."

Mrs. Cabrera looks at her husband. "We'll see what we can do, Miguel," she says. "Maybe there is a way out."

"I'm going," Mickey says. "Maybe I can get into an Officers Training program."

"And maybe you should get in the car and drive to Canada," his mother says.

—

We agree to call each other once we are back in school, get together at Christmas, have one last hike to try and find Lone Pine, but Mickey enlists rather than go back to college and is in South Carolina in basic training before Christmas.

"He said if he had to go, he wanted to get it over with as soon as possible," his mother tells us. "I have his address. Please write to him."

"Every week," Hannah says.

I nod in agreement. "I swear," I say.

*

Part Three

OUT OF THE WOODS
1972–1975

– 21 –

It has been thirteen years since Jason Talbot vanished. On trips back to Haydon, one look up DeWitt Street, one glance at his front yard as I drive by, and it all comes roaring back. If I close my eyes, I can see Jason, his face reddened, the imprint of his father's hand outlined on his cheek.

—

In March 1972 Mickey returns from Vietnam and receives his Honorable Discharge. He spends time at the local VA hospital, resting, his parents explain, and is back on DeWitt Street a few months later. Shortly after his release from the hospital, as a favor to his father, Lou Wade hires Mickey to work in his insurance agency. That job lasts less than three weeks.

He starts—and leaves—three or four other jobs—none lasting more than a few months. The last time I see Mickey, the Studebaker Lark picture is hanging in the bathroom of his efficiency apartment. I help him pack his belongings and move them into a U–Haul van. The picture of the Lark is among the last things to go.

"I loved that car," Mickey says as I wrap the picture in some newspaper. "I wish we still had it. It has to be worth more than we paid for it by this point." He pauses. "What did we do with it, Grant?"

"We got fifty bucks for it at the junkyard, Mick. Don't you remember?"

"I guess," he says.

We finish packing and stand outside next to the fully loaded van. "I'll follow you," I say. "We can have this unloaded before dark."

"No thanks. I'm going to drop some of this stuff off at my folks' house, before going to my new place."

"You still haven't told me about your new work, or even where you're going to live," I say.

"I have something lined up in Albany with a guy I know from the VA hospital," Mickey tells me as he gets in the van. "I'll call you when I have a new number." It is the third move of this type in the last year.

"I'll wait to hear from you," I say as he drives off.

—

A few months later Hannah tells me Mickey sold his uncle's Ford and cashed in his modest inheritance. The furniture we loaded on the van never made it to DeWitt Street—it has been sold as well. Mickey is obviously strapped for cash—that much I know from Hannah—but he never asks me for anything.

A few days after learning that Mickey is selling everything he owns of value, Hannah tells me he is back in the VA hospital—again. "He needs more time, Grant." She hesitates. "And he is clear about one thing: no visitors—not even his mother and father—no one." When I ask for more information, Hannah is not open to discussion. Finally, she says: "He is hurting, Grant—all the time—and neither he nor anyone else can make it stop."

—

My copy of the Studebaker Lark picture hangs on the wall in the waiting room of my law office on Seneca Avenue in Albany, New York. My law degree from Albany Law School, granted in May 1973, hangs behind my desk.

A framed sketch of Lone Pine, however, is what I see when I first enter the office. The pencil drawing of the tree and shelter is next to my door. It is as accurate as memory allows.

I made the sketch one morning during my second year of law school. I was in the law library on the third floor of the Albany Federal Building researching some urgently important topic I no longer recall. From my carrel next to the window, I could see snow falling on a rusting statue and a few small trees that survived the rigors of Albany's winter in a courtyard sixty feet below. The lawn and sidewalks were white and the trees and statue brown—nothing but those two colors were visible from where I sat—and I started drawing.

I had been working as a law clerk in a large firm in Albany. The work laid waste to any vestige of creativity I might have possessed. I labeled, organized, and filed documents, wrote research memoranda, photocopied cases, and never saw—much less met—a client.

I had a headache that lasted from late September 1971 until April 1972, when I parted ways with the firm. Such was my second year of law school.

—

During my final year of law school, I spent 20 hours a week working as a "student lawyer" with Albany Legal Services Program, a legal aid office in the heart of Albany's one and only Latino community. We were there to help with civil cases, landlord-tenant problems, debt management, immigration, divorce, child custody, and occasional criminal cases. Despite four years of Spanish taken during high school and college, my interviewing style was halting, but language differences were not an issue at Legal Aid for one reason: Señor Juan Cabrera—the same Señor Juan Cabrera with whom I grew up—Mickey's father ... that Señor Juan Cabrera.

Given our clients, it made sense that a translator would be available to assist with communication. What did not make sense was the identity of the translator (who served also as an administrative assistant in the office). It was not that Mr. Cabrera was unqualified—quite the contrary. It was more that he seemed wildly out of place.

"Home" is our family house on DeWitt Street where the neighborhood familial class structure is fixed. Hannah, Mickey, and our various friends and siblings are a loose coalition joined by age, upbringing, Caulfield County schools, the war in Vietnam, music, movies, and far too much cheap beer.

My parents' generation socializes with martinis and Manhattans and follows the progress of my generation as we enter the adult world. They attend weddings, mourn the passing of loved ones, receive birth announcement and send gifts, and joke about becoming grandparents. With this clear generational separation, there was something deeply unsettling about the prospect of working with Mickey's father.

While translators and legal assistants in legal aid offices are poorly paid, I set aside the troubling remunerative aspects of this relationship after my supervisor explained that Mr. Cabrera owned several valuable rental properties in the city. While this did not render him wealthy, it was stable revenue and had been his main source of income for many years. Last year, he hired a management company to handle the properties and approached the director of Albany Legal Services. Mr. Cabrera had been clear: it was time to become involved in the U.S. legal system. Legal aid was his only viable entry point.

Our initial exchange was surprisingly formal, considering that I have known Mr. Cabrera for most of my life. We talked about Mickey—but only briefly. And while his accent and cadence were familiar, for the most part we spoke as colleagues, as professionals, not as neighbors.

Despite the heat that day, for our first meeting, Mr. Cabrera wore a three-piece suit with a dark red tie that stayed firmly knotted throughout our discussion. I wore khakis and a blue short-sleeved shirt with a thin knit tie (loosened at the neck) my mother gave me for Christmas my senior year in high school.

Mr. Cabrera's cuff links were thick, thumbnail-sized gold squares—no engraving or gem stones. I have one pair, a hand-me-down from my grandfather. I have worn them at weddings—but that's about it. As we spoke, he took notes with a fountain pen that put my dime store ballpoint to shame. Anyone observing our discussion would have concluded that he was my supervisor—and yet, that was not at all the case. He was, he made clear, the office translator and legal assistant.

In the months that followed, I came to understand that Mickey's father was far more than a translator and an aid to the lawyers and law students with whom he worked. He was the most experienced professional in the office.

Juan Cabrera has lived a complex and courageous life about which I knew almost nothing—until now. Slowly, with great care, he shared with me his past.

He was a lawyer of some renown who fled Havana during Fulgencio Batista's reign. Offended by Batista's excesses and misuse of power, he made a catastrophic error and aligned with Castro in the early 1950's. He was counsel to the pre-revolutionary Moncado Army and an armed combatant during the ill-fated attack on the military barracks in Oriente Province.

The incident was a disaster; a number of the Moncado "freedom fighters" were killed or imprisoned by Batista's forces while others, including Raúl and Fidel Castro fled ("like jackals," Juan notes when he tells the story) to Mexico. "They knew Ernesto Che Guevara—thought they knew what was best for 'the masses'—and walked away from all we had built in Havana—all that was good and successful. Castro and Batista were out for themselves, though at different ends of the political spectrum—and I was in the middle of that spectrum. I was a member of a professional class about to be extinguished—and so my wife and I—and little Miguel—sought out a new home."

His flight to the United States cost him his Cuban license to practice law, but not his judgment, skill, knowledge, ambition, or dignity. He has been in the United States for almost twenty years but has not taken the New York bar. He is intensely proud—and although his rental properties would allow him to do so, there are some expenses—including his own re-education—he refuses to incur. He is unwilling to subject himself to U.S. law school classes, the profoundly infantalizing bar review course, or the bar exam itself. His work at Albany Legal Services, however, allows him to reinstitute contact with his chosen profession—but that's about it.

—

After calling him Mr. Cabrera for a month, he began to insist on being called Juan. "You and I are colleagues," he said. "In public, I will call you Mr. Harper and you will refer to me as Mr. Cabrera—but in this office, Grant, you may call me Juan—

and you, soon to be a licensed member of the bar, will be Mr. Harper to your clients. There is no choice." I argued with him over this reshuffling of names but he was resolute. In the end, I knew he was right: the other law students referred to him as Juan and he referred to them by their last names. It made little sense for me to address him any other way. Still, it took many weeks before it became second nature.

—

By spring of 1973 it is clear: when I graduate, I will open my own firm joined by Señor Juan Cabrera, Esquire, a once-prominent Havana lawyer—and an unlicensed attorney in the State of New York. He will be my mentor and colleague.

The conventional wisdom is that there is almost no chance of success for sole practitioners who go into private practice directly from law school—but Señor Cabrera changes the odds.

It is Juan who first brought up the idea of going into private practice. "I have watched you this year, Grant. You took time with every client—I'm now talking about Hispanic clients. You were patient with the senior members of this community. You explained Social Security and pensions. You went with our youngsters to the Juvenile Court—you believed in them, comforted their families—the other lawyers had no time for us. You are about to become a distinguished member of the bar and I promise you there are many in this community who will want you to be their lawyer."

—

In November 1973, with the bar exam behind me, I lease an office and, by agreement, Juan takes over. It is a dingy but decent-sized suite. "This door, the frosted glass, looks too much like a government office. The doorway is important. Clients must feel success the moment they cross the threshold. A dark wood—with a brass nameplate off to one side—I will arrange that later today."

"And how will we pay for that?" I ask.

"Let us not worry about money for now." He grasps my hand and shakes it firmly. "You and I will have a fine future together, Grant. There is great potential—for both of us. Now, a thorough cleaning is in order. A client will not have confidence in a lawyer who works in surroundings that lack dignity." A few minutes later, a cleaning crew arrives—followed by a painter. They greet their employer, Señor Juan Cabrera, and begin work. It is all I can do to stay out of their way.

—

On DeWitt Street, Mr. Cabrera was—and is— Mickey's father, personal friends with my parents— a quiet and well-liked member of the Haydon PTA. However, here in this neighborhood of Nicaraguans, Mexicans, Guatemalans, El Salvadorans, Peruvians, Panamanians, and Cubans, in this one Hispanic enclave in the City of Albany, he is so much more. Here, Señor Juan Cabrera strides through the community with such confidence that walking alone, he is a parade.

—

My books are still in boxes when our first clients arrive. They are hard-working residents of our neighborhood, very much like those served at Legal Aid, but these individuals—attracted to my office by Juan—are prepared to pay for our services. We have more work than we can handle from the outset—and that is very good news.

—

Hannah's copy of the Studebaker photograph hangs on the wall behind the cash register in Blake's Pharmacy where she worked part-time in Haydon for ten straight years—a record for student workers, Dr. Blake said. My father saw Hannah regularly at that drugstore. During these visits, as they discussed evolving pharmacological miracles, my father would glance at that picture and smile.

Hannah did not resign from Blake's Pharmacy until she completed the grueling four year part-time law school program.

In the summer of 1974, Juan and I attend graduation at Albany Law School and sit with Mr. and Mrs. Weiner, waiting for Hannah to cross the stage. When we hear, "Hannah Weiner, Juris Doctor, *cum laude*," I applaud, Mrs. Weiner whistles using two fingers (an art form she refused to share with Hannah, Mickey, and me), and Mr. Weiner holds up a sign saying "That's My Daughter—The Woman Lawyer!"

As she crosses the stage it strikes me that she will soon be able to play the grand jury game she invented with more skill than she did fifteen years ago.

For many law students, the last year of law school is overwhelming not just because of the academic challenges but because they face an uncertain job market. For Hannah, while the course work and bar preparation loom large, there was never a question about her employment. Juan and I have been waiting a year for her to join us in practice at our law firm. She will be my partner when she passes the bar. She is also my first non-paying client.

Hannah is straightforward: she wants to change her name from Weiner to Wein, despite the anger this generates with her father. Peace does not return until Hannah explains that "Harper and Weiner" would never do—too awkward, she says— while "Harper & Wein" has a nice ring to it.

Unlike Hannah's parents, Juan has never come to terms with Hannah's name change. He has always been very fond of Hannah otherwise, but on this topic there is nothing but friction. "A person does not defile her ancestry for convenience," Juan said on more than one occasion. "In the Spanish tradition, a woman never gives up the name of her family."

Hannah is not easily intimidated and responds to Juan uniformly: "And if your name was Juan Carapene—not Cabrera—you wouldn't change it?" Carapene, in Hannah's understanding of Spanish, means penis face.

—

Just before Thanksgiving, with the bar behind her, Hannah and I order a new brass door plaque that will read: "Harper & Wein." Since the rules of the state bar do not permit recognition of Juan's Cuban law degree, the nameplate cannot reveal our true partnership—but the sign should read "Harper, Wein & Cabrera."

Hannah and I spend hours, in private of course, talking through how completely bizarre it is to be in business with Mickey's father. Juan maintains separation on all things pertaining to DeWitt Street, family, and Mickey. While he is a member of my parents' cohort—and those lines do not cross—at work, in our firm, he is at once my more than a colleague—he is *primus inter pares*. No lawyer we meet comes close to Juan when it comes to competence as judged by strategic insight and the ability to prevail on behalf of a client—and yet he is barred from the legal tasks and recognition he deserves.

– 22 –

Summer 1975

In terms of demand for our services, to say that Juan was prescient understates it: business at Harper & Wein is booming. More often than not, we work late into the evening and frequently seven days a week. Juan has an endless array of contacts—and contacts produce and become clients.

Our biggest personal injury case involves a cook at our favorite restaurant, Nuevo Leon. Our client was nearly decapitated by the blades of an expensive and, as it turns out, defectively designed commercial blender. The manufacturer settled for a small fortune (both for the cook and for us), and the case makes headlines on the financial pages. Of course the paper does not report that the cook came to our office because of Juan—not Hannah or me. Nevertheless, the article brings us more clients— and more substantial contingency fees.

———

After an extended negotiation, I return to the office like a victorious Argonaut to report our first settlement to exceed a half-million dollars. I appreciate Juan's firm handshake but it is Hannah's powerful hug that defines the moment.

Hannah has long brown hair and green eyes, and males pursue her shamelessly. She is determined to wait until she is thirty to get married— though not for a lack of offers. When she started law school in 1970, she was one of a handful of women in her class—and in that group she was the most compelling by any measure. While my college girlfriend Lisa Montgomery was right—I am attracted to Hannah—who wouldn't be?—we are in business together and common sense dictates that we maintain separate social lives, and we do.

———

In under a year, we have an enviable fiscal base. I issue bonus checks to Hannah and Juan, apply for "key employee" life insurance, buy three new IBM Selectric typewriters, and hire a second full-time assistant. The life insurance requires a physical—and the results are not what I expect.

———

"Your blood pressure is 160 over 85, your cholesterol is problematic, and you look like you haven't slept in a week." The doctor, who probably cranks out physicals by the score for insurance companies, closes her file. "You'll get insurance—they'll tweak your premium because of these tests—but if I were you, I'd take better care of myself. How's your sex life?"

"You assume I have one," I say.

"Well, do you?" She is not smiling.

"Isn't that a bit private? I hardly think my sex life is relevant to a life insurance physical."

"You fit into a pattern, Mr. Harper. If I had to guess—and I don't—I'd say you spend too much time at the office. You skin is pale, there are dark circles around your eyes, and you check your watch every few minutes. There is more to life than work. Here," she hands me a form. "Sign this." She shoves a consent form in my direction. "And Mr. Harper—take a break."

—

I discuss with Juan and Hannah the doctor's unsolicited editorial comments and the results of the physical. "I'm with the doctor," Juan says. "A little time off sounds like an excellent idea." A few days later, I am given my temporary walking papers by Juan. "Enjoy yourself, Grant—catch a few fish and get rested." He hands me an envelope with keys and a map. "The cabin is a short stroll from Lake Placid. It is owned by the proprietor of Nuevo Leon, the employer of one of our most grateful clients—he was happy to be of service."

"Maybe I can get Mickey to come with me—I'll give him a call," I say.

In a low voice, Juan says, "Miguel is lost, Grant—you know that. He needs more time to readjust. He rarely speaks to me—or anyone in the family for that matter. I very much doubt he will respond—but call him if you like."

"I don't have a working phone number," I say.

"Nor do I," Juan says. "You must take care of yourself, Grant. Miguel must figure this out on his own."

—

The last leg of the trip to the cabin takes me down a winding dirt road and I get a sense of the complete isolation of this hideaway. The cabin is larger than I expect and while there is electricity, the closest phone is half an hour away.

The first night I expect to sleep until noon and am disappointed when I am up at 5:30. I have spent the night with one eye open, thinking of nothing but the day that I entered the Talbots' house and was attacked by a man I believed to be the late Hack Talbot—knowing full well that is just plain impossible. That happened 17 years ago and I have considered asking to have his body exhumed, but have instead kept silent.

More than once, I have wondered if it really happened—as Mickey once said, sometimes you think you remember something, but instead it is something someone said. The thing is, no one ever said anything about this to me—and I found two tin cans shot straight through on my windowsill the day before my testimony in front of the grand jury that ended the inquiry into the disappearance of Jason Talbot.

My as-yet-unpacked suitcase sits at the edge of the bed. I stumble into the main room of the cabin, get coffee going, and open the door to inhale woods and lake smells. I cannot see the water although it is less than a quarter of a mile from the cabin. The forest, thick with evergreen, barely lets through light.

At some point today I will drive to the local bait and tackle shop and buy a couple dozen night crawlers—I plan on freshly caught yellow-striped perch for dinner. For now, I am content with the aroma of the coffee as it joins the unmistakable smells of the forest.

The evergreen near the cabin are short-needled and consistent, one to the next. Their sameness is disconcerting. The uniformity is not natural and I wonder if each tree has been planted, its location selected by a tree farmer who will return one day and harvest his crop. These woods are not like mine. My woods are wild and random.

I wipe the dew from the green Adirondack chair that sits on the lakeside of the cabin's deck and begin my watch. The rewards that flow from staring into a forest are unpredictable. I sit motionless and scan from left to right, my physical effort limited to eye movement, quite content to be alone. A few minutes pass before I begin to hear the sounds.

There is no true quiet at our office in Albany. Even with the doors and windows closed, it is impossible to escape the sound of a bus accelerating and car horns. The continuous presence of street noises dulls one to the delicate. Freed from urban clatter, I begin to hear the forest. It is full of life and movement, of things that fly and crawl and scamper on tiny feet. I have been longing for that special peace only woodland brings.

My desire for fresh perch is unrequited. In three hours, I catch two bluegills and an infant large-mouth bass, hardly a dinner. I have not spoken to a soul in twenty-four hours.

After a meal of canned spaghetti and green beans, I return to the lake, conserving my flashlight batteries as I make my way down the path and out onto the dock. I hear the washing whisper of small waves on the rocky brown shore, watch the last moments of the sunset, and am witness to the beginning of night. I have a star chart, binoculars, and a goal: to see Callisto or Ganymede, Jupiter's largest moons. Unlike many who scan the skies solely to find a shooting star, I was brought up to find the rare but permanent parts of the sky. It is a victory to count more than ten stars in the Pleiades, to find the tiny pin pricks of light that are the other moons in our solar system.

I light two citronella candles, lie on my back on a bench on the dock, and take in the great arc of the universe. There is an occasional splash as fish collect their evening meals. Just why they are more interested in eating water spiders and mosquitoes when earlier today they could have had my luscious night crawlers is beyond me.

I find Jupiter and begin to move the binoculars. I go slowly—moving quickly will spook my prey. With the binoculars in place, I begin to focus. The planet gets clearer as I adjust the lens, but I see no tiny moons. I remove the binoculars and wonder whether I have identified the right heavenly body. I pick up the star chart in my left hand and turn on the flashlight with my right and begin the process of looking from the chart to the heavens and back. Before I can refocus the binoculars, I hear the unmistakable sound of a car rumbling down the dirt road that leads to my cabin. A car door closes and I pick up my flashlight.

I enter the woods, flashlight in hand, and am not surprised when I hear the first call. "Grant!" It is Hannah.

– 23 –

I have practiced law long enough to know there is no point in calling out: "Is everything okay?" The forest floor, including the path on which I walk, is covered with roots and it is dangerous to run, but I know how to move fast through the woods. I catalogue the various catastrophes that might have occurred, beginning with the well-being of my parents. It goes through my mind that the threats made against my parents in the Talbots' house that sweltering afternoon in August 1959, have been carried out—maybe that's why I spent last night reliving that horror.

I am fifty yards from the cabin when Hannah and I begin our discussion.

"What are you doing here?" I call to her.

"You're lucky I found this place," she says. I am relieved this is her first concern. "This is the middle of nowhere."

"Hannah?"

"It's Mickey. He is in trouble. He's been arrested, Grant. Actually, he was picked up several weeks ago."

"How is that possible? We would have heard." When she does not respond I ask: "What did he do?"

She walks to the long wooden steps at the front end of the cabin's porch and sits. Her skirt and white blouse make clear—she left directly from the office.

"Hannah?"

She looks up at me, takes a deep breath. "I know very few details, but the essence of it is this—he is charged with killing a clerk during a robbery of a bookstore at the university."

"What?" Again, no response. "Who knows?"

"Up until early this afternoon, no one outside of the prosecutors' office and the public defender. Mickey had no identification on him when he was arrested and refused to give a name. They took their time with the fingerprints. I guess they figured there was no rush. This morning, the D.A. got the fingerprint report, learned their prisoner was Mickey, and guessed he was the son of Juan Cabrera—and half the D.A.'s office knows Juan."

"Do they have the robbery on a security tape?" I ask.

"No. This is a college bookstore," Hannah says. "They have one security guard for the building—and the guard was not in the store at the time the crime took place."

"Any witnesses?" I ask.

"The worst kind, Grant. When the police arrived, they found Mickey lying unconscious on the floor. The clerk had been shot through the chest, but was still talking. He gestured toward Mickey and said something like: 'He attacked' . . . 'or he's the one.' "

Hannah stops, and I know what happened next. "The clerk passed away at that moment, right?" I say.

"Right," Hannah says.

"Has Mickey signed anything?"

"I doubt it," Hannah says. "From what we have been able to learn, the robbery was a debacle. At some point someone bashed Mickey in the head with a fire extinguisher and knocked him cold."

"Have you spoken with Mickey?"

"No—but Juan has," Hannah says. "I called him earlier from a payphone." She hesitates and continues. "Grant, Juan told me Mickey's head injury is quite serious. He said Mickey has received very limited attention in the jail and later, the infirmary—he was upset, as you might expect."

"He should be in a hospital," I say. "Is Juan getting him medical attention?"

"This is his son, Grant. Mickey will get the care he needs." She stops. "He asked me to think about municipal immunity as I drove up to find you."

"Municipal immunity?" He is already thinking about a lawsuit against the city and understands a suit against the city will require penetration of the qualified immunity accorded to different governmental entities. "What's the bail situation?"

"Juan knows the clerks. Mickey was in front of a magistrate this evening before I called. Juan put up his house as collateral."

"I'm surprised he got Mickey out so easily," I say. "Bail in a murder case is a fight."

"I did not say it was easy, Grant—I said it was Juan. I don't know any lawyer who could have done that on such short notice."

—

Repacking my belongings takes only a few minutes. I check the cabin lights and empty the cardboard container of night crawlers off of the side of the deck. Hannah and I will drive back in tandem. It will be after midnight when we get back to Albany and tomorrow will be a demanding day.

*

Part Four

IN COURT
1975–1976

– 24 –

It is before eight when I arrive at the office. Hannah has been in since seven. The Cabreras will get here in an hour or so.

"The police report is on the table in the conference room," Hannah says as I walk in. "I spoke with the desk sergeant before the shift change. They think it likely that Mickey had an accomplice."

"Do they have ideas on a second suspect?" I ask.

"None—they based their opinion on the absence of a murder weapon," Hannah says.

"Then why not assume there was a single actor who kills the clerk, clobbers Mickey, and flees?" I ask. "Were there powder markings on Mickey's hands?"

"I asked for a residue report but there was none," Hannah says.

"What about the clerk's last words. What does the report say?" I ask.

"I looked through the file," Hannah says. "They seem convinced that the clerk identified Mickey as his assailant—as I said last night, the clerk said either, 'He attacked' or 'he's the one.' "

"Neither will help us," I say.

We hear Juan's voice from the hallway. "Not so fast," he says. "There is much to be examined." Despite the unthinkable family horror that has just transpired, Juan has come to work—dressed impeccably as usual. His comments suggest unexpected professional detachment. "The clerk's statements lack in clarity—they are inconclusive. On cross-examination, we can show this to be unreliable."

Hannah stares at Juan and says softly. "You should be with your son, Juan—Miguel needs you."

Juan stiffens. "Miguel needs to navigate the criminal justice system in Albany, in my city, and he needs medical care. A civil suit against the city should be prepared. That is what Miguel needs. His mother will give him all the affection he can handle. I am his father—and guiding his legal affairs is the way I can help him most."

—

When tragedy strikes, there are those who grieve, those who act, and infinite combinations of both. These are mechanisms to cope with foreseen and unforeseen disaster. It is clear how Juan will proceed.

—

"Let us talk about the cases—the criminal case and the civil case." Juan looks at Hannah and reveals the hint of a smile. "Hannah, I know you think it odd that I am focused on Miguel's legal problems. I know this concern comes from your kindness and your fondness for my son. A man can love his children in many different ways." Juan takes a deep breath. "The law is the best way for me—it does not overshadow my love for Miguel. It *is* my love for him. If these cases are not thought through carefully—and concluded successfully—Miguel will be forever lost. Do you understand?"

A silence follows. I know what Hannah is thinking—this is Mickey, Juan's one and only beloved son, the son who went to war and returned so lost and hurt.

Hannah pulls it together, clears her throat, and begins in a whisper: "There is a problem beyond the clerk's statement. According to the report, Mickey was found with almost a hundred dollars in small bills stuffed in his pockets and the bookstore cash register had been cleaned out," Hannah says.

"And so there is an apparent motive," Juan says. "Miguel had no money or identification—and, as I have learned, no known current address."

"I should have done more," I say.

"That is both wrong and not the question," Juan says. "We must have a good picture of the State's case and find the right slogan for my Miguel."

"A slogan?" Hannah asks.

"Perhaps I used the wrong word," Juan says. "Miguel needs a simple story, a few words that provide a way for a judge—for a jury—to understand him—magical words that will become our theory of the case."

Juan stands, professorial. "Grant," he says, "what do you see as the case theory?"

"He was an innocent bystander. Jurors understand how fate can deposit you in the wrong place at the wrong time."

"That is a theory—but quite vulnerable. The identification by the clerk, the cash—other evidence that may turn up—can undo that message in the blink of an eye," Juan says.

"What about the public defender?" I ask. "Did you get anywhere with them?"

"We spoke," Juan says. "Until they knew he was my son, they saw Miguel as a vagrant—another returning vet who cannot adjust to civilian life. They gave me what they had yesterday and it was almost nothing. Let us not worry about lawyers who do not want my son, your friend, for a client. Miguel is not high on their list. He refused to speak with them and refused to identify himself. He was headed for a catastrophic plea bargain."

"They have no idea what he went through in Vietnam," Hannah says. "None."

Juan picks up the police report—a three-page document, rife with law enforcement jargon and stick figures. "This tells us the physical location of Miguel and the decedent but resolves no mysteries." He walks to the window. "Miguel is found unconscious, the clerk gestures, points to Miguel, uses incriminating language before he dies, a gun is never found, no witnesses surface. The District Attorney has an easier task in prosecution than we do as defense counsel—but their case is not perfect. They are without a murder weapon—someone else was there."

"So what is our case theory?" Hannah asks.

Juan turns to her. "There is your theme: Miguel is a veteran of war not yet fully recovered from his wounds. . . ."

"He is a veteran of an unpopular war and even if we succeed in showing him as a victim of Vietnam, sympathy won't produce an acquittal," I say.

"The circumstantial evidence suggests Miguel's participation" Juan says. "He was—and is—destitute. Despair leads him to take action. Miguel was set aside by the society that sent him to war."

Hannah and I are silent for a time. Finally she says. "We can handle this, Juan. You do not need to do this."

"He is my son," Juan says and turns to me. "Your father would never leave your care to another. You cannot expect me to abandon Miguel."

—

I place the scant documentation on the conference table and read aloud each line. Finally, I say: "Why concede his involvement in the crime at all? Mickey is simply not capable of this kind of behavior."

"Grant," Hannah says, "that was before."

Juan closes his eyes and rubs them. "Think about this crime—these facts. Try not to think about Miguel as he was." He turns to Hannah. "A judge—a juror—will have to understand how a seemingly homeless man, weak from hunger, ends up in a college bookstore with money jammed in his trousers." Juan stops. "He has probably sold his license and other identification—a market exists for those documents in our community—and reached the end of options he was willing to exercise. Does one under such circumstances set out to buy a textbook—or typing paper?"

We continue discussing various theories when Mickey and his mother arrive. Mickey is unshaven—his dark hair is filthy and hangs in his face. His eyes are almost closed. There is a white bandage on a shaved section of the right side of his head.

Mrs. Cabrera hugs Juan and then Hannah and me. "Will they take Mickey? He is sick. Please."

"You know we'll do everything we can, Mrs. Cabrera," I say.

As Mrs. Cabrera releases me from her embrace, Juan leads Mickey to a seat at our conference table. "You can be truthful here, my son." He kisses Mickey on the forehead and takes a seat at the table.

I walk to Mickey, kneel next to his chair, and place my arm around his shoulder. He does not move at my touch. "Mickey, it's me, Grant." He continues to stare.

"He's been that way since yesterday," his mother says.

"We will be your lawyers, Mickey," I say. "What you say is confidential, a secret, like when we were growing up."

Mickey lifts his head slowly. "I need Jason."

"Jason Talbot?" his father asks.

"He keeps asking for Jason," Mrs. Cabrera says. "I cannot explain it."

"He is confused," Juan replies. "He mentioned Jason Talbot in the bail hearing yesterday as well."

"Mickey, do you know who I am?" I ask.

Mickey continues to stare across the table.

I point to his parents. "Mickey, tell me, who are these people?"

Mickey continues to stare across the table. "Do you want to go back to the jail?" I ask.

Mickey turns his head and shouts: "Don't say that."

"Then you remember jail?" I ask.

"Awful," he says softly.

I barely recognize his voice. His pronunciation is odd and his tones hoarse. "Did you talk to anyone while you were in jail?" I ask.

"No," he says in a whisper.

"Grant," Mrs. Cabrera says, "you remind me of your father when he was a young man. He was always there when someone needed him. He still is."

Mickey turns to me. "Is Jason coming?"

"You know Jason is gone. Why did you talk about him in the bail hearing?"

Mickey nods and then rubs his face with both hands. "Jason always has answers. He knows where things are."

"We don't know where Jason is, Mick." Hannah says. "You remember how Jason got lost?"

"Where is he?" Mickey asks.

"He isn't here, Mick. You are with your parents, with Hannah and me," I say.

"Find him," Mickey says.

"We tried," I answer.

"Then Arthur—what about Arthur?" Mickey asks.

"Arthur?" Hannah asks. "Is he a friend?"

Mickey shuts his eyes and slams the table with his fist. "I need Arthur."

"Is he someone from the Army—a friend from Vietnam?" Hannah asks.

Mickey slams the table again. "Help us, Mick. We don't know Arthur," I say.

Mickey doubles over in his chair, holding his stomach. "Arthur . . . now."

The request for Arthur is all we hear from Mickey from that point forward. From time to time, Juan speaks with him in Spanish. When we were kids, the only time Spanish was spoken in the Cabrera household was when Mickey was in serious trouble.

———

There is a long silence after Mickey and his mother leave. Finally, Hannah turns to Juan: "Why Jason?"

"You tell me," Juan says. "What secret could he unlock for my Miguel? Think back—he was the older boy. He knew all things from your perspective, including the greatest secret of your childhood—the location of the place you called Lone Pine."

"What puzzle does Mickey want Jason to solve?" I ask. "At this point, I doubt it is finding Lone Pine."

"Mickey faces other challenges," Hannah says. "He is a casualty." Juan and I wait for her to say more but Hannah picks up some papers on the table.

"A part of him is in the past—perhaps his childhood, perhaps in Southeast Asia," Juan says. "It's not for us to untangle Miguel, however. I pray that will happen, but we must be his advocates, not his doctors. We must understand his needs in terms of the court system."

"He has shut down, closed everyone out—even you," Hannah says.

"You think this silence is a conscious choice?" Juan asks. "You of all people know that is not so."

"I am sorry, Mr. Cabrera—so very sorry," Hannah says.

Juan nods. "Miguel has been through too much."

"Here's a theory. I don't think Mickey has a grasp on reality and certainly no ability to formulate criminal intent. No criminal intent—no *mens rea*—no homicide," Hannah says.

"We're not looking at an insanity defense," I say. "The injury affecting Mickey's ability to speak or think clearly happened in the course of the crime. Unless he lacks mental capacity at the time of the crime, his deficiencies are no defense—they only make his defense more difficult, and that's the real problem. We can't defend Mickey at all."

Before both Hannah and Juan can react, I move ahead with my idea. "If Mickey can't communicate with us, can't participate in his own defense, doesn't understand the charges against him, he can't be tried. Our case theory—our strategy—at least for now—involves his competency to stand trial."

"Let us consider if that's a desirable posture for this case," Juan says. "If Miguel is found incompetent, he will be confined in a state hospital until such time as he is deemed mentally fit. He would then be tried for murder." Juan pauses. "Of course, over time, the State's ability to prosecute him will decline."

I look at Hannah. "What do you think?"

"Grant, are you willing to have him committed to a hospital for the criminally insane? Those are horrible places. The longer he stays in such a facility, the less likely it is he'll ever get out."

"So what do we do?" I ask. Juan and Hannah are silent. "The State has a dying declaration of the clerk coupled with some cash in Mickey's pockets."

"It's more than that. This is *my* son, Miguel Cabrera." Juan says the name slowly. "He is Hispanic, a Cuban, born in a country with which the great United States of America has no diplomatic relations—the closest homeland of communism in this hemisphere—Cuba—the home of the dreaded and despised Fidel Castro. Do you think a jury can look beyond that?''

Juan moves away from the table, stands erect, and straightens his tie. "Grant is right. Our case theory, at least for now, is clear. Mickey is incompetent to stand trial." He backs away another few steps. "My son is a veteran who served with honor and distinction—and now he is so sick he cannot be tried in a case he does not comprehend. It is a principled position."

I fall into a chair at the conference table as Juan leaves the room. "I'll explore the possibilities for civil confinement in a first-rate private hospital," I say. "Our goal should be a placement that avoids the horror of a state hospital."

Hannah gathers the paper from the table. Without looking up she says, "Mickey needs help— not months of waiting in some hospital. I know you think it's better to suffer delay than defeat, but we have to come up with something, Grant. Something that turns this around."

– 25 –

I met Dr. Victor Starling during my first year in practice. I represented a pedestrian run over by a U.S. Post Office truck. My client needed a neurological assessment. I spoke briefly about the case with my father who suggested I call Victor, a classmate of his who had gone on to become one of the pioneers in the field of neuropsychology.

In the last 36 hours, since our first meeting with Mickey, at Juan's and my request, Victor has seen Mickey several times. After the last visit, Juan invites him to stop by our office and discuss his findings. Juan asks Hannah and me to join them after Victor arrives. Victor lays a printout from Mickey's electroencephalogram on the conference table in my office. "Take a look at this," he says, pointing to a series of erratic lines.

"Is this is the result of the head trauma from the night of the crime in the bookstore?" Juan asks.

"This tells us there is a medical problem. It doesn't tell us precisely how or when it occurred," Victor says. "The overwhelming probability is that an injury occurred on the night he sustained the head trauma. I have him scheduled for a CT scan this afternoon. My guess is that we'll find a subdural hematoma—he will need surgery." Victor draws an oval on a sheet of yellow paper. "This is Miguel's head." He continues to draw as he speaks. "Here is his neck, and moving up from the base, his brain stem, the medulla and pons and the corpus callosum. So far, so good. This is the cerebellum and the cerebrum. It's well-protected—covered with a thick leathery skin, the dura, and insulated with cranial fluid. Here is the apparent point of impact."

I get up from my chair, stand behind Victor and Juan, and look at the picture. Victor shades in an area on the front portion of the drawing. "In all likelihood, a surgeon will have to clean out this area. It's a standard but risky operation. They peel back the scalp, remove a section of the skull, remove the hematoma, and then try to put him back together. If everything goes well, he should experience considerable improvement."

Juan nods. "Dr. Starling, you give me reason to expect a surgical miracle. If there is a successful operation, tell me—what I can expect of my Miguel?"

"We hope for comprehensive recovery—but I can't say with certainty that will happen." Victor looks at Juan. "It's appalling he was not given a thorough neurological examination when he was incarcerated. A man is found unconscious, a bleeding wound—a depressed skull fracture—and then thrown in a cell? That is barbaric. Let me know when the trial is scheduled. I want to hear how the State explains its non-treatment of your son. In the meantime, I'll set the wheels in motion to get him a first-rate neurosurgeon—I'm hoping to have him in the hospital tomorrow morning. If my hunch is right, there is no time to waste."

– 26 –

It is almost nine when Juan and I finish the paperwork needed to secure VA health insurance for Mickey's hospitalization and upcoming surgery. "I will hand-deliver these in the morning," Juan says as he puts on his overcoat.

After Juan leaves, I settle into my office and begin to go through a growing stack of mail and messages. Before making much progress, the phone rings. It is Lieutenant Wallace Huntington of the Caulfield County Police Department, and he catches me completely off guard.

Lieutenant Huntington has news and needs just a short time with me. He is down the street—

only a block or two away—and wonders if I have a moment. Under normal circumstances, Juan and Hannah would be with me in a meeting of this nature, but there is no time and I have no reason to alarm them.

—

Lieutenant Wallace Huntington could have taken early retirement in 1973—his finances were in order, his children grown, his record of service with the Caulfield County Police Department beyond reproach, his connections with other aspects of the community life—including his church and the Haydon Township Kiwanis Club—strong, all giving hope for rich and rewarding golden years. These parts of his life were made public when an article appeared in the CAULFIELD COUNTY JOURNAL on the anniversary of his thirty-fifth year as the county's chief law enforcement officer. My mother sent me a copy without her characteristic note. She still has nothing good to say about the Lieutenant after all these years—and with nothing good to say, she says nothing at all.

Contrary to my concerns about gangsters seventeen years earlier, Caulfield County is not exactly a hotbed of organized crime, and in his years on the force, Lieutenant Huntington and his able associates have maintained order—few criminal acts go unpunished. Between 1958 and 1975, as Haydon tripled in size and new roads were built, there were concomitant law enforcement responsibilities—particularly traffic control—all addressed impressively by Lieutenant Huntington, or so said the article. Perhaps a lesser public servant would have been content with these accomplishments, but Lieutenant Wallace Huntington is not such an official.

With all its detail and effusive praise, the article left out the driving force that prevents the Lieutenant from the repose he apparently deserves. As former girlfriend and psychologist-in-training Lisa Montgomery pointed out to me the day I was deleted from her list of possible mates, it is impossible to compete with an obsession, and—like Hannah and me—Lieutenant Huntington is obsessed with a single unsolved case, the disappearance of Jason Talbot, as his visit to my office makes clear.

"In my office, I have an entire wall covered with pictures of your woods," he explains. "Thirty square miles is a vast area but not infinite."

"The woods seemed infinite to us when we were kids," I say. "I imagine one day they will be developed—turned into tract housing—and that will be a terrible loss."

"I did not come up here to discuss the possible development of that area. I read about your big settlement—the one involving the chef who claimed an electric blender attacked him—quite a story—but then again, stories are your specialty—this one made the front page of the JOURNAL. I wanted to see your office." Lieutenant Huntington coughs several times—clearly, cigarettes have taken their toll. "You're a lucky young man, Grant. You managed to avoid the draft and now, while most people are struggling to make a buck, you have struck it rich. Your buddy—Mickey Cabrera—isn't doing so well as I understand it."

Mickey's arrest was reported in our local paper today, and Lieutenant Huntington's comments do not come as a surprise. "We represent Mickey, as you probably know, and I can't discuss anything about his situation. Is that why you're here?"

"You're very good at keeping secrets," Lieutenant Huntington says. "I know that better than most."

"Then you know I'm not going to discuss Mickey Cabrera. How can I help you, Lieutenant?"

"Mind if I look around?" he says. He stands up and walks behind my desk, looking at the various certificates hanging on the wall and then walks to the door and stands in front of my sketch of Lone Pine. "I'll be darned." He turns to me. "I just happen to have a warrant issued by a judge in the Superior Court of Caulfield County to seize this drawing." He turns to the conference table, extracts a search warrant from his brief case and hands it to me.

"Lieutenant, I'm tired and it's late—otherwise I'd be happy to play along with you. This warrant can't be legitimate. No judge would sign off on something like this."

"I just needed a signature, counsel, and I got one," he says.

"How did you know about this picture?"

"Just a coincidence—one of your clients is a former cop—he mentioned that he saw this picture on your wall. It's important to my investigation— hence, the warrant."

"Investigation of what?" Lieutenant Huntington raises his eyebrows but does not respond. "This is about Jason Talbot, isn't it? You've come up with something new?"

"You still hold all the cards, Grant," Lieutenant Huntington says. "I've been trying to put together a puzzle for seventeen years and most of the key pieces are still missing. When I was able to pry you away from your mother during the initial investigation, I was sure I could get to you—but for some reason, you would not talk. When the District Attorney told me he wanted to go forward with a grand jury investigation, I told him that he'd get nothing from you—and I was right. People who do, or see, terrible things have a way of locking up and you locked up but good."

"Don't you think I would have said something if I had any idea where Jason was?" I notice that Lieutenant Huntington has taken his small note pad from his lapel pocket. "Are you reopening this investigation?"

"This investigation was never closed and, to be blunt, I never believed you."

He pauses. "You know Hack Talbot was a friend. This was his son."

I had heard the Lieutenant and Hack had a falling out a month before Hack died—but Hack has been dead for nearly fifteen years. This is not about Hack—or friendship. My guess—and it's just that— is that this is about an internal torment, a maddening, festering, relentless, and powerful sense of incompletion.

"Am I a suspect?" I ask.

"Did you know we ran grappling hooks along the base of St. Clare and Willis Creeks?"

"When?" I ask.

"After the snows melted—during April and May, 1959. There was nothing there, Grant, nothing at all. The gang hooks we used will pick up the remains of even a small boy, but he was not there."

"You did not answer my question. Am I a suspect?"

"I've kept an eye on the Talbots over the years. Long after my friend Hack died, I kept looking. They're an interesting bunch, particularly Hack's brother, Luther—but they haven't seen Jason since December 1958—I'm sure of that. On the other side of the family, I thought Jason might turn up at his aunt's home—the same place where Valerie Talbot lived—but it did not happen. The grandfather, Connor Clarke—now there is an interesting character— very successful—worth a fortune—owns a number of munitions factories, a thriving company that sells athletic equipment. You'd think he'd use all that money to nail you, Grant, but he doesn't even like to talk about Jason. As far as I can tell none of them have had any contact with Jason." He stares at my pencil drawing before continuing. "That leaves me—and you. Where did he go, Grant?"

"If I knew, I would tell you. Children do disappear. It's tragic but true. I wish I could help you, Lieutenant—more than you know."

"Tell me something—did you have a backpack with you the day that you and Jason went on your famous expedition?"

"I didn't, but Jason did. You knew that—I testified about the knapsack before the grand jury."

Lieutenant Huntington pulls from his briefcase a snapshot and hands it to me. "Is this it?" he asks.

Set on a gray laboratory table are the tattered remains of what might have been a knapsack. I can see an evidence tag attached to what appears to be a strap. "Where did you find this?" I ask.

"Where do you think?" Lieutenant Huntington says.

"I assume in the woods behind my house."

"That would be a reasonable assumption," Lieutenant Huntington says. "Unfortunately, I can't tell you whether you're correct or not." He takes back the picture. "This was turned over to my office a month ago. A family on DeWitt Street has a beautiful liver-colored Lab who wandered off. They figured that the dog was lost or hit by a car and a day or two later he reappeared—with this backpack in his mouth."

"Is this the basis of a renewed investigation?" I ask. "You have no idea whether that was Jason's backpack—and from the picture, neither do I."

"That—and your client making reference to Jason Talbot in his bail hearing—was enough to get the search warrant."

I stand up, hand Lieutenant Huntington his coat, and begin the process of showing him the door. "I never lied to you about any of this. Do you want me to take a lie detector test?"

"Skilled liars, counsel, are not caught in lie detectors. We both know that."

"What is your problem, Lieutenant? Jason is gone—I don't know if he is dead or not."

"People don't just disappear. It would be a sad state of affairs in this country if small children simply vanished." Huntington leans forward. "I am not done with this—or with you. You are protecting someone—or yourself—and I will be goddamned if I let you get away with it. You don't get to play God—not when you're ten—and not now."

"Get out, Lieutenant."

"I have spent more time in police work than you have been alive. I resolve disputes. I solve hard cases. I let this one go once—I'm not letting it go again."

"Fine—have at it. In the meantime, I'm going home and having dinner—and I want my picture back when this is over," I say as I show Lieutenant Huntington the door.

– 27 –

By 7:15 a.m. Mickey is shaved, anesthetized, and whisked away into the operating room at Albany General.

Mrs. Cabrera and other members of the family huddle around Juan in the hospital waiting room. He stands off to one side of the room and holds forth. "I've checked the credentials of the surgeon thoroughly," Juan says. "There is no one better suited for this operation." I watch as Juan reassures his family. They listen to him because his very presence inspires calm—the same cannot be said of me. After a final testimonial regarding the surgeon's brilliance, Juan returns to his seat.

"It was nice of you to come here today, Mr. Harper." Mickey's younger sister, Teresa, is standing next to me. "We did not expect you to come to the hospital. We thought you would send Hannah Wein—or is it Weiner? Mickey must be very important to your firm."

"He isn't just a client, he is my friend," I say. "You know that. Hannah would have come as well but there are things that must be taken care of in our office—for Mickey as well as our other clients." Teresa was born when Mickey was eight and while Hannah and I spent many hours in the Cabrera home, we barely knew her.

"Of course," she says. "My mother tells me that when the criminal case is over you and my father will sue the city for failing to treat my brother when he was in jail." She folds her arms across her chest. "Your firm gets one-third of my brother's money. Do I have that right?"

"Our concern is Mickey's well-being. If he has a legitimate claim, we will pursue it—if that's his choice," I say.

"And if you do," Teresa says, "he will have to give your firm one-third of anything the city gives to him. Doesn't that bother you? Mickey will need every penny he can get. If this operation is not successful, he may never be able to work, to study, to read. Do you think we are stupid people? Mickey won't be the same man he was before this. Your interest, Mr. Harper, is mercenary."

"You know that isn't true," I say.

"You took him on, Mr. Harper, because he can make you quite wealthy." Teresa turns and starts to walk away.

"We took him on because he is one of our oldest friends. Mickey, Hannah, and I were inseparable before you were born. He needs our help," I say.

"Everyone is scared," I hear Juan say. He guides Teresa to a chair and kisses her forehead. Her head drops in her hands and she is sobbing. "She loves her brother very much," Juan says as he sits beside me. "You just had a minor collision with her anxiety."

"It came out of nowhere," I say.

—

The surgery seems to go on forever. It is 5:00 p.m. when the surgeon appears. Hannah joins Juan and me in the waiting room to hear the news.

"The subdural hematoma was the size of a tennis ball," the surgeon says. "It's amazing Mickey could function at all. The compression in the left frontal lobe may prove to have very unfortunate consequences."

"How long does it take for something like that to form?" Juan asks.

"Hard to say," the surgeon responds. "Given the texture and composition, the size ... maybe a few weeks."

"Had you operated sooner, could this have been avoided?" Juan asks.

"Again, I can't be sure. Certainly, it would not have achieved this level of mass."

"How long before we'll know the full extent of his deficits?" Juan asks.

"One to two years—maybe more," he responds. "The brain heals slowly. There is also the possibility that we could end up with another bleed. Hundreds of tiny vessels ruptured in the impact area. I did what I could to seal them, but as they heal, they can develop mass. Additional bleeding may take place and another clot may form. The brain might respond by attaching a web of tiny capillaries to the new clot—the longer that goes on, the larger the mass—the greater the downstream risk."

"Is that what you expect?" Hannah asks.

"It's a risk. Let's hope for the best. I'll monitor him closely," the doctor answers. "He is in the recovery area—a few family members can go in and visit." I watch as Juan directs his family to the recovery room where they will stand at the bedside and pray. After Juan returns, the surgeon continues. "There is a confidential matter, Mr. Cabrera—I should speak with you alone."

"Please," Juan says, "we have no secrets. What is it, doctor?"

"Very well. Are you aware that Miguel's body has been affected—weakened—by his narcotic addiction?" When Juan says nothing in response, the surgeon continues. "His initial blood series shows elevated levels of quinine."

"Quinine? Like tonic water?" I ask.

"Sellers use quinine to cut heroin—it affects the bitter taste. I have to report this."

"Not if it's just quinine," Hannah says. "Quinine can come from many sources. I know those rules, doctor...."

"Well, good for you," the surgeon says. Neurosurgeons, I have discovered, are remarkably talented—but not necessarily the most sensitive members of the medical community. "Listen, he is positive for methadone and it's possible when the full lab report is complete, they will find traces of diacetylmorphine—heroin—as well."

"What about needle marks on his arm? Did you see any?" I ask.

"No—he uses his legs—his hips, actually. It isn't all that uncommon. Unless you see him with his pants down, you would not notice. By the way, did you know the derivation of the term "hippie" comes from addicts who shoot up using the upper thigh?" the doctor asks, as if we are discussing a crossword puzzle.

"But he's been off the street for more than a month," I say.

"I can't be precise based on his blood levels—but he has taken methadone in the last thirty-six hours. Now heroin—that's in your system for three days—in rare cases a few more. After that, it becomes somewhat speculative. Similarly, quinine passes out of the system in under a week—however, the markers for quinine were unequivocal."

"Where is he getting it?" I ask.

"That will become your problem, I suppose."
He slaps his knees with both hands. "Well, I have
other patients." He delivers his parting line flatly:
"Heroin addiction is common with returning Vietnam veterans—it's a national tragedy."

Juan shakes the surgeon's hand and walks
away with him. "Juan will try to get the doctor to
hold off on reporting this," Hannah says. "I hope
he succeeds."

We leave after Hannah hugs most members of
the Cabrera family—including Teresa. Hannah
takes my arm as we head to the parking lot. "We
need to talk," she says as we reach her car. "Not
here. Meet me at Nuevo Leon in an hour."

—

Hannah is in a booth in the rear of the restaurant when I arrive. "How are you holding up?" she
asks as I sit down.

"I'm fine. What's this about?"

Hannah looks at the pressed tin ceiling of the
restaurant and takes a deep breath. "I should have
told you a long time ago, Grant." She takes hold of
my hand. "I tried to stop him. I even got your
father involved. He agreed to help and had him
hospitalized a few times but Mickey could not stay
with the programs."

"I don't understand. You knew about Mickey's
addiction? My father knew?"

"I was more than Mickey's old friend over the
last few years," Hannah says. "I worked in a pharmacy that handled the needs of many returning
Vietnam veterans. We had a substantial supply of

methadone. Dr. Blake was nearly blind—and Mickey was suffering. I took advantage of my position. I couldn't stand to see Mickey in so much pain. I was his methadone supplier, Grant. Week in and week out, for a long time."

"Jesus Christ, Hannah! You can get disbarred for that—you can end up in jail. You can't keep things like this from me."

"That was Mickey's call. He didn't want you to know. He put on a show whenever you were around. You and I have professions, Grant. In Mickey's eyes, we have done all the right things. He doesn't want to be seen as a failure, especially by you," Hannah says.

"And you couldn't have told me at some point? You're my partner—and my friend. There aren't supposed to be secrets between us. I had a right to know Mickey was in this kind of trouble. Don't you think I could have helped?"

"There is more, Grant. When Mickey came home from Vietnam, I was the person he came to see first. He wrote me letters, very private ones, when he was overseas and made clear he was anxious to see me."

"I felt the same way—I remember we...."

She hesitates as I catch up. "They were special letters, Grant. He was lonely and it was natural that he wanted to have a girl back home. I was that girl. The three of us have been so close for so long— he thought he loved me." She hesitates.

"You don't tell me much," I say slowly. "I had no idea." I have to ask. "Did you love him, Hannah?"

"It was easy in the letters—it kept me in control and gave me a way to fend off other guys," she says.

"Are you two still . . . ?"

"No—of course not. We never were—I have always loved Mickey—but not in that way." She stops. "The three of us," she says, "what we have is love, isn't it?" I nod. "But Mickey wanted more— maybe I led him on—but we never. . . . " She stops. "Really, Grant, we were not intimate, if that's what you're thinking."

"I wasn't asking that, Hannah." This is a lie, of course.

"I could tell—the first day—after he got out of the VA hospital. Mickey was not himself. I was overwhelmed with law school and work at the pharmacy, but that was not the problem. Mickey was barely there half the time. He had lost interest in so many things that used to be important to him—he was in no shape to start a serious relationship."

"Had he been healthy, is that what would have happened—a serious relationship?"

"Goddamn, Grant, enough." She pauses. "Actually, no. That was never going to happen." Her tone softens. "I think—I hope—at some level, you know that—so stop asking."

At least three times I start to ask what she means and stop myself. This is Hannah—my law partner. We share all aspects of our business and one key to our success is that we are tough with each other, just as we have always been. I can take—and use—her criticism on all things pertaining to our clients—but the potential of rejection from her at a personal level is too grave a risk.

After I fail to follow up on her comment, she continues. "Mickey is more than a friend and I would do anything for him—and I did. Even after I left the pharmacy, I took enough methadone to last until Mickey got things turned around. A few months ago, I turned all of it over to Teresa after she convinced me that she would take care of her brother. Mickey signed an admission form to a rehab center where patients are not free to leave. Teresa was convinced he would kick it this time. Next thing I heard, he was in jail."

"You should have included me, Hannah." I say, struggling to stay focused.

"I made him a promise, Grant—I swore I would not tell you." She stops and looks away. "I don't break promises."

"I'm not sure I would have handled things any better than you did," I say. "If Mickey had asked me for money, I would have given it to him and I would have been compounding the problem, not helping." I look at Hannah. "Teresa is still supplying him with methadone?"

"She swears the carton is empty."

"Do you believe her?"

Hannah shakes her head. "I am not sure what happens next," she says. "Each time Mickey was in rehab, he would sign himself in, stay until the withdrawal was too much, and leave. Even if we can get him into a private rehab program, I have no idea who will pay for it—or if he'll make it. Juan paid for the parts of each hospitalization not covered by the VA—and he just posted the house as collateral for Mickey's bail—the Cabrera family must be close to tapped out."

"Hence, the civil case," I say.

Hannah leans forward. "Damn right," she says quietly. "They need money—tens and tens of thousands of dollars. Juan saw this possibility immediately...."

"Of course he did," I say. "So did you, I assume. I, on the other hand, had no way to know about the addiction...."

"Mickey was strong, smart, funny, athletic, and ambitious when he left for Vietnam. Look what they've done to him." She pauses and I can tell this is hard for her. "Look what he's done to himself. Grant, at some level, you had to know."

—

Our law firm foyer is dark when we return. Hannah stands behind me as I unlock the door to my office. "I can't believe Huntington took the Lone Pine sketch." I told her about the Lieutenant's visit last night after he left but we have not been in the office together until now. She looks at the space on my wall where the picture was hanging until yesterday. "Did he leave you a copy of the backpack photograph?"

"No—it's hard to believe a warrant would issue based on Mickey's ramblings about Jason and a rotting backpack."

"My guess is that Huntington has been around long enough—and is on good enough terms with the local judges—that he can get a warrant to do pretty much whatever he wants at this point." Hannah hesitates. "Is it clear that you're the target of an investigation?"

"I asked him if I was a suspect and he evaded the question."

"This is serious," Hannah says. "We don't need any distractions right now—and we don't need bad publicity."

"I don't have anything to hide, Hannah."

"I know that," she says. "The problem is, we are about to launch into a trial. Our strategy could entail getting a sympathetic assessment of Mickey's situation from the media. We'll want them to focus on his service to his country, not on the fact that his lawyer is the subject of a seventeen-year old murder investigation."

– 28 –

December 1975

An article in THE CAULFIELD COUNTY JOURNAL regarding the resurrected investigation into the disappearance of Jason Talbot causes phones to ring throughout Haydon. My mother calls the moment she sees it.

"Were you listening when I read you the article, Grant?" she says. "While your name is not mentioned, Lieutenant Huntington says: 'I have my sights set on the prime suspect. It's a matter of time.' He's after you—you need to protect yourself."

"Lieutenant Huntington is as perplexed as he was years ago—and with the decayed backpack, he figures he has the first piece of tangible evidence since Jason's disappearance. I would like nothing better than to get to the bottom of this."

"You're being naïve, Grant," she says. "For Wallace Huntington, a solution exists when he has a suspect in custody—not when he has Jason. You are that suspect. He needs someone to blame for his failure to find Jason and it will be you if you aren't careful."

"Then I'll be careful," I say. "Hannah and I can handle Lieutenant Huntington—you need to trust me on this. In the meantime, I need to stay focused on Mickey."

———

It has been a month since Mickey's surgery and, despite the removal of the subdural hematoma and careful monitoring, he continues to be uncommunicative. This could be attributable to his injury or to a combination of other factors, including his use of narcotics. Hannah and I have confronted Teresa who swears that Mickey is clean, and we try to impress on her the importance of things staying that way. An incompetence defense, like an insanity defense, will fail if the reason for the incapacity is self-administration of narcotics. Narcotics aside, Mickey is completely incapable of participating in his own defense on the first day of his competency hearing.

—

Albany's bitter cold contrasts with the stifling heat in the courtroom. The large windows on the left side of the room are masked with condensation. Hannah holds Mickey's arm and guides him to his seat. We are the only case on the docket. The State will rely on Dr. Alvin Merton, the psychologist hired by the city, who will testify that Mickey is competent.

I intend to call Victor Starling as my only witness. I will not call Mickey unless ordered by the judge. If Mickey testifies, I have no way of predicting what he will say. For the most part, he exists in an angry dream state.

Mickey sits between Hannah and me in the courtroom, his white shirt washed but not ironed. The knot on his tie is far to one side and almost buried beneath the floppy collar. His pants, two sizes too large, are belted high, above his navel, exposing his white socks and black shoes. The cuffs of his shirt hang almost to his fingertips and are buttoned. It is a clown-like appearance—carefully tailored by Hannah.

The bailiff calls, "All rise," and the Honorable Judge Miles Prentice enters the room. "Competency hearing, *In Re Miguel Cabrera, People of the State of New York versus Cabrera*," the bailiff announces.

"Is the defense ready?" Judge Prentice asks. I nod. "The State?" Owen Hollister, the Assistant District Attorney assigned to the case, nods as well.

Owen Hollister is a few years out of law school and despite his heavy caseload—and contrary to our hopes—has been unwilling to plea bargain. When

we raised the matter of Mickey's mental state,
Hollister flat out rejected our claim. He seems anxious to have a trial on the merits, and not pleased
about being dragged into a competency hearing, a
proceeding in which he bears the burden of convinc-
ing the court that Mickey is sufficiently sane to
understand the charges against him.

"Pursuant to my earlier ruling, you will begin
Mr. Harper," Judge Prentice announces. "That
doesn't alter the burden of proof which rests with
the State. It is your task, Mr. Hollister, to convince
me by a preponderance of the evidence, that Miguel
Cabrera is fit to stand trial. Assuming that is clear,
I suggest we begin. Mr. Harper?"

"I have an opening statement, Your Honor," I
say and wait for Judge Prentice to nod in my
direction.

"Any time, Mr. Harper," he says without looking up.

"Some weeks after the commission of the crime
with which Mr. Cabrera is charged, a massive subdural hematoma was removed from his left frontal
lobe. Both before and after that operation, I have
been in contact with my client but not in communication with him. I considered withdrawing, unsure
how to represent an individual with whom I could
not communicate, but that would solve nothing.

"Until such time as there is a significant
change in Mr. Cabrera's condition, a fair trial is an
impossibility. My client lacks coherence, his short-
term memory is corrupted—he has no recollection
of the day on which the offense occurred.

"Your Honor, the State has contended this competency hearing is a maneuver designed to avoid a criminal trial. Nothing could be farther from the truth. We are here seeking commitment, confinement in a psychiatric institution, and that is hardly the easy way out."

"Mr. Hollister?" Judge Prentice asks.

"Mr. Harper would have us believe he has come before this Court to insure the imprisonment of his own client in a state mental hospital. I'm quite sure Mr. Harper understands this Court has many options regarding the fate of Mr. Cabrera, should a determination of incompetency be made. Thank you."

"Thank you, Mr. Hollister. Now, Mr. Harper?"

"Dr. Victor Starling." I stand while Victor is sworn in. The radiator underneath the window closest to the bailiff hisses and then shakes violently. "It does that sometimes," Judge Prentice says as Victor takes his seat, looking nervously to his right. The radiator hisses again, threatening a second eruption but the fit stops as suddenly as it starts.

The smell of rust and old water hangs in the air and Mickey reaches his left hand to the far end of the table and he pushes himself, chair and all, away from me. Juan is up immediately and places his large hands on Mickey's shoulders, as if to keep him from rising up in the air. Mickey tilts his head backwards, his eyes wide, and stares at his father. Juan says, "Sweet boy," in Spanish, leans over and kisses Mickey on the forehead, and returns to his seat.

My direct examination of Dr. Starling is focused entirely on Mickey's present condition, since the question is whether, at this moment, he is fit to stand trial. It takes most of the morning to describe the physiology of the head injury. To move from that to competency, I ask about the standardized tests Mickey has taken in the last month.

"I've run the gamut with Mr. Cabrera, and as I stated in my report, it has been a difficult assessment. There are times when Mr. Cabrera seems able to carry on a conversation and times when he does not. For that reason, he can't perform appropriately on a number of the standardized tests, and those we can score are troubling. The extent of his problems becomes even more apparent in light of the description of his behavior before the injury provided by his family, as well as other pre-morbid data."

"Pre-morbid?"

"Testing data from before his injury. We have his high school grades, a college transcript, his military record, and examples of his writing."

"Based on that pre-morbid data, are you in a position to make a judgment regarding Mr. Cabrera's capacity prior to the injury to his brain?"

"Mr. Cabrera was a 'B+' student across the board. His writing was rather eloquent and organized. From what I can tell, he was fully bilingual. While it is difficult to evaluate personality, based on the information I have received, it would seem he was a relatively normal individual."

"And now?"

"There are many ways to describe Mr. Cabrera's condition, Mr. Harper. Normal is not one of them."

– 29 –

Owen Hollister's cross-examination of Victor Starling is thorough. It seems to take forever and I hear Juan's sigh of relief when he finished. He whispers to me: "There is not enough money in Albany to buy excessive and irritating cross-examination like that. The judge stopped listening an hour ago."

"I wish I had your confidence," I say.

"So do I, Grant," Juan says.

We join the Cabrera family in the hallway. "Was any harm done?" Teresa asks. "Why didn't you object more?"

"Mr. Harper was giving Hollister enough rope so that he could hang himself," Juan says.

She looks at her father. "You're sure?" she asks.

Juan puts his arm around her and says, "Just watch."

We recess for lunch at 11:45 with the instruction that the hearing will commence at 2:00 p.m., giving us an unusually long lunch period.

"We must remember, if all goes well today, Miguel will be declared incompetent to stand trial, and will be institutionalized for a period of time," Juan says as we wait at the elevator with the other members of the Cabrera family.

"It is better than going to jail," Teresa says.

"I believe this is the best course for now," Juan says. "This has never been a good case for the State. When our prayers are answered and Miguel is again well, the State's interest in a second trial may be limited. Such a trial might take place in a year or two. Much can change in that period of time. The family of the bookstore clerk will still be grieving the loss of a loved one, but life will have moved on. Information gets lost, witnesses are difficult to locate, and the State's interest in prosecuting Mickey may well dissipate."

"I think Jason's coming," Mickey says.

"Jason isn't coming," Hannah says evenly.

"Then Arthur—now."

It is the first time Mickey has spoken clearly in days and we all turn and look at him. Juan responds first. "Do you mean Arthur Soto?" Mickey nods. "Arthur Soto will not be here today, Miguel. You want help because you feel so sick—and you think the friend you seek can make you better." Mickey nods. "Now I understand."

"I do not understand, Juan," Mrs. Cabrera says. "Who?"

Juan looks at Mickey. "You look ridiculous, my son. Straighten your tie."

Mickey takes the short end of his tie in his left hand and holds the knot of the tie in his right and pulls with such sudden force that his head is thrown back. His father grabs him and Mickey continues to pull as they fall to the floor. Teresa and I grab at Mickey's collar and tear open his shirt at the neckline. Juan removes the tie completely and Mickey lies on the floor, his body shaking. Mickey's eyes are wide open and the shaking becomes more violent.

Teresa is on her knees next to her brother. "It will stop in a moment. The key is to keep him from hurting himself."

We watch as Mickey's body quiets.

"The stress of the hearing is too much for him," Juan says.

"I thought he was taking phenobarbital?" I turn to Teresa. "I thought that was to prevent seizures."

"Maybe he hasn't taken it for a few days," Teresa says softly. "He says it makes him like a dead man."

"He said that?" Hannah asks. "He said 'it makes me like a dead man?'" Mickey's sister is silent. "I haven't heard him use such complex language for months."

"You know he can speak that way sometimes," Teresa says to Hannah.

"Not recently," Hannah says.

Two police officers wait with us until the ambulance arrives. There will be no continuation of the hearing this afternoon. Hannah and I navigate the back hallways to Judge Prentice's chambers where we find his law clerk and inform him that Mickey Cabrera has had a seizure and will need rest.

Mickey is on a stretcher surrounded by his family and paramedics when we return to the hallway. "You must be brave, Miguel." Juan pats Mickey on the cheek.

As the Cabrera family and the medical entourage leave, I notice Lieutenant Wallace Huntington leaning on the hallway wall adjacent to us, watching. "Did you bring my picture back, Lieutenant?" I ask.

"I wanted to watch you in court," he says. "I wondered if you would be distracted by all the attention in Haydon—you're the talk of the town. I guess you are able to compartmentalize things—the Jason Talbot investigation goes into the root cellar while you defend your friend, Cabrera. Compartmentalization is a mark of amorality."

"Don't you have something better to do with your time, Lieutenant?" Hannah says, moving between the Lieutenant and me. "Why don't you go back to Haydon and track down some unlicensed deer hunters?"

"Hannah Weiner—or I guess it's Wein now—all grown up. Are you always that impolite? I guess it goes with the profession," Lieutenant Huntington says.

I grab Hannah's arm—a knuckle punch from her would do neither of us much good. "There is a respect and dignity in my profession that you could not begin to understand," she says, pulling at my grip, although not all that forcefully.

"You're still new at this business, Ms. Wein. Wait a few years—I'm sure you will be singing a different tune." He pauses. "Maybe it won't take that long. Your partner can explain. You see, he has decided to let a family suffer—for seventeen years—

rather than putting himself at risk. The Talbots have gone too long without an answer—but your partner doesn't seem inclined to help them by clearing up Jason's disappearance ... hardly respectful or dignified, is it Ms. Wein?''

I pull Hannah back a few inches and reply before she can respond. "Do you think insulting me—or Ms. Wein—will further your investigation? When are you going to get it through your head that I know nothing more than I knew seventeen years ago? I'm not going to try to stop you—or even slow you down. You didn't lose Jason in the woods that afternoon—I did. You haven't lost a thousand nights' sleep trying to figure out what happened— right under your nose—but I have, Lieutenant. Now, if you have something to say—or another unlawful warrant to execute—go for it. If not, then I suggest you find something more productive to do with your time.''

As I turn Hannah and steer her down the hallway away from Lieutenant Huntington, she says, quite audibly: "One of the worst toupees I've ever seen.''

Lieutenant Huntington, as far as I know, does not wear a toupee, opting instead for a comb-over that fools no one. As we turn the corner, I notice him looking at his reflection in a glass-covered bulletin board, rearranging his remaining locks.

– 30 –

Juan, Hannah, and I sit in a booth at Nuevo Leon sipping strong black coffee from small cups. "I really thought you were going to pop Lieutenant Huntington in the nose," I say to Hannah.

"I knew you'd grab me," she says.

Juan interrupts. "I appreciate your dispute with this noxious official, but we have more important things to discuss, beginning with the upcoming testimony of this Dr. Merton. His written report is very basic—superficial—Judge Prentice will see through it."

"We don't know that," Hannah says. "Depending on Judge Prentice's view of the report, he could agree with the State—find Mickey sick—but competent—and then what?"

"Then we go to trial on the merits—and at present, we have no real case to present." I take another sip of coffee and look at Juan. "We have one distant possibility, assuming we can find the other person in the bookstore."

"Who might that be?" says Juan.

"We know he is the one who picked up the gun and ran," I say. "We know Mickey did not have it on him. There had to be someone else at the scene. Is it likely that another student, another customer, enters the store, sees two men lying on the floor, bleeding, picks up what would appear to be a murder weapon, and leaves? Who would take that chance?"

"No one—the only one likely to touch the gun at that point would be someone who does not want it to fall into the hands of the police," Hannah says.

"This is speculation," Juan says. "We cannot concern ourselves with phantoms. The State is looking for a trial, for a culprit, and Miguel is all they have."

"He is not all we have," I say, turning to Juan. "Who is Arthur Soto?"

"You do not want to know," Juan says.

"I certainly do," I say.

"Very well. Arthur Soto is a drug dealer—a pusher," Juan says. "Let me assure you, Arthur Soto is nothing but trouble." Juan looks around the restaurant, but we are the only ones there. "At one point, before you began practicing here, Soto was a major figure in the Latino community, but his star has fallen."

"Do you think Soto was involved in the robbery?" Hannah asks.

"That is possible—but not my point. Miguel wants to see Arthur Soto because of his illness. His memory may be disrupted but his addiction is powerful and he does seem to recall how to secure drugs. It would be best if this information is not disclosed. It would support the thesis that he is only selectively incompetent."

There is a long pause. Finally, Hannah says, "The civil case seems solid. His condition mandated more aggressive treatment. We can prove that with the neurosurgeon's report and Dr. Starling's testimony. I am ready to file. Maybe this will push the State in the right direction in the competency proceeding."

"Quite the opposite," I say. "We wait. When the competency hearing is over, we can file."

"We should start discovery now," Hannah says.

"We'd get nothing, Hannah. The State would shut us down in a heartbeat. They are mid-stream in a criminal case. The whole thing would be stayed. We wait."

I spend the afternoon reviewing the notes from the hearing and preparing for the next session. This is not complicated. I have not had a single useful discussion with Mickey regarding strategy and tactics, nor has he ever appeared to understand when I explain to him his basic rights.

I close my trial notebook and begin to sketch on a pad. I always use the same simple thin lines. It is Lone Pine in the dead of winter. When I finish, I tape it to the wall next to my door, filling in the space left by Lieutenant Huntington's seizure of my picture. It will be the first thing I see each morning as I hang up my coat until Wallace Huntington returns my framed drawing.

—

By morning, I have pages of questions for Dr. Alvin Merton. Hannah has started drafting an opinion for Judge Prentice in the event he asks for a proposed order at the conclusion of the competency proceedings. This must be a carefully written document, making reference to the exhibits that have been admitted as well as case and statutory material. If we can get the judge to sign it, it will greatly aid us on the civil side of Mickey's case. The order should make clear that it is not what the State did when Mickey was in their custody—it is what they failed to do that has led to his tragic deterioration. We will finish the proposed order after all witnesses have testified.

We load a cart to bring to the courtroom with the texts we need to address any argument or contingency that arises when Juan walks in carrying a picnic basket. Two thermos bottles protrude from either end of the basket, and I know they are full of the best coffee in Albany. "Mrs. Cabrera prepared breakfast for us," Juan says. "She has gone to Mass. She will be praying for Miguel—and for you, Grant—this morning."

He places the food on the conference table and the smell of fresh homemade Cuban breads and breakfast rolls competes with the rich coffee from the Cabrera kitchen. While it is a tempting morning feast, I can eat only a few bites. "What kind of strategy is this? We're defense lawyers, marshaling every asset at our disposal so that we can get our client incarcerated in a mental hospital. This can't be the right thing to do."

"We reviewed every alternative, Grant," Juan says. "This is still our best option for my son."

The phone rings and Juan answers. "I'm going to take this in my office," he says and leaves the room.

He is back in less than a minute, his coat already on. "I must go out. It will take some time."

"We have a hearing today—you can't leave now. What could be more important than this?" I ask.

"Arthur Soto. I shall meet with him." Juan is out the door before I can stop him.

I have to concentrate on the hearing. I cannot accompany Juan—even assuming he wants me to join him—without compromising Mickey's interests. Yet, Juan heads toward danger, to meet a known criminal. My friend and senior colleague will confront risk and I do not know how to help him.

I yelled till my throat hurt the day Jason disappeared and there was no response.

I bolt down the office stairs and stand on the street. I shield my eyes, turning from left to right, looking for Juan. I am too late. Juan is gone.

– 31 –

The hearing begins with Owen Hollister introducing the State's only expert witness, Dr. Alvin Merton. Dr. Merton moved to Albany fifteen years ago with the hope of setting up a family counseling practice. In the late sixties, he became friends with the head District Attorney in Albany, a contact he nurtured. At present, half his income is derived from the city, the remainder coming from his private practice.

Hollister spends an inordinate amount of time qualifying Dr. Merton as an expert witness. After ten minutes Judge Prentice interrupts. "Mr. Hollister, we now know everything about Dr. Merton except for the size of his suit coat."

"Forty-two-long," Merton says.

Judge Prentice looks at Dr. Merton. "The court appreciates that information, Doctor."

Before Hollister responds, I say, "Your Honor, we have no objection to Dr. Merton testifying as an expert."

"I did not think you would, Mr. Harper," Judge Prentice says. I turn and look at the chair Juan occupied when we were last in this courtroom. The Cabrera family sits behind me. They have placed a coat on Juan's seat, in the event he appears during the course of the hearing. I have no doubt his absence is as disconcerting to them as it is to me.

Hollister does not hide the fact that Merton has spent all of two hours with Mickey Cabrera. During that time, Merton testifies, he administered a standard battery of tests. The scores Mickey received were, for all practical purposes, identical to scores discussed by Victor Starling. It is finally Hollister's great moment.

"Based on your observations and the tests given, have you formed an opinion regarding the competency of Miguel Cabrera?" Hollister asks.

"I have," Merton says.

"Can you share with us that opinion, Doctor?" Hollister asks.

"Mickey Cabrera is a drug addict." I watch as Judge Prentice stiffens. Dr. Merton continues. "During the course of his confinement, he went through some form of withdrawal. In addition, Mr. Cabrera received a blow to the head that resulted in a subdural hematoma that was operated on about one month ago. However, the behavior of Mickey Cabrera is not fully consistent with addiction or with what might be feared, given the nature of the brain injury he sustained. At times, he appeared not to understand a single word I said. His responses were meaningless. At other times, his responses were not only appropriate, but somewhat sophisticated.

"At one point, I showed him a two-minute clip of a movie in which a lead character dies. Mr. Cabrera's response demonstrated empathy and sadness. While his test scores suggest incompetence, his overall affect did not. I have no choice but to conclude that Mr. Cabrera has determined his best course is to convince the State he is unfit to stand trial. Based on my professional judgment, my assessment of his performance and his behavior, I am of the opinion he is fit to stand trial. Mr. Cabrera has willed himself into an almost catatonic state. It's a remarkable performance, quite frankly."

"Your witness," Hollister says.

Merton is docile during my cross-examination. He does not waiver from his basic position—that Mickey is competent to stand trial. Yet, he has not spent the time required to support his diagnosis.

After an hour, Judge Prentice begins to lose patience. "Mr. Harper, how much longer?" Judge Prentice does not cover his irritation. "Unless you have something to ask that sheds new light on this testimony, I want it brought to an end."

I have more questions, but they are unlikely to be fruitful and this is a critical moment. I could stay with the current line of questions and run the risk of losing the attention of the court, or I could leave things where they stand—and lose the opportunity to ask the perfect question.

"One moment, Your Honor."

I hate this familiar, hollow feeling. Had I stayed at Lone Pine after Jason disappeared, he might have come back—but I left. To this day, I live with my fear, my indecision, not knowing whether to stay or go. I was alone—ten years old—but I am not alone now. I look at Hannah—she has great litigation instincts. "Enough," she whispers.

"Competency is complex and two hours is a very short time. You spent only two hours, doctor. Is that correct?

"Yes, but . . . ."

"No further questions."

—

After I finish with Dr. Merton, Judge Prentice asks: "Do you have any other witnesses, Mr. Hollister?"

"No, Your Honor."

"We're going to recess until tomorrow. We will have closing arguments when we reconvene in the morning. Before we do that, I have a question for you, Mr. Harper. This is a competency hearing. Your client has the right to make a statement."

"I have explained to my client everything about this case, Your Honor. For the record, my co-counsel and I have known Mickey Cabrera for many years. Up until two months ago, we had no difficulty explaining things to him, nor did he have difficulty speaking with us. Now everything is different. He has been informed of his rights, but I'm not sure he has understood one word I have said."

"Objection." Mr. Hollister stands. "Mr. Harper is testifying."

"Really," Judge Prentice says. "I thought he was explaining why Mr. Carbrera would not testify. Overruled."

"Do you want to say anything, Mick?" I ask him.

Mickey sits, his eyes closed, his head tilted forward.

"Your Honor, I believe my client will not be making a statement."

"Very well. We are recessed."

When I turn, Mrs. Cabrera is standing directly behind me. "Grant, you did a fine job." She shakes my hand. I turn to Mickey and notice he has fallen sound asleep. His arms dangle toward the wooden floor and his cheek rests on the wooden surface of the table. Hannah, who has been sitting on his left side, helps me prop him to a standing position. We drape his arms over our shoulders and drag him from the courtroom.

In the hallway, we walk passed Lieutenant Wallace Huntington. "We have a fan," I say to Hannah as we slide Mickey down the hallway. "Did you enjoy the show, Lieutenant?"

"I hope your trial comes to an end soon—you'll be spending some time in Haydon." The Lieutenant catches up with Hannah and me and grabs my arm. "Don't walk away while I'm talking to you."

"Get your hands off me." He lets go and we stop. Mickey is awake enough to stand on his own. "What is it this time?"

"This time? This time a group of twenty-three honest Haydon residents are about to learn Grant Harper's secrets."

"You talked the District Attorney into another grand jury?" Hannah asks. Grand juries consist of twenty-three members.

"Contrary to your partner's beliefs, children do not simply vanish."

"What a waste of time and money," Hannah says. "You're like a dog with a bone." She turns to me. "Let's get out of here."

We pick up the pace and leave Lieutenant Huntington wheezing on the steps of the courthouse.

– 32 –

Back at our office, I begin work on my closing argument while Hannah works on the proposed order. On and off all afternoon we make calls all over the city to see if we can find Juan. It is after six when I speak to Hannah again. "I've spoken with half the community asking if anyone has seen Juan—and no luck," she says. "I did find Mrs. Cabrera."

"And?"

"She hasn't heard from him," she says. "I told her we'd give her a call if we hear anything."

"If Juan isn't back at the office before we leave, we're calling the police. He's been gone too long."

"And say what?" Hannah says. "We can't tell them about Arthur Soto—that's confidential client information." When Hannah does not respond, I say: "Juan wouldn't take off like this on his own volition, Hannah. We need to find him."

———

I make a pot of coffee while Hannah heads to Nuevo Leon to pick up our dinner. I am in the waiting room studying the picture of Mickey, Hannah, and me in front of the Studebaker Lark when Hannah returns and sets the food on the conference room table.

"Did you ask at Nuevo Leon?"

"Of course," she says. "They haven't seen Juan all day."

"I called Mrs. Cabrera again. No news," I say.

"You're scaring her. Juan can take care of himself. He knows how to handle people like Soto," Hannah says.

"And Jason knew the woods," I say.

"Juan is not lost, Grant."

"I'm not so sure."

———

I see Juan trying to cut a deal with Soto for Mickey's benefit. Juan discloses his suspicion that Soto was behind the robbery at the bookstore and reveals one piece of information too many. He does not notice as one of Soto's thugs come up behind him, covers his mouth with a gloved hand, his other arm across his chest, and drags him to a corner. He does not see as Soto pulls a gun. I hear the sound of Soto's gun—Juan is struck but does not fall. His suit coat is soaked with blood. He staggers into daylight and is surrounded by those who know him. He is taken to a hospital where, from the loss of blood, he loses consciousness. He lies in a bed, his heart rate and breathing monitored electronically, his wife at his side.

—

A dozen more calls to friends, clients, and community contacts produce nothing. Juan Cabrera has vanished. It is almost 9:00 p.m. when Hannah shoves a typed draft in front of me. "This is the proposed order," she says. "I'll keep calling—you need to finish the closing argument."

"I'm set. I'll use the Starling excerpts. . . ."

"I think we're good on the competency question, Grant. We have other goals. First, get permission for a private placement, and second, secure our position in the civil litigation. You will need to persuade Judge Prentice to sign the proposed order I wrote. This is how Mickey is going to pay for first-rate medical care. This is how Mickey is going to be supported for many years to come." She hesitates. "These are the subjects at hand—not Juan."

—

By 3:30 in the morning, Hannah has reviewed my closing argument and I have edited her draft proposed order. If Judge Prentice accepts our position, he will declare Mickey legally incompetent and will excoriate the State for its unconscionable maltreatment of our friend.

I spend the night in the office sleeping on the waiting room sofa and Hannah lays claim to the couch in my office. I am in a dreamless sleep when I hear voices in the hallway and smell the rich coffee that comes from the Cabrera kitchen.

– 33 –

I tumble off the couch. Mrs. Cabrera wears a full-length black coat, and I am quite sure she has just come from Mass. She pulls the cover off a platter of pastries and sets it on the conference table.

"You only take cream, right Grant?" she asks.

"Yes, thank you." I cannot read her expression. She hands me a cup of coffee and a folded napkin. Her dark eyes are clear and her demeanor professional.

"Juan asked me to make sure I brought you coffee and rolls this morning. I hope I have brought enough."

"More than enough, Mrs. Cabrera," I say. "When did Juan speak with you?"

"After dinner ... last night," she says, her tone matter-of-fact. "Juan told me he was in a negotiation involving a confidential matter of great importance. He said he expected it to run all night." She buttons her coat and turns. "I'm sure he will give you a call when he has concluded his affairs."

"Did he mention the substance of the negotiation?" I ask.

"Juan and I never discuss his legal business— even now, when it involves our son." She pauses. "When we were in Havana, it was not unusual for him to be gone for a day or two when handling an important client."

—

"What would possess Juan to call his wife but not leave a message here?" I ask Hannah after Mrs. Cabrera is gone.

"Juan did not want his wife to worry," she says.

Neither Hannah's measured response nor Mrs. Cabrera's surface calm provide reassurance. "We can't wait any longer. Juan has been gone for 24 hours. We need help."

"Mickey needs your help today. Let me take care of Juan," Hannah says. She rubs her eyes and forehead. "I've left messages in every precinct in Albany. Every officer in this city has an eye out for Juan."

Hannah and I assemble all the documents for our case on mobile carts. It takes two trips to move everything to the sidewalk. To save time we forego the trunk of the car and throw the boxes in the backseat. We have almost finished loading the car when I hear him.

"You must complete your tasks quickly. It's starting to snow and your papers will get wet."

I drop a cardboard box filled with medical records. As Juan gets closer, I see he has neither shaved nor changed his clothes since yesterday morning. "I thought you were dead. Where have you been?" I shake his hand and give him a hug. He is stiff and grudgingly pats me on the back.

"You must get to court right away. I will explain while we drive."

Hannah has already begun to take the boxes out of the backseat and move them into the trunk so that we can all fit in the car.

"Don't you think you could have called?" I ask.

Juan ignores my question and surveys the boxes. "In our business, you must prepare for infinite variables, always with the realization that things may not go according to plan. A great lawyer, Grant, understands that implementing a preconceived plan is less important than securing the legitimate interests of a client. You are becoming such a lawyer." Juan lowers himself into the front seat of the car. "Grant, what are you waiting for? Judge Prentice and Mr. Hollister await." He closes the door, leaving Hannah and me standing on the sidewalk, motionless.

"Well, what *are* you waiting for?" Hannah says as she jumps in the car.

"As I'm sure you have surmised, there is a significant piece of new evidence," Juan says as I pull away from the curb.

"Soto?" I ask.

"Yes, Mr. Soto, courtesy of the FBI crime lab and Owen Hollister. We recall the crime scene provided little evidence. My Miguel, seemingly without recollection, the clerk dead, no gun found—a perplexing problem. The police sealed off the area and the morning following the crime, our Mr. Hollister arrived on the scene. He had the good judgment to exercise care in removing the fire extinguisher from the crime scene. He had it taken to the evidence room at the police station where it sat on a shelf for a month."

"There was blood and hair on the fire extinguisher at the point where it made contact with Mickey's head," I say. "We've known that all along."

"Indeed," says Juan. "When you became the attorney for Miguel, you caught Mr. Hollister's attention." Juan pauses. "Mr. Hollister observed the intensity of your commitment, personally and professionally, to Miguel. He knew, from the outset, that Miguel was your lifelong friend.

"Perhaps it was your friendship—perhaps Hollister is a more competent fellow than we surmised. On a hunch, he sent the fire extinguisher to Washington for further analysis and received the results the day before yesterday. Arthur Soto's prints were on the inside of the handle of that fire extinguisher. This had been missed by our local forensic laboratory.

"Based on that information, Hollister has decided to move on Soto—a narcotics dealer, a suspected killer, a man of interest to the government—and an embarrassment to the Latino community. Without a murder weapon and in light of the clerk's dying declaration, the best he could get was a material witness warrant that would allow him to hold Soto until more evidence surfaced—but Soto knows many people in the city government. He was tipped that the police were coming for him and left his home before they arrived. He went to the apartment of a friend, located not far from our office, and called me."

"Why you?" Hannah says.

"Arthur is Cuban," Juan says. "He trusts me. I have helped his family over the years. I secured green cards for his cousins. He believed I would help him." Juan straightens his tie and fluffs his lapels. "He was convinced I could balance my son's interests with his and form an agreement with Hollister. It was a serious misjudgment on his part."

"Juan," I say, "you didn't tell Soto that you could help him?"

"And why not? I'm not a licensed attorney in the United States, Grant. Soto has information of great value to my son. I was not about to scare him off—ultimately, I convinced him to appear in the case pursuant to the warrant—he will be in court today."

"Under false pretenses—his appearance will be the result of your deception," I say.

"He will be under oath—he is free to be truthful—and we now know with certainty he was in the bookstore," Juan says.

"And you related Soto's 'conversation' with you to Hollister?"

"Soto confided in me, but I'm under no binding obligation to respect his confidence. I am not a prosecutor. I am not a lawyer in this country. Consider that your system of law and lawyers has seen fit to exclude from the practice of law those of us who were educated outside of the United States.

Insularity of this nature has unanticipated consequences." Juan pauses and clears his throat. "It is
not for me to psychoanalyze Mr. Soto. Perhaps he
wanted to unburden his troubled soul. In the eyes
of the law, I am just another citizen, employed as a
simple clerk, without professional responsibility,
without the ability to establish an attorney-client
privilege."

"You know that's nonsense," I say. "I am fully
responsible for what you do. I am bound by the
Code of Professional Responsibility and, as my employee, so are you—and you know it."

"I am aware of your responsibilities—and I
know that if you solicit knowingly false testimony
from a witness, you commit a felony—subornation
of perjury. Thus, my friend, the less you know, the
better." I hear cars honking behind me and realize I
have slowed to a near crawl. I pull over to the
curbside and turn off the ignition. "It took some
time for Soto to tell me his story," Juan says. "It
did not take 24 hours, however. I met with our Mr.
Hollister and several senior officers in charge of the
narcotics unit in this city—as well as the homicide
investigator who worked on this case. You will
understand more when we get to court. I suggest
you continue driving and when we get to court, do
your job. I trust you, Grant. Now, I would hate to
see you held in contempt this morning for being
late." Juan tilts his head back and closes his eyes.
"I will rest for a brief time, until the hearing
begins."

Juan remains quiet despite the barrage of questions from Hannah and me. When we arrive at the
courthouse, Juan tells me to stop by the main door

and wait. A few minutes later, he returns with several clerks who work in the main filing room. "We are in Courtroom 714," Juan says to the clerks. He shakes hands with each, carefully moving ten-dollar bills from his palm to theirs.

We are in the courtroom when our porters arrive with the boxes. Mickey watches as they line them up behind Hannah. "I can help," Mickey says.

For a moment, no one speaks and then Juan says: "Then you should help, Miguel. This box should be next to Mr. Harper." Mickey stands and then begins to walk slowly toward the carton. He lifts it with two hands. The carton rises past his knees and his abdomen. With a small sigh, he raises the carton over the top of his head and then rests it on his shoulder. With it properly balanced, he walks like a longshoreman around the front of counsel table, stops at my chair, slowly removes the carton from his shoulder, and lays it on the floor.

Owen Hollister moves from behind his table and stands next to Mickey. "What building is this, Mickey?" he asks. Hannah stands, ready to silence Hollister. It is unethical for him to speak with Mickey at this juncture—but Juan places his hand on her arm and she returns to her seat. Mickey looks around the room, pausing as he focuses on me. "The law offices of Harper & Wein," he says quietly.

"These are your old friends, Grant and Hannah," Hollister says.

Mickey takes time to process this statement. "Hannah Weiner and Grant Harper are my friends." Mickey leans across the table. "Jason Talbot might be here," he says quietly. "Maybe he came home."

"That would be wonderful," Hannah says.

"That would be a miracle," Mrs. Cabrera says. Owen Hollister turns to Mrs. Cabrera. "It sounds like this is the beginning of getting your son back," he says.

"You have not helped," Hannah says turning her back to Hollister.

"Quite the contrary," Juan says. "Mr. Hollister has the interests of justice and the State of New York first and foremost." He turns to his wife. "You will see. Now, there is much to be done in this courtroom today. Let Mr. Hollister and Mr. Harper do their jobs."

Mickey returns to his seat next to Hannah. "Is Jason going to help?"

"We're going to take care of you, Mick," Hannah says. "Jason is gone. We can talk more about him if you like, but not now."

"Tomorrow?" Mickey says.

"Sure," Hannah replies.

I open my briefcase and take out the text of my closing argument and the proposed order for Judge Prentice. Hannah removes the two heavy hearing notebooks containing the motions, briefs, and pre-hearing orders issued over the last month.

Owen Hollister leans in our direction and says: "Before we get to closing argument, I'll be asking for permission to call an additional witness—Arthur Soto. Hopefully you won't object."

"You are putting Arthur Soto on the stand? Now? You spring this on me...."

"We have no objection," Juan says, cutting off my response. He holds up his left palm in a quieting motion and I lean toward him. "There are two choices," he whispers. "I can tell you everything that happened over the last 24 hours, in which case you would be compromised in terms of your ethics and your professional responsibility—not to mention the possibility of a subornation charge. My other choice is to treat my discussions as private and let you examine this witness, as you are trained to do. I prefer to rely on your questioning."

Before I can respond, the bailiff quiets the courtroom. "All rise," he says.

Judge Prentice makes clear he is looking forward to efficient and informative closing arguments. After he concludes his remarks, Hollister stands. "Your Honor, the State would like to call a rebuttal witness."

"A rebuttal to what?" Judge Prentice asks. "You concluded your case-in-chief yesterday. You are an enigma, Mr. Hollister. Presumably, you're calling a witness to rebut the testimony your witnesses provided?"

"No, Your Honor. In the last twenty-four hours, we were able to locate a witness who was present at the crime scene. This witness is sufficiently important to the State that we secured a warrant pursuant to Section 618(B) of the Code," Hollister says. "The witness appeared in our office earlier today and is in custody."

"You mean to tell me you arrested a witness—wouldn't a subpoena have sufficed?"

"There is a flight risk with this witness, Your Honor," Hollister says. "In fact, initially the witness sought to avoid law enforcement officials."

"Is that surprising? You sent officers after a person, guns drawn, who has done nothing wrong—flight is not an irrational response." Judge Prentice says.

"Your Honor, this is not your run-of-the-mill witness...."

"I have an idea, Mr. Hollister—let's allow the testimony of the witness to speak for itself—assuming I let the witness testify at all. How does that sound?"

"Of course, Your Honor. I'll have him brought...."

"Silence, Mr. Hollister," Judge Prentice says. "Mr. Harper, were you aware the State intends to call another witness?"

"I learned of it this morning, Your Honor. We have no objection." I know Juan is nodding without turning around to check.

"No objection," Judge Prentice mumbles. "Mr. Hollister, while you bear the burden of proof in this proceeding and while Mr. Harper is not objecting, I question the necessity of this witness. There is no contention that Mickey Cabrera was incompetent on the night of the crime, but rather, as a consequence of his injury, sustained at the scene of the crime, he is experiencing significant deficits. I am hard-pressed to see what purpose would be served by calling a witness to testify about the crime itself."

"After Mr. Harper's cross-examination of Dr. Merton, the State believes that more information regarding the night of the commission of the crime is critical to the State's case. We will not need much time, Your Honor."

"Is this where we are: you want to put a witness on the stand to testify about the night of the crime, a time when the defendant doesn't claim incompetence—and defense counsel has no problem with this testimony?" Judge Prentice pauses. Hollister and I nod. "You two lawyers make me wonder whose competency is in question in this proceeding." Judge Prentice turns to the bailiff. "How about you? Do you have any objections to this witness?" The bailiff smiles, but stays silent. "Very well, Mr. Hollister. You get your witness—keep it brief."

"The State calls Arthur Soto."

Two deputies escort a middle-aged male through the courtroom doors. He is wearing black slacks, a blue oxford button-down shirt, and a char-coal-gray crewneck sweater. I notice the bailiff is standing, his right hand on his revolver. I look to the far side of the bench and notice a second officer, also at the ready. I survey the audience. There are four uniformed police, all standing against the wall, attentive.

I turn and look at Mickey. His eyes are open wide. Soto walks through the swinging gate that separates the audience from the well of the court-room and stops for a moment next to me. He leans forward, looks at Mickey, and points at him with his index finger. A marshal grabs his arm and they continue their march to the witness stand.

"Arthur is here," Mickey says quite audibly, "not Jason. Maybe Jason can't help." I notice his hands are shaking and I turn to Teresa, who is sitting next to Juan.

"Is he up-to-date on his medication?" I whisper. She nods.

Soto speaks quietly as he takes the oath and seats himself. "For the record, please state your name," Hollister says.

"Arthur Soto," he says.

"Good luck, Grant," Juan whispers. "You'll know what to do."

"Where are you going now?" I ask.

Juan squeezes my shoulder. "You do not want me in the courtroom while this testimony is given." Carrying his overcoat over his left arm, he is out the courtroom door in a matter of moments.

Hollister runs through the preliminaries with Soto and within five minutes has him at the crime scene. "What did you observe when you entered the bookstore?" Hollister asks.

"I was minding my own business, looking for a gift for my godson. I was thinking of buying him a sweatshirt from the great New York State University at Albany when I heard shouting."

"He has conceded his presence at the crime scene under oath—add to that the prints," Hannah whispers to me, "and the State has him set up perfectly."

"For what?" I whisper back.

"Accessory—or perjury. . . ." She stops as we both notice Judge Prentice leaning forward toward us.

"Should I recess so you two can finish? How impolite it would be to interrupt your private discussion," he says.

Hannah stands quickly. "I am sorry, Your Honor."

"For God's sake, pay attention to the witness," Judge Prentice says. He leans toward the bailiff. "If you see them passing notes, cuff both of them. Mr. Hollister, continue."

"Who was shouting?" Hollister asks.

"The guy behind the counter was yelling for help. He was being robbed—and that guy had a gun," Soto says.

"Do you see in this courtroom the person who had the gun?"

"Of course I do, there, next to one of his lawyers." Soto points at Mickey.

"Miguel Cabrera?"

"Yes," Soto says.

"What happened then?" Hollister asks.

"He demanded money and then told the clerk he was going to kill him."

Hollister raises his eyebrows. "He announced—in advance—'I'm going to kill you?' "

"I don't know—I think so—he wasn't brain damaged yet, if that's what you're asking."

"Actually Mr. Soto, I wasn't asking that at all. You do know you are under oath?

"I discussed that with Juan Cabrera—of course I know that."

"That didn't take long," Hannah whispers.

"Ms. Wein...." Judge Prentice warns. "Mr. Hollister—can you please proceed."

"Mr. Soto, what did you do as these events were unfolding?" Hollister asks. I see he is reading from the script of prepared questions written neatly in a thick dark-blue ink. I turn to Soto to listen for his answer.

"I'm no longer a young man, and was concerned for my own safety. I could not let this event take place without doing something, so I pulled a fire extinguisher off the wall and charged at him."

"At whom?"

"What do you want me to call him? The assailant—the veteran—the addict—that guy—the defendant."

"You can call him Mr. Cabrera," Hollister says. "What happened next?"

"Before I could get to him, he fired at the clerk. I knew if I did not get him, he would shoot me as well and so I swung the extinguisher—caught him on the side of the head and he fell over. I dropped the fire extinguisher and ran out the door to get help."

"What a crock," Hannah whispers. Before she is sanctioned by Judge Prentice, Mickey yells, "You liar!"

"Mr. Harper, can you keep a lid on things at your table," Judge Prentice says.

"Again, I apologize, Your Honor."

Hollister looks up at the Judge. "Should I continue my . . . ."

"Now, Mr. Hollister," Judge Prentice says.

"Mr. Soto, were you successful in getting assistance?"

There is a long pause. I write a note to Hannah: "Either Hollister or Soto has gone off the script," and carefully slide it across the desk. She looks at it and nods.

"Well," Soto says, "I was quite upset—and fearful—in shock. I left the Student Union and I think I drove home. I am not sure."

"Take a moment, Mr. Soto," Hollister says.

Soto nods and then, as if in a discussion with himself, he says: "I was terrified by these events, but what more could I do? Mr. Cabrera was there— on the floor—easy for the police to find—there was no reason for me to complicate the situation further."

"Getting back to the events in the store—Mr. Soto, this is a competency hearing. For that reason, it's important that you tell us what you heard the defendant say."

Soto pauses and rubs his finger across his upper lip. "I think he said he needed a fix real bad."

"To whom was this said?"

"You would have to ask him," Soto replies.

"Was there anyone else in the bookstore at the time this was said?"

"Not that I recall," Soto answers.

"When he asked for, as you put it, 'a fix,' is it possible Mr. Cabrera was speaking to you?"

"What the hell are you talking about? Juan Cabrera. . . ."

"Mr. Soto, watch your language—and answer the question," Judge Prentice says.

"Maybe he was talking to God," Soto says. "Maybe to me—maybe to the clerk—I don't know."

"Yes—well—Mr. Soto, did he say anything else?" Hollister asks.

"Not that I recall," Soto says.

"Your witness, Mr. Harper."

"That's it?" Judge Prentice says, his voice higher than normal.

"It's all we needed," Hollister says.

"Needed? This was needed?" Judge Prentice asks.

"Yes, Your Honor," Hollister responds. "It was."

"Mr. Harper? Is it possible that you want to cross-examine this witness?"

"I do, Your Honor."

"Why, Mr. Harper?"

"I'll be brief, Your Honor."

"Quickly, please."

I turn to Hannah. "Do you think he's lying?"

"Of course." She hands me her notes, taken during Soto's testimony. "I don't understand why Juan left."

"I do," I whisper. "You have just heard a carefully developed fairy tale Juan created for Mr. Soto."

"Mr. Harper, do you have any questions for this witness or would you prefer to chat quietly with Ms. Wein while we wait?" Judge Prentice asks.

"One moment, Your Honor." I look at Mickey. He is staring at Arthur Soto and for the first time since all this started, Mickey has a look of pure fury on his face. Hannah has her left hand on Mickey's shoulder to prevent him from standing.

"You testified you heard Mr. Cabrera demand money from the bookstore clerk and further announce he would kill the clerk. Were there other phrases spoken by Mr. Cabrera?"

"I told you—he said he wanted a fix," Soto says.

"And by a 'fix,' you mean Mr. Cabrera was seeking heroin."

"I don't know what drug he was seeking. It could have been heroin. He's an addict, can't you see that? Addicts are a blight on the Latino community," Soto says. "But since he was suffering from this serious illness, he needs medical help."

"What illness?" I ask.

"The illness of addiction," Soto says. I hear Juan's phraseology in Soto's testimony. "Where's your partner, Mr. Cabrera senior?"

"I get to ask the questions, Mr. Soto," I say. "Since the time of the crime at the bookstore, did you have an opportunity to visit with Mickey Cabrera?"

"What difference does it make?" Soto says.

I ignore his question. "Have you ever sold narcotics to Mr. Cabrera, either before or after the robbery?"

Soto looks at Hollister and says: "What the hell is going on here?"

"Just answer the question, Mr. Soto," Judge Prentice instructs. "And watch your language."

"I have nothing further to say."

"Did you come to court voluntarily?" I ask.

"You know why I'm here," Soto says. "I was told things were worked out—then they arrest me. I am here to testify today so you could get your client into a classy rehab hospital—where is Juan Cabrera?"

Hannah looks up at me and whispers, "Juan is direct, I'll give him that."

"To the best of your knowledge, has anyone been in your home in the last twenty-four hours?" I ask.

"Mr. Harper," Judge Prentice interrupts. "While Mr. Hollister seems disinclined to object to any of your questions for reasons that escape me

completely—is this going to the matter at hand—
Mr. Cabrera's competency?''

"It is, Your Honor."

"Well get there expeditiously," Judge Prentice
says, and then adds, "and what is going on, Mr.
Hollister?" Owen Hollister is deep in discussion
with his deputies. "Mr. Hollister, would it be too
much to ask if *you* could pay attention to the cross-
examination of your witness?"

Owen Hollister spins around. "My apologies,
Your Honor. The State is most interested in Mr.
Soto's testimony, including the possible occupants
of his apartment in the last day."

"His apartment? Yesterday and today? That
interests you? You have no problem with this line of
questioning, Mr. Hollister?" Judge Prentice asks.

"No, Your Honor," Hollister says.

"I thought not. Very well, Mr. Harper—where
are you headed?"

"Mr. Soto was the last person to see Miguel
Cabrera before his injury. The contrast...."

"Contrast? Before and after?" Judge Prentice
asks.

"After, Your Honor."

Judge Prentice shakes his head. "Well, that
seems to have something to do with this case. Let's
move this thing along."

"You testified you saw Mickey Cabrera fire a
revolver in the course of the commission of this
crime. No revolver was found at the scene of the

crime, however. Did you pick up the revolver, Mr. Soto?" I ask.

"That's a ridiculous question," Soto says. "Where is the old one—Juan Cabrera?"

I hear Hollister whisper: "He does not deny possession of the firearm—he's under oath—this should do it."

"Your Honor?" I ask.

"Just answer the question, Mr. Soto," Judge Prentice says. "Mr. Hollister, eyes front."

"I don't remember," Soto says. "Anything is possible."

I notice Hollister turn and sign several documents. The attorney and the detective with whom he has been speaking have left the courtroom.

"On the night of the murder did you hear Mickey Cabrera speak sentences clearly?"

"Yes. Is that what you want to hear? He was talking like Winston Churchill. Now he's a complete idiot," Soto says.

Owen Hollister stands up quickly. "Move to strike, Your Honor."

"For whose benefit, Mr. Hollister? There is no jury here," Judge Prentice says.

"The answer was non-responsive," Hollister says slowly.

"Well, at least you're paying attention, Mr. Hollister. Overruled."

"What leads you to believe Mr. Cabrera is 'a complete idiot' at this point, Mr. Soto? I thought you testified you did not speak with him after the commission of the crime?''

Soto stares at me, his eyes narrowing. ''I heard from your associate that his son—Miguel Cabrera—had brain damage—but he caused it—by committing the robbery—but now . . . . ''

''The question,'' I interrupt Soto, ''is whether you spoke with Miguel Cabrera after the robbery.''

''This must be the moment,'' Soto mutters. He reaches in his shirt pocket. A marshal and a bailiff both step forward, but Soto pulls out only a small sheet of paper. He holds it away from his face and begins to read. ''Since the robbery, Mickey Cabrera's condition has declined significantly. I know that personally. I swear it is true. This is a terrible tragedy. I regret that my actions caused him harm, but I acted both in self-defense and in the interest of public safety.'' He folds the paper back up and puts it in his pocket.

''May I see the piece of paper from which you were just reading, Mr. Soto?'' I ask.

Soto takes the paper out of his pocket and I approach the witness stand. I glance at the paper and recognize the ink from Juan's fountain pen and his handwriting. ''Thank you, Mr. Soto,'' I say and hand him back the script Juan prepared.

I walk around to the front of the counsel's table and lean close to Mickey. ''How are you doing?'' I whisper. Mickey looks at me.

''I didn't shoot in the store,'' he says. ''Grant, why won't Jason tell them?''

''Mickey, Jason is gone,'' I say.

"What are you doing—talking to him?" Soto asks from the witness stand.

"Remember, Mr. Soto, I'm the one who gets to ask questions." I check my notes—I do not know what Soto and Juan cooked up. I look to Hannah but she shakes her head.

"Any time, Mr. Harper," Judge Prentice says.

"Yes, Your Honor. Sorry. Mr. Soto, you had a clear view of the shooting in the bookstore. Do you remember the gun being fired?"

Soto again looks at the chair in which Juan had been sitting. "I'm not answering any more questions until Juan Cabrera returns."

"I'm afraid you do not have that option, Mr. Soto," Judge Prentice says. "In my courtroom, if you don't answer questions, I hold you in contempt and you stay in jail. It's really quite simple."

"Then that's it—I'm done. It's the Fifth Amendment, right?"

"There is a privilege against self-incrimination," Judge Prentice says. "Since you are neither charged with a crime nor are, as far as I have been told, even under investigation, I am hard-pressed to see why you would want to assert that privilege at this point."

"I got nothing further to say," Soto says.

"Your Honor, I have more questions for Mr. Soto," I say.

"If he takes the Fifth Amendment, counsel, I'm not sure I see any point in continuing. We're going to take a 30 minute recess." Judge Prentice looks at his watch. "The witness is instructed to remain in the courtroom. Counsel, meet me in chambers a few minutes before we reconvene."

Hannah, Mickey, and I stay at counsel table during the recess. "Mickey," Hannah asks quietly, "help me understand—why bring up Jason?"

Mickey turns to her. "Miss him—miss you."

"I miss him, too, Mick," Hannah says.

Mickey looks at her. "Do you miss me?"

Hannah puts her hand over his. "You are my very good friend, Mickey Cabrera."

"Can you help?" Mickey asks Hannah.

"Grant and I are going to get you help, Mick," Hannah says.

"Nothing?" Mickey says. "I need something."

Hannah shakes her head—and Mickey screams a string of obscenities and knocks a stack of paper to the floor. The bailiff and Teresa are at his side immediately. "Stop it, Mickey," she says, grabbing his arm. Mickey tries to pull away from his sister but Teresa holds on tight. "No more."

—

Judge Prentice closes the door after Hollister enters and turns to me. "What are you doing in my courtroom, Mr. Harper?" he asks.

"I am trying to cross-examine Mr. Soto, Your Honor," I say. "Based on the shreds of a discussion with my client, I have reason to think Mr. Soto provided Mickey Cabrera with heroin—and that. . . ."

"You can't tell me what your client said, counsel. Did either of you take the ethics course when you were in law school? Let me ask you the same simple question, Mr. Hollister: what are you doing in my courtroom?"

"Your Honor, the State has been involved in a long-term undercover operation. We have a strong suspicion that Arthur Soto was, until recently, a central figure in a drug ring. But he is also a thug— and he was cash poor. We think he had been involved in a series of armed robberies—including the robbery at the bookstore. As of a few days ago, we learned Soto was present the night the clerk was killed. After listening to a few minutes of cross-examination this morning, I signed off on a request for a warrant to search Mr. Soto's apartment."

"Soto didn't give you cause for a warrant," Judge Prentice says.

"He did not deny possession of the suspected murder weapon, Your Honor—and he testified that he has not been home in the last day. In conjunction with fingerprint evidence as well as a well-developed undercover report from an operative, his testimony, under oath, will be sufficient. I would guess the magistrate signed off on the warrant because I asked a colleague to let me know if there were any problems and I haven't heard back yet. We have investigators standing by outside of Soto's apartment in the event the warrant did issue—it will only be a matter of a few minutes until they're inside, if they're not there now," Hollister says.

"Just what do you expect to find, Mr. Hollister?" Judge Prentice asks.

"The gun used to kill the bookstore clerk, drugs, and drug paraphernalia," Hollister answers. "If Mr. Soto was centrally involved in the robbery— in the murder—that could change the position of the State vis-à-vis Miguel Cabrera."

"Why does Soto keep asking for Juan Cabrera?" Judge Prentice asks.

"Mr. Cabrera met with Mr. Soto yesterday," I say. "I saw him briefly this morning and he would not disclose the content of his discussion."

Judge Prentice turns to Hollister. "Were you aware of this meeting with Cabrera?"

"As I said earlier, Your Honor, we are in the middle of an undercover investigation and I am obligated to protect the identity of our operatives," Hollister says.

"Have you lost your mind, Mr. Hollister? You are in a judge's chambers, in a confidential discussion. I am at a loss to know whether to advise you of your rights or simply kick you out of my office. Now answer my question," Judge Prentice says.

"Juan Cabrera provided us with a wealth of information, Your Honor. We spoke with him at length before the hearing today regarding Mr. Soto," Hollister says. "We are in the process of verifying his assertions."

The door opens a crack and Judge Prentice's clerk peeks inside the Judge's chambers. "Your Honor, someone from the D.A.'s office is on your line. They say they need to speak with Mr. Hollister right away."

"Oh, by all means, Mr. Hollister," says Judge Prentice. "Why don't you take my chair?"

Hollister starts to walk behind the judge's desk. "I was not being serious," Judge Prentice says. "Take your call in the hallway. We will wait here."

———

With Hollister out of the room, Judge Prentice sits down in his chair and puts his feet up on his desk. "Juan Cabrera is quite something," Judge Prentice says. "He and I have crossed paths before—a fine, fine legal mind—but not a member of the bar." Judge Prentice says: "He's going to end up in trouble one of these days."

"Do you know his history?" I ask.

"I know his track record in the city—it is enviable," Judge Prentice says. "Still...."

"With your permission, let me tell you a bit more." Judge Prentice nods. "Juan Cabrera is a very proud man," I begin. Thinking back to my first few weeks at Albany Legal Services, I repeat the highlights of Juan's story.

After I finish, Judge Prentice sits quietly for a full minute. Finally, he leans forward. "Off the record?"

I nod.

"I agree with you—he is a most impressive man," Judge Prentice says. "After this case is over, tell him to stop by my chambers. Maybe I can help."

"I appreciate that, your Honor," I say.

—

Owen Hollister knocks once and then enters the chambers without waiting to hear from Judge Prentice. "They found the gun and a few grams of heroin," he says. "The gun is the same caliber used in the robbery. We won't have a ballistics test or know about the prints on the gun for a few hours, but it only makes sense that the gun will be covered with Soto's fingerprints."

"Thank God," I say. I turn to Hollister. "Are we done?"

"There is more to work out," Hollister says.

"Your Honor, will you consider dismissing charges?"

"We're not quite there, Mr. Harper. It is quite possible that Mickey Cabrera shot the clerk and Soto picked up the gun and stuck it in his pocket. If Cabrera was his partner, this becomes a felony-murder case—whether the gun was fired by Cabrera or Soto may not matter all that much if they conspired to commit this crime. I will see you both in the courtroom in a few minutes," Judge Prentice says and we are dismissed.

In the hallway, Hollister takes my arm and stops me before I enter the back door of the courtroom. "It's clear Mickey Cabrera is getting better. Both Merton and Starling suggested this would happen. As he recovers, Merton told me he could regain most or even all of his memory. Promise me his complete cooperation and we can cut a deal."

"I can't counsel him to enter a guilty plea under these circumstances," I say.

"We need Soto off the street, Mr. Harper. This has been a central project in our office for more than a year. If we nail Soto using Mickey Cabrera, we'll reduce the charges."

"I can't tell you how long it will take for Mickey to recover. Quite frankly, you know more than I do about the discussion between Juan and Soto." Judge Prentice walks by us without speaking and bursts into the courtroom and we follow.

"All rise." Arthur Soto has been sitting in the witness stand speaking with one of the bailiffs. I have not made it to my seat when I hear Judge Prentice, "Mr. Hollister, did you want to comment on the assertion of the Fifth Amendment privilege? Soto is your witness."

Owen Hollister rises. "Your Honor, based on information and belief, based on evidence secured in a search that took place earlier today, the State charges Mr. Soto with unlawful possession of a firearm."

Two marshals and the bailiff approach Soto on the stand and bring him to his feet. "Mr. Soto," Judge Prentice says. "You have the right to remain silent. You have a right to a lawyer. If you cannot afford one, a lawyer will be provided. From this point forward, anything you say can and will be used against you. Do you understand these rights?"

"You're all screwed," Soto says. "By the time my lawyers are done with you, we will own this building."

"I'll take that as a 'yes,' " Judge Prentice says.

"Your Honor, I have not finished cross-examining this witness—and we would like to make a closing argument," I say.

"We are recessed, Mr. Harper. I strongly suggest you and Mr. Hollister get together and see if you can formulate a resolution." For the first time in the course of these proceedings, Judge Prentice slams his gavel on the bench and exits the courtroom.

"We should have the fingerprints and a preliminary ballistics report by the end of the day," Hollister says to me. "I'll give you a call in the morning."

I drop into my chair and listen as the entire Cabrera family asks, both in English and Spanish, what just happened. I do my best to explain and ask Hannah for help.

Hannah takes Mrs. Cabrera by the arm and says: "I understand your confusion. I have a feeling this will get resolved. Grant and I need to speak with your husband. In the interim, I have a very important question." Mrs. Cabrera turns to Hannah. "I am of the opinion that Mickey must face his addiction and that will not happen unless he is hospitalized in the right setting. Do you agree?"

Mrs. Cabrera gives Hannah a hug and says quietly: "Can you and Grant help with this—can you find the right place—a hospital that understands Vietnam veterans? This is what Miguel needs—and you, dearest Hannah, and I both know that."

I turn to my left and notice that Mickey has taken a yellow pad. On the top of the pad, in large and shaky letters, Mickey has written, "**MIGUEL JUAN CABRERA**."

"He writes," Mrs. Cabrera says. "Teresa—look—he writes."

—

As we exit the courtroom, Lieutenant Huntington approaches. "It looks like another DeWitt Street resident is about to get away with murder," he says. I feel Hannah grab my arm tightly. "Hollister had Mickey Cabrera in his crosshairs and missed. I won't make that same mistake with you, Grant."

"Bailiff!" Hannah calls. "We're being harassed. Can you give us a hand?"

A uniformed officer and the bailiff exit the courtroom and approach the Lieutenant. "Back off, sir," the officer says.

"Get your hand off me, jackass, I'm a cop."

"Jackass?" the officer responds. As Lieutenant Huntington reaches into his pocket for his badge, the officer grabs his wrist and spins him against the wall and pats him down. "He's armed," he says to the bailiff. "You recognize him?" The bailiff shakes his head.

As the Lieutenant swears at the officer again and demands to be freed, we hear the click of handcuffs and the recitation of the *Miranda* rights over the Lieutenant's angry protest.

"Firearms are not allowed in the courthouse," Hannah says as we exit the building. "Wallace Huntington should know better than that."

– 34 –

Back in our conference room, Juan gives Hannah and me two affidavits, each captioned: "The People of the State of New York v. Arthur Soto" followed by "Affidavit of Señor Juan Cabrera, Abogado, Havana, Cuba."

I read the affidavits aloud. They are devastating. In the first, Juan explains how he was contacted by Arthur Soto after the initial material witness warrant issued for Soto's detention and then recites how Soto confessed responsibility for the murder of the clerk in the bookstore.

According to the affidavit, Mickey was not central to the plan to rob the bookstore. Mickey had begged Soto for heroin and was told to meet Soto at the bookstore. Soto's plan was to rob the store and stick Mickey with the gun on the way out.

Mickey arrived on schedule and walked in as the robbery was in progress. Soto had a gun pointed at the clerk. Just as Mickey reached Soto, the clerk grabbed a fire extinguisher off the wall and threw it—catching Mickey in the head, rendering him unconscious and knocking Soto off-balance. Seizing the moment, the clerk attempted to get the gun from Soto and in the ensuing struggle, Soto's gun discharged and struck the clerk in the chest. Stunned, Soto picked up—and then dropped—the extinguisher. As the clerk lay bleeding, Soto cleaned out the register, stuffed some of the money in Mickey's pockets, and fled.

In the second affidavit, Juan states he discussed a deal with Soto. Juan and Soto would tell

the State that Mickey was the assailant—and Juan
would make sure Soto ceased to be the primary
target of the State's narcotics probe—and Soto
would be off the hook for the death of the clerk.
Juan agreed to this—at least in his meeting with
Soto—in exchange for Soto agreeing to help Juan
persuade the State—in open court if necessary—to
place Mickey in a private treatment facility. The
affidavit ends as follows: "The affiant did not make
promises on behalf of attorney Grant Harper, attorney Hannah Wein, or Owen Hollister or any other
officials working on behalf of the State of New
York."

———

"Have you read through my affidavits?" Juan
asks as he walks into the conference room.

"Has anyone seen these—other than us?" I
ask.

"A copy is being delivered to Mr. Hollister as
we speak."

"You set up Soto. You let him think the State
was anxious to get his testimony regarding Mickey.
You made up a story for Arthur Soto—and he told it
in court, apparently believing you arranged a deal
with Hollister. Do I have it right?"

Juan does not reply. "What did you tell him,
Juan?" I ask.

"I gave him reason to think they were going
after him on drug trafficking and murder charges."
Juan pauses. "As I surmised, the State was not out
to get Miguel, Grant—they wanted Soto. Dr. Merton convinced Hollister that my son would come

around, at which point, they would give him a
reduced sentence in exchange for the head of Arthur Soto. They used Miguel. Why do you think Dr.
Merton only spent two hours on him? Dr. Merton
knew he couldn't make a legitimate diagnosis of a
head injury in one visit. Dr. Merton's job was to
make an educated guess on the probability of Miguel's recovery. Assuming Mr. Hollister accepts my
affidavits and uses them before a grand jury, all
they will need from us is an assurance that we'll
make Mickey available to testify as he recovers his
memory."

"So now what?" Hannah asks.

"Now we sue the City for failing to treat my
son. A favorable settlement will be reached quickly," Juan says. "Mr. Hollister has read Dr. Starling's report—and an early draft of your proposed
order for Judge Prentice." Hannah begins to speak
but Juan continues. "Mr. Hollister knows Miguel's
condition went from treatable to nearly fatal during
the time he was in jail. He has contacted the City
Attorney—there will be a settlement."

—

I spend the remainder of the day writing and
editing, and when I am done, I have a proposed
disposition for the criminal case against Mickey. I
also review the civil complaint against the City
drafted by Hannah, make a few changes, and end
the day at the clerk's office where I file suit against
the City of Albany and State of New York on behalf
of Miguel Juan Cabrera.

– 35 –

Owen Hollister and I have little difficulty agreeing on the wording of those documents required to dispose of the criminal case against Mickey. The presentation in front of Judge Prentice takes five minutes—I am sure he is pleased to be done with both Hollister and me. As I am packing up, his clerk hands me a file. "Have Mr. Cabrera read through these documents. They pertain to bar membership for lawyers educated outside the United States. Tell him to call our chambers when he has a moment."

—

In the hallway, Hannah informs me that we are heading to Nuevo Leon to celebrate.

Mickey rides in the front of my car while Hannah is stuffed in the back seat with Mr. and Mrs. Cabrera. Although it is bitterly cold, Mickey opens the window and smiles as the icy-cold reddens his face. "Close the window, Miguel," his father commands from the back seat.

"Oh, let him enjoy the fresh air," Mrs. Cabrera says. I turn the car heat to the maximum and then open my window. Hannah, who is sitting next to Mrs. Cabrera, opens her window and sticks her arm out in the cold air. I hold my left hand straight up and feel the frigid air push against my palm. I turn to my right and watch as Mickey extends his right hand out the window, his fingers spread wide. I look in the rear view mirror and see the broad smile on Juan Cabrera's face. The day we bought the Studebaker Lark, we drove up DeWitt Street with the windows wide open and our arms straight up in the air screaming at the top of our lungs.

As we approach the restaurant, two boys direct us to a parking spot that has been reserved, adjacent to the awning of the restaurant. The restaurant is packed. The moment I enter, I am grabbed by my sister and then my mother and father. I look around the room and recognize nearly every face. These are the families from DeWitt Street—Hannah's parents and a dozen others. There is applause as Mickey comes in, then handshakes and embraces.

I work my way through the crowd, greeting old friends, when I hear, "Grant, I hear you did a good job."

I turn and notice an exquisite woman with reddish-brown hair wearing a fringed leather jacket and when she smiles, I have no doubt about her identity. It is Valerie Talbot. I hear Denise shriek as she comes flying across the room, grabs Valerie and they spin.

"Your mother found her," my father says. "It took a month—but it was time to bring out the troops. Here we are."

"Where was she?" I manage to ask.

"She's a veterinarian in Bangor, Maine. Quite something, isn't it?" my father says. "We had breakfast this morning. She's a lovely person, Grant. She and her husband run an animal hospital. He stayed up in Bangor with their kids, but she decided to come."

"She didn't have any news, did she?" I ask.

"About Jason?" he says. I nod. "We didn't bring up the topic. I'm sure if there was something she wanted me to know, she would have told me," my father says.

"You going to give me the afternoon off, Boss?" Hannah says. She is holding a glass of beer. Her cheeks are still red from the car ride, her hair is wind-blown, and she cannot stop smiling. "Grant, you're staring at me," she says.

I fight the urge to hug Hannah—after all, she is my law partner. I take several steps back and in a loud voice ask: "Did you have anything to do with organizing all this?"

Hannah raises her eyebrows. "Why are you raising your voice—and where are you going?"

"Nowhere," I say.

Her smile broadens. "Come closer."

"What?" I say.

"I think there something we need to discuss," she says.

"Hannah," I say, now whispering, "maybe at some point we should talk. I—you...." Her smile turns into a laugh and I run out of courage.

"Later," she says. "What a party." The subject has been changed. "The amazing part is that neither Juan nor I orchestrated this. Mrs. Cabrera called your parents, your sister got involved, and after that, I lost track. As far as I can tell, they've been planning and praying for about two months solid." She touches my cheek and her smile softens. "We're a good very team, Grant ... you and me."

My moment with Hannah is cut short as Juan knocks a spoon against a glass, calling the crowd to order. "I will not try to thank all of you, because I do not know the words in English or Spanish to say what is in my heart."

"Juan, no speeches," Hannah says with a smile.

"No speeches it is," he says. "Simply the love of the Cabrera family to all of you."

Hannah is next to me. "I should have gotten the case dismissed," I whisper. "Without putting Mickey through this process—he's going to end up locked in a hospital because of my strategy."

"And you and I both know he needs just that," she replies. "Stop beating yourself up." She turns to me and whispers: "We'll talk more when we're alone—I think we both have much more to say." She touches my shoulder and nods with a smile. "Later," she says—and then: "Where's Denise?"

After graduation from the University of Vermont, Denise dove head-long into a Masters in Social Work program. She finished grad school before Hannah and I started law school and works for the State of New York. She is one of a small number of licensed social workers in Caulfield and Montgomery Counties—the wooded vast brown-gray region northwest of Albany—and, to the delight of my mother, concentrates on eldercare.

Despite her specialization, Denise knows the programs that provide public assistance—minimal though they may be—to veterans and consults periodically (confidentially, of course) with Hannah and the Cabreras. Like the rest of us, though her recommendations sprang from the best of intentions, they were rejected summarily. Until the crisis that gave birth to this moment—a celebration of an escape from incarceration that would have been the end of him—Mickey let no one interfere with his downward spiral, turning away all offers of assistance, pushing aside all outstretched hands.

—

The tables in the restaurant are arranged in a long line, the food served buffet style. Mickey sits with his parents, holding his plate on his lap and I watch as one person after the next spends a moment with him, wishing him well. He seems to recognize some, but the commotion has caused him to turn inward and he says little.

This is my first opportunity to speak with a member of the Talbot family in seventeen years and I do not show the restraint my father exhibited. I wait for a pause in the non-stop chatter between Denise and Valerie.

"I've thought about you and your family more than you could possibly know," I say to Valerie. Denise takes a step back and listens.

"I know things were hard for you after Jason disappeared," Valerie says, just like that. If there is a set of rules that prohibits discussion regarding Jason Talbot, they have just been broken. "There were reasons things happened the way they did."

"Tell me about the rest of your family," I say. "It was as if somebody drew a curtain and you all disappeared, not just Jason."

"I came here to congratulate you. You had a friend in trouble, the most serious kind of trouble, and you did what had to be done."

"Did you ever go to Lone Pine?" I ask, bypassing her compliment.

"Lone Pine is ancient history, Grant," she says.

"Not for me," I say.

"What do you want me to say?" she says.

"I just want to know if you've been there."

"Do you know why I left home?" she asks.

"Not really."

"Grant, enough," Denise says.

"I had no choice," Valerie says.

"I'm not asking you to discuss that," I say.

"Of course you are, Grant. There were awful problems in my family and no solution for Jason or for me. Getting out of that house was the best thing I ever did—and the hardest. You agonize over the fact that Jason disappeared when he was with you. I think you overlook the fact that I left home a day earlier." She hesitates. "You wish, somehow, you could have brought Jason back that day. I do understand."

"How is it possible we could not find Lone Pine? Half the New York State National Guard looked for it. Hannah, Mickey, and I went back, over and over again. It never made any sense to me. After a time, I started wondering whether I imagined it."

"Maybe what you remember is part imagination. Over time, we fill in the blanks left open by uncertain recollection."

Denise takes Valerie's arm and they head toward Hannah for what I believe will be long overdue DeWitt Street gossip. Half an hour later, Valerie picks up her leather fringe jacket, walks across the room and says to me. "It's just a big tree, Grant." She kisses Mickey on the top of the head and is the first to leave the celebration.

As I open the front door of the restaurant to say good-bye, she enters the back seat of a small silver-gray limousine and a moment later is gone.

– **36** –

The civil case against the City of Albany and the State of New York floats through the legal system. A final report prepared by Victor Starling ends any question of the State's liability. Had Mickey been given appropriate medical care, the hematoma that nearly killed him—and now affects his future—would have been dealt with long before it could do such awful damage. The heart of the settlement provides Mickey more than enough to cover all current and future medical costs as well as annuity that will yield monthly income for the next 30 years.

"We should have held out for more," I say to Hannah and Juan as we leave Hollister's office.

"Miguel's interests are well-protected," Juan says. "It's his needs that count. Remember that."

—

On the same day we settle with the State, my mother calls. "Listen to this. This was in the CAUL-FIELD COUNTY JOURNAL this afternoon." I hear her rustling the paper. " 'After almost four decades of distinguished service with the Caulfield County Police Department, Lieutenant Wallace Huntington announced his retirement last night at the County Council meeting. "I'll take a few days off—but I'm not ready for the hammock," Huntington noted. "I've accepted an offer to work in the private security sector pursing a matter of considerable importance—I'm not at liberty to discuss the nature of my work—maybe it's time to sock away a few extra dollars for a rainy day." I hear more paper rustling. "Thank God," she says.

"Did he say what he was pursuing?" I ask.

"No, but later in the article, there is reference to the Lieutenant expressing dismay over a grand jury investigation that had been 'cut short'—whatever that means. The article talks about Lieutenant Huntington making an appearance before the grand jury last week and then being celebrated in an event at the office of the District Attorney."

"It sounds like he was pushing for greater investigatory powers and was denied," I say. "Did it mention if he was staying in the area—or perhaps moving to Albany?"

"His consulting work, or whatever it is, will take him abroad. Their house is on the market—they're moving, Grant."

My mother is rarely jubilant—and this is no exception. "I distrusted that man," she says. "The very thought of taking you back into the woods after midnight the day Jason disappeared—he had no judgment whatsoever." I wait for her to say that she never should have let me go back in with the Lieutenant the next day, an angry little discourse I have heard before in which my father does not come out smelling like a rose, but she restrains herself.

"I'm surprised," I say. "Not about the travel but that he retired at all and that he makes mention of money—he isn't over Jason's disappearance and never seemed to me particularly interested in accumulating wealth. It just doesn't make sense."

"Someone must have made him a good offer," my mother says. "Think of it as an early Christmas present, Grant."

– 37 –

March 1976

In the end, I probably could have gotten Owen Hollister to drop the charges completely—but Juan had a different plan. All proceedings would be suspended for one year. Assuming no further misconduct, the case will be dropped and the records expunged on the condition that Mickey spend three months in residential treatment.

—

The time Mickey spends in rehabilitation goes by slowly. He receives the full treatment: detoxification—and physical, occupational, cognitive, and speech therapies. The only visitor permitted is Denise. She tells us he misses his family—and Hannah and me—but otherwise treats her visits as part of her professional mission, thus, strictly confidential.

Some time after a briefing from Denise—that lasted all of five minutes—Hannah comes into my office. "One day, you will go home for Thanksgiving dinner and there will be nothing but silence at your family table—your lay-clergy mother, your Hippocratic Oath-bound father, your social worker sister, and you—all dead silent. The meditation hour at the Trappist Monastery in Genesee would be a cacophony compared to a November afternoon with the Harper clan."

"You should join us—after what happened with Mickey, you'd fit right in," I say.

"Don't start with me, Grant," Hannah says. "I kept quiet about Mickey because he begged me to say nothing to you—you would have done the same thing." She looks at me. "Are you still jealous?"

"About you and Mickey?"

"Of course about Mickey and me—are you?"

I am still searching for words when I see Hannah smile. "You're jealous." Her smile broadens. "And a fine lawyer. And staggeringly dense."

—

On the day of his release, Juan picks up Mickey and drives him to the apartment complex that will be his new home. Denise, Hannah, Teresa, and I are waiting for them in the lobby as Juan pulls up to the apartment building.

Teresa will live with Mickey in the apartment at least through the end of the summer. Denise will continue her visits—though God knows what they will discuss.

Teresa introduces us to the security guards and desk clerk. No one, we are told, is permitted in the building without the approval of one of the residents.

We take the elevator to the fourth floor, walk down the hallway, and enter Mickey's new home. It is a three-bedroom apartment with a wonderful view of City Park. The living room and kitchen are larger than the comparable space in the home where I grew up.

"You'll like it here, Miguel," Teresa says. "There is a game room, an exercise room, and indoor and outdoor pools."

"This is nicer than my place," I say.

Mickey stands at the window looking across the trees at City Park. "I want to go home," he says.

"You are home," Juan says. "You live here now."

"Home, not here." Mickey turns and looks at me. "I want to go home, Grant. Maybe we'll see Jason."

"To DeWitt Street?" I ask.

"DeWitt Street," Mickey says. "We can look for your pine tree."

"Once you're settled in here, you can go home," Juan says. "You're going to be busy for the next few weeks. Denise, do you have the therapy schedule?"

She nods. "I need to call Dr. Starling. He wanted to see you the moment you returned from the hospital."

"Hannah and I need to get back to the office," I say. "I'll check in with you this evening."

—

I sit with Juan and Hannah in the conference room. "The apartment will work out fine," I say. "I don't think Mickey grasps that it's his new home."

"He will adjust," Juan says. "Are you going to finish the vacation you started months ago?"

"I might," I say. "I'll wait a few weeks."

"You are not going back to the cabin, are you?" Juan says.

"No," I say. "Juan, let us take Mickey home."

"In good time," he says.

*

Part Five

REDISCOVERING LONE PINE

1976

– 38 –

I place the call to Valerie—to the North Bangor Animal Hospital—from my parents' living room. After brief pleasantries, she says, "Grant, are you up here—in our neck of the woods?"

"No, I'm home—on DeWitt Street. I've been here with Hannah and Mickey for the last week."

There is a long pause. "This isn't about Lone Pine, is it?" she asks.

"I've been haunted by this for too long," I say. "I've studied maps of Haydon—of Caulfield County for that matter—and there is no Lone Pine . . . yet, I was there." I hesitate for a moment. "You aren't interested in going for a walk in the woods with Hannah, Mickey, and me this weekend, are you?"

"For God's sake, Grant, let it go." She hangs up without saying goodbye. Hannah, who has been studying U.S. Forest Service maps, laughs. "I told you she didn't want to talk about this." Without looking up, she continues: "What if we—what if

everyone—has been looking in the wrong place,"
Hannah says. "What if Lone Pine isn't in our
woods?"

"Jason and I went in the woods just before the
DeWitt Street dead end—there is no other area," I
say.

"Maybe you and Jason only started in our
woods—it took you hours and hours to get there.
You left just after eight in the morning. If you
walked for six or seven hours—that is easily fifteen
miles. And consider this—when you walked to Lone
Pine, you had no idea you would have to find your
way back on your own."

"So what? I remember. . . . "

Hannah ignores me. "I see roads . . . intersec-
tions and landmarks . . . differently when someone
else is driving—when someone else is responsible
for knowing how to get to and from an unfamiliar
place and I am just a passenger. It is a whole
different matter if I drive—it is a common experience. That's what happened to you—Jason was
leading . . . and you were just a passenger." She
pauses. "Everyone assumed you knew where you
had been—you assumed that as well—but Grant,
you have no idea where you went with Jason that
day."

Hannah looks down at the county map. "What
if you went in the woods—and you and Jason circled around—completely—and went due south—not
north or east—you could have walked right out of
Haydon Township."

"We would have walked into the orchards," I
say.

The area south of DeWitt Street is privately-owned and mostly orchard and corn fields. Cason Orchard, located a mile or two south of the DeWitt Street dead end, is one of the largest orchards in the state. The crop is harvested each fall and is used to make apple sauce, cider, and juice. The apples are neither crisp nor tasty and the orchard is loaded with bees. Other than swiping an occasional apple when we were desperately hungry, we stayed away from that area.

"Maybe ... or maybe you were walking along the side of the orchard. Given the snow, the icy cover, everything looked the same." She examines the map again. "For our hike, what if we head south from the DeWitt Street dead end—and go away from our woods—toward the orchard and farm properties.... "

"So, Meriwether Lewis, Sacajawea, and what's-his-name Clark are planning the great expedition," my mother says as she comes into the room.

"William Clark," I say.

"Why don't you just pitch a tent in the woods behind our house?" she says. "This is a crazy idea. If something happens to Mickey, you two will never forgive yourselves."

"I discussed this plan with Victor Starling," I say. "He thinks it's a great idea."

"I have a hard time believing that," my mother says. "Did you explain to him that our woods aren't like a tame city park, that they are hilly and dense, that you could end up miles from civilization with no way to get help."

"Not in those terms," I say. "I did say that this was a long and demanding hike and that didn't seem to faze him. He told me that there is quite a debate about recovery from a traumatic brain injury. Other than the necessity of rest, there is not much agreement on therapy or medication. In Victor's view, recovery or regeneration may be activated by experiences, challenges that urge reconnection of those regions of the brain that have been bruised or even partly sheared. He talked about awakening from a coma—there is no agreement about what prompts the revival, but some basis to think that a comatose person can be affected by external stimuli. For conscious brain-damaged people, the same should apply."

She smiles at me. "There is a difference between an experience that stimulates a person and one that puts them in jeopardy. What is your plan?"

"We'll walk for the better part of one day, set up camp and spend the night, and come back the following day. It isn't as if we're tackling the north slope of Everest."

"I won't breathe easily until you three are back," she says.

"Mrs. Harper, do you know how far south the orchards and cornfields go?" Hannah asks.

My mother squeezes between Hannah and me and looks at the map. "Down here?" she asks. Hannah nods. "Miles and miles. That land belongs to the Cason Corporation—the apple people. Why would you want to go there?"

"At some point, the orchards have to stop," Hannah says. "If you head south and pass the orchards, it looks like there is nothing but woods—and a corner of the State Park—for at least a dozen miles—maybe more—before you get to the Interstate."

"Way down here?" my mother says, pointing past the township line.

"Exactly," I say.

My mother leans over to get a better look at the county map. Looking over the top of her glasses, she says: "Bring a compass."

—

Hannah and I spend Friday working on our framed backpacks. Mickey will carry a day pack, with his sleeping bag tied below. We are in the last week of March and while we have had snow at this time of year in the past, it has been in the mid–50s all week. The forecast for the weekend is continued mild weather with a chance of showers, and we include ponchos in our packs. By late afternoon, the packs are complete. "You have the hatchet, compass, camera, pocket knife, and canteen," Hannah says. "I have the mace, a first aid kit, the maps, a second compass—and a small screw-top of bourbon. Did you ask Dr. Starling if Mickey was allowed to have a drink?"

"I didn't need to ask. They're hesitant to let Mickey have coffee, much less bourbon."

"I'm going to take it anyway. It just might hit the spot in case we're in need of a disinfectant." I see Hannah smile.

"Right," I say. "Disinfectant."

– 39 –

The home-building boom on DeWitt Street that produced jobs for Mickey and me sputtered and died in the mid–sixties. Evidence of that period of careless growth is apparent as we walk by the three red posts marking the dead end point on DeWitt Street. There are piles of tree stumps and construction debris on all sides. Rotting plywood is thrown together with cement block; twisted reinforcement rods poke through cracked hunks of concrete. This part of our woods is an unauthorized burial ground used by home-builders who moved on to other projects or perhaps dissolved into bankruptcy. We walk along the deeper ruts left by the dump trucks that produced this abomination. Their actions were common at the time and it crosses my mind that Mickey and I loaded some of the trucks that dumped this mess.

"Let's keep hiking—I'm ready—now," Mickey says.

"Take it easy, Mick. I don't want anyone to fall and twist an ankle," Hannah says. Like me, she is huffing slightly. I hope this initial breathlessness is the consequence of adjusting to our heavy packs and not an indication of our lack of conditioning.

"Hannah is right. You end up with pain along the antero-lateral portions of the ankle and you can experience syndesmosis," I say. Hannah and Mickey both stop. "I had a case involving a sprained ankle. I remember those terms. That's all."

"Your mind is cluttered," Hannah says.

We survive the construction dumping ground without injury and enter woods indistinguishable from those behind my house. There are no paths on this route, at least none we know. Based on the map, heading south should bring us to the edge of the orchards before we work up a good sweat.

"We head to the apple trees first," Mickey says. "I know the plan."

Hannah turns and gives me a huge smile. "You lead the way, Mick," she says. We pass elm, beech, oak, maple, birch, and sinewy stands of hickory and I am reminded how much I love the random and wild nature of these woods. Hannah hefts her backpack as if repositioning will lighten her load. "How do your feet feel?" she asks me.

"Fine—so far," I say. "I'm not sure we should have been talked into buying these boots."

Mickey looks at his feet and then turns to me. "We needed the hiking boots. I like mine," he says.

As was the case when we were young, we walk attentive to the latent risks and benefits the woods provide. Apart from footpaths and horse trails, the forest floor is deceiving. Ruts and collapsed abandoned burrows are filled with leaves and easy to miss unless one pays careful attention. At eye level, in any direction, we are likely to see pheasant or white-tail fawn. Given these visual obligations and opportunities, our discussions are limited. I remember being in the woods with Mickey and Hannah, walking for hours, communicating only with hand signals, barely blinking.

We head south toward the Cason Orchard and walk for some time before Mickey says: *"Magna itinera."*

"Caesar's Gallic Wars," I say. "Forced march, right?" Mickey nods and trudges forward without commenting on the apparent return of what we all believed to be memories forever lost.

We come to the end of a section of mature trees and enter dense undergrowth littered with vine-covered rotting stumps. Between the dead roots and branches grow junk trees of dubious pedigree— fruitless mulberry and acacias, locust, hostile buck- thorn, and prickly sassafras. "The orchard must be just ahead," Hannah says. "When they cleared the fields, they dumped the remains along the perime- ter."

We break free from the jumble of bushes and vines and come to a chicken-wire fence. On the other side are tens of thousands of apple trees. "This is their attempt to keep out the deer," I say. We walk west along the fence for a short distance and at the western edge of the orchard turn south. After a mile or so, we stop for a drink. I open my canteen and hand Mickey a cup of water.

He downs it in two gulps. "More please, Grant," he says. He downs the second cup, belches, and asks, "More?"

Victor Starling explained to me some time ago that Mickey's sense of satiety was affected by his injury. His brain and his stomach do not communi- cate efficiently and there are times when he is unaware he is overeating. I decide two cups is enough. "Sorry, no more water for now. We need to save water for the remainder of the hike." I take the cup from Mickey's hand and he does not argue.

"Too much water and we have to find the bathroom," Mickey says. This is more humor than we have gotten from Mickey in many months and I know, without looking, Hannah is glowing.

After another hour of uninterrupted marching, I am forced to accept that while the practice of law has been physically and emotionally demanding, the stresses of the profession do nothing to maintain one's conditioning. "I feel this in my knees," I say.

"I feel it everywhere," Hannah says.

Mickey, who is in the front position, stops. He extends both arms and holds his palms out parallel to the ground. Hannah and I freeze. He lowers himself to his knees and moves his hands up and down, just once, in a silencing motion. Hannah takes a step forward and again Mickey gestures with his hands. It is a full minute before Mickey gives us the "all clear."

"You listen to the point," Mickey says. Hannah and I both understand this reference. Mickey had been a ground infantry officer and told us his platoon would proceed through the jungle in a diamond-shaped formation. All were in danger—but the man at greatest risk was the one at the front of the diamond who was referred to as the point.

"Time for a break, Mick," I say. Mickey is still on one knee, arms extended. "No noise," he says, his voice an urgent whisper.

"We're alone in the woods," Hannah says. "We're four or five miles from DeWitt Street, Mick.

Do you understand?'' Mickey does not turn his head but continues to look from side to side. "You're near home, Mick. Stand up and look at me.'' When Mickey does not move, Hannah walks around and stands in front of him. "You don't need to worry about the enemy on this trip. I promise.''

"You walk point,'' Mickey says. He takes off his backpack and throws it on the ground.

Hannah looks at me and then unties the sleeping bag and hands it to me. She takes Mickey's daypack and throws it on top of her own. "We brought this stuff for a reason,'' she says. "Let's go. Are you coming, Mick?''

After another half-hour, we are in an area of unusually tall trees with sparse undergrowth. Openings in the canopy create blue-gray shadows that obscure the forest floor. We are in near darkness when Mickey trips over a root covered with leaves. We are at his side in an instant. "I feel shaking,'' Mickey says.

"This is an echo of withdrawal,'' Hannah whispers calmly. "How bad is it?''

Mickey shakes his head angrily. "Not a good thing,'' he says.

"No, Mick, not a good thing,'' she says.

"Do you have any?'' Mickey says, looking at Hannah.

"Just some aspirin,'' Hannah says. "Give it a try.'' She begins to dig through her pack for her first aid kit.

"We need to stop and eat,'' I say. The distraction works and a few minutes later we are on the forest floor, sitting on our supposedly waterproof drop-cloth. Hannah engages Mickey with a steady patter of calming talk, selecting the most innocent of topics. She steers clear of our mission, Jason, Vietnam, and anything related to the last six months, focusing instead on baseball. She does not push Mickey's memory by reliving our time as ballplayers. It is skillful healing chatter. "Albany could support a second triple-A team," she says. "I could see going to games, meeting you guys there." Throughout this discussion, she checks to confirm Mickey is paying attention. As I listen, it strikes me that Hannah is a first-rate storyteller—and I am glad she is my partner.

———

We are finally beyond the orchard, on the edge of a marshy field—and it is too soon in our trip to proceed with soaked socks. A compass check reveals we are headed southeast—our predetermined route. We traverse several small mounds and stop at the top of a ridge. Two hundred yards in front of us is a stand of fifteen or so pine trees.

"Is that your pine?" Mickey asks.

"No, Mick. My pine is larger and near a hillside," I say.

"Let's go to it," Mickey says. "This walk is too long."

We discover a creek small enough to cross by jumping from stone to stone and walk up the bank into a section of forest with a musty smell. Rotting trees are strewn on the forest floor and a shelf of mushrooms a foot and a half wide protrudes from a stump. In those few places where light penetrates, lime-green ferns grow in small groups.

I run my foot across the forest floor making a small trough through dark, rich peat, a mixture of all that has died in this place. The ground is home to countless millions of microscopic organisms converting the forest remains into a substance that is fertile and potent. The hardened toe of my hiking boot picks up several sticky white forest grubs. While this is old forest, it is in some ways a nursery producing nutrients for all that surrounds us.

With Hannah walking point, we shuffle forward, often breaking the branches in our path. Moisture has hastened the deterioration of most of the fallen limbs and they crack easily making barely a sound. Above us the leaves are more brown and gray than green.

"Look at the sky," I say. "The wind is picking up."

Hannah scans the tops of the trees. "We're in for a storm."

"Are we close to your pine, Grant?" Mickey says.

"I hope so."

Hannah looks at me. "You would remember a place like this. So, does this ring a bell?"

"The day I came here with Jason, everything was covered in snow. We walked across the frozen surface. It is possible we were in here—but it wouldn't have looked anything like this. In the winter, this place would be indistinguishable from any other part of the woods."

"Raining," Mickey says.

It starts like a mist, penetrating the branches and spring leaves but in a few minutes, we are in a downpour.

"I have the ponchos." Hannah has to shout to be heard over the rain and wind.

"These go over your pack first, then your head," Mickey says. "Make sure your piece doesn't get wet."

Hannah and I know *piece* refers to a rifle and that Mickey is momentarily somewhere between this forest and South Vietnam. We follow his directions and use the ponchos to cover both our equipment and our bodies. The plastic is stiff and while it provides some protection from the rain, we are quickly getting drenched.

– 40 –

The sky explodes with thick cold rain as we emerge from the ancient section of forest and look across a field of rocks. On the best of days, footing in such places is treacherous. Some of the rocks are jagged, while others are smooth as the skin of a watermelon, their surfaces exfoliated by tens of thousands of years of rain and wind.

"We have to go around," I yell.

"Go around where?" Hannah yells back.

There are usually options when walking through the woods but in this instance there is no easy alternative. The forest we have just left is saturated and dark, the field in front of us seemingly impassable. "I'll lead," I say. "Mickey, grab onto my backpack and follow me. Hannah will be right behind you, holding tight." I edge to my left, trying to stay on the muddy grasses instead of the slippery rocks. We inch forward like circus elephants, trunk-to-tail, barely progressing.

After twenty minutes of sliding across muddy grasses and rocks, the boulder field begins to thin. "We should set up the tent here," I say.

"This is too exposed," Hannah says. "We need to find some type of natural protection, like a hill or a more heavily wooded area. We'll never get a fire going out here."

"Look around you," I say. "I'm open to suggestions."

Hannah lifts the binoculars to her face with her right hand, and shields the lenses from the rain with her left. "Holy cow!" She adjusts the binoculars. "Look at that."

She hands me the binoculars and I focus as directed. "It looks like the back end of the Sphinx," I say. As we walk toward the rock across saturated ground, I am grateful for our stiff high-top hiking boots—the suction of the mud would pull off any pair of sneakers.

"What do you think, Grant—is that the Cedar Dome Mountain?"

"I can't tell from here," I say. "We'd come through heavy woods, swamp, and then around a lake when I saw it last time. The terrain was nothing like this."

We stumble forward for ten minutes and through the gray steady rain can see the outline of the rock formation. We push our way through undergrowth, at one point plowing into a prickly bush resembling British gorse, until we come to the base of the rock and begin to look for a way around—or through—the rock.

The first major fissure in the rock is about fifteen feet deep. At its entrance is a pile of rocky material, as if the rock was hit by a giant hammer from above. The crevice provides no protection for us, however, and we continue our march.

The second irregularity is not as wide as the first, but travels deep into the rock's center. "This could go all the way through," Hannah says. "This could be the crevice you walked through with Jason." She pushes her way in and I follow, instructing Mickey to stay at the base of the rock and wait. Hannah takes a few steps before the frame of her backpack becomes wedged between the two walls of the crevice. I grab her pack with both hands, pull, and we crawl in reverse out of the crevice. Mickey has taken a few steps away from the baseline and is facing into the woods.

"Is that your pine tree, Grant?" he asks, pointing ahead.

Even with the rain and fading light, even with the spring foliage that obstructs my view, I can tell. Before us, several hundred yards away, towering above the trees, is the top of Lone Pine. I was here eighteen years ago with Jason.

"There is no question about it. That's Lone Pine."

I feel Hannah's hand wrap around the top of my head as she pulls me to her. "We found it, goddamn it," she says. "Great eyes, Mickey," she says. "Clarence Darrow and I would have walked right by it." She raises her fist in the air and screams. Rivulets of rain run into my mouth and eyes as I yell.

The noise we produce nearly drowns out the sound of a shotgun being fired. It is only when I see Mickey lying on the ground, hands covering his head, that I know. Someone has taken a shot at us.

– 41 –

Through the rain we hear the boom and echo of the second shot and hit the ground.

I pull my face off of the saturated leafy forest floor. "Hey!"

"Quiet," Mickey commands, his voice a jet-propelled whisper.

"I don't see anybody," Hannah says.

"Behind those rocks," Mickey says. "Someone moved."

"What do you want?" I yell. Mickey tells me to shut up again.

"This is private property. Now get up, turn around, and get moving. Do what I say and you won't get hurt." The voice is hoarse but clear.

"We need a place to camp," I say—and then: "We're unarmed."

A gunshot explodes through the water-soaked air.

"No choice." Mickey turns his head and whispers: "Hannah, go left. I go right. Grant, you charge—dive, twist and roll. Stay very low. When I say go."

"No, Mick," I say. "Let's not do something to...."

"Go!" Mickey yells. In one motion, he stands and is running to his right. Hannah follows immediately and runs left, and I charge, hitting the ground, rolling, screaming at full volume.

Another shot. I hear the boom and echo. I am up for a second, leaping sideways, and then down again, yelling, rolling in soaking wet mud and leaves. Mickey flies through the air—a moment later, Hannah—howling like a warrior princess—sails in from the opposite direction, and we are on top of the shooter.

In seconds, Hannah is holding the rifle and Mickey has the shooter's right arm behind his back in a hammer-lock. "What the hell is the matter with you? Are you crazy? You could have killed us," Hannah screams.

I pull back the hood of the shooter and hear Hannah gasp. He is tall, with long, thin white hair and milky blue eyes. His skin is wrinkled and red. Hannah keeps the rifle trained at his head.

"I wasn't going to hurt you," he says—and then, softly: "This is private property." He turns sideways and stares down the barrel of the gun Hannah holds. "You look comfortable holding that, Hannah."

"How do you know my name?" Hannah takes a step back.

"You're the famous Hannah Weiner—still out hiking with your chums," he says. "Valerie said you were a darn fine girl—she admires you."

I move closer to his face. "I know you," I say. "You're Jason's grandfather."

"Valerie called me—said you three might be headed in this direction. I told her to tell you not to come. You shouldn't be here. This is my place. Now, turn around and head back where you came from."

"No." Mickey lifts up the bound arms. "Take me to Grant's pine tree."

As we walk toward Lone Pine, I have an image of electrical circuits flipping on in Mickey's brain. We have just had an experience that flooded each of us, particularly Mickey, with adrenalin. The strategy to disarm, with its demands on instinct and cunning, planned and executed by Mickey, while a throwback to his military experiences, was a cognitive jolt—and he is a changed person.

"Connor Clarke," I say as we head toward the clear area under the tree where pine needles are a foot deep.

"You have a good memory, Grant," he says.

Over time, I have learned that some childhood memories are at best inexact. Not long after Mickey returned from Vietnam, Hannah and I took him to the Fourth of July Carnival held behind the Haydon firehouse. It was the first time I had been there since high school. As we walked down the woodchip path and entered the fairgrounds, I realized the

Ferris wheel was nowhere near as tall as I remembered. Other objects as well as distances have had to be adjusted to conform with my adult sense of space. No such change is required with Lone Pine. As Jason said when he first whispered to me the secret of its existence, it is bigger than any pine I have ever seen.

"This is Lone Pine, Mickey," I say as we stand at its base.

"I'm glad you found your pine tree, Grant," Mickey says.

Hannah peers down at St. Clare Creek—or at least I once thought it was St. Clare Creek—and shakes her head. "It's exactly what you described— and even so, had I not been with you, I might have walked right passed it." She turns to Connor. "What do we do with you?"

"We talk," I say before Connor can reply.

I turn my back to Lone Pine, Connor, and my friends and walk towards the hill that slopes down to the forest floor. Undoubtedly anticipating our arrival, Connor has placed leafy branches to camouflage the wooden door but I am sure of its location. I drop to my knees and begin to brush away undergrowth and forest waste piled hastily in front of the opening. It does not take long to clear all four sides of the door. I reach for the handle and it opens.

– **42** –

It has been eighteen years since I was inside the shelter at Lone Pine. It is unchanged. Mickey and Hannah give me a minute to take in the discovery, but the weather is a persuasive force and they join me in the shelter, Connor Clarke in tow. The cot, buck saw, ax, cans of food—including the Sardines of Norway—and traps are as I remember. We light the lanterns and take off our wet clothes. Hannah gives me the gun and retires to the fire-pit, her private dressing room.

"Give me the piece," Mickey says to me as Hannah emerges from the fire-pit.

"They're blanks," Connor says. "I would not fire live rounds." He sighs. "This is my place—you have no right to be here."

"Why do you want the rifle, Mick?" Hannah asks.

"Inspection," Mickey says. "It isn't safe to have a loaded weapon inside a dwelling."

"It's empty," Connor says.

Mickey's sentences, his reactions, are stunning and I am increasingly sure Victor Starling was right: experiences prompt changes in the quality and nature of thinking, perhaps in overall capacity, and Mickey is moving in leaps and bounds. Hannah and I watch as Mickey sits down on the cot, grasps the stock and inspects the rifle.

"Not air-cooled or gas-operated. A simple spring mechanism," Mickey says. "I trained on the M–14 and then had to use the M–16 in Vietnam."

Jason once said that Connor Clarke ran a business that manufactured rifles—and Mickey's comment prompts a response from Clarke. "The M–16 was versatile—and deadly—but unreliable."

Mickey nods and points the barrel of the rifle at the dirt floor of the shelter and pulls back the bolt. "There is nothing in the chamber," Mickey says.

Mickey holds the rifle in the air above his head with both arms and looks at its underside. "Is this the magazine?" he asks.

"It is," Connor says.

Mickey removes the magazine and hands it to Hannah.

"I have a right to preserve what's mine." Connor looks at me carefully. "What do you want, Grant?"

"I want answers," I say.

"I own this land—as far as you can see in every direction—and I own this shelter," Connor says. "I built it, I maintain it, and I have no intention of letting you—or anyone else—make use of it."

"You know what happened to Jason, don't you?"

He does not answer.

"Why do you think that?" Hannah asks.

"He knows," I say. "Connor, it's time for the truth."

"What the hell are you talking about?" Connor says.

"I expect you to tell me the truth." I have learned that asking direct questions is potent. Lawyers who place conditions in questions, providing information that leads witnesses, tend to get poor results. Most people are not fooled by a loaded question. I will treat this like a hearing—and of course, I will not tell Connor that is my plan.

"I don't know any more about Jason than you do," Connor says.

"You must," I say, and my thoughts turn to Mickey's father. Juan would approve. The moment for questioning is perfect. In the few years I have practiced law, I have learned that interrogation is all about timing, getting a witness to move with the cadence of the inquiry, to become part of your mission. My goal will be to get Connor to buy into the mission of disclosure and for once, I feel well-suited to the task.

"If you think I'm going to answer your questions sitting here in sopping wet clothes, you're not the bright young lawyer Valerie said you were."

"Of course." I see Connor shiver. "You must have dry clothes stashed somewhere in here."

"In the large brown cupboard in the wall in the fire-pit room."

A few minutes later, Connor emerges from the fire-pit wearing denim overalls and a sweater. He rubs and flexes his hands.

"My mother writes to Martha—Mrs. Talbot—every now and then," I say, hoping I have a conversant and willing witness.

"Martha? My daughter?" he asks. "She changed her name back to Clarke. She was a decent girl who married poorly," Connor says.

"She was nice to me," I say. "I wasn't in their house all that often—particularly when Mr. Talbot came home from work."

"You didn't need to be Carl Jung to know what was going on in that place," Connor says.

"I heard a lot of yelling, saw Valerie cry a few times. I knew Jason wanted to get away from home—he said that the day he disappeared." I see Connor raise his eyebrows.

"So you figured he was running away from his father." Connor shakes his head and continues. "The boy might have had it in his mind to run away. It's a shame he never made it."

"That is so hard to accept," Hannah says. "Jason knew the woods better than any of us. We have always assumed that—for whatever reason— he took off on his own."

Connor and Hannah lock eyes. "My grandson disappeared. It's a tragedy, but I have had to learn to live with it. I suggest you do the same." He turns to me. "Is that what this is all about? You want to know what happened to poor Jason all those years ago? He is gone. It was a freezing cold day and he was miles from home."

"You must have followed the search carefully," I say.

"Well, of course," Connor says. "Jason was a wonderful boy and I was hoping he would be found."

"Even if Jason didn't make it out of the woods that first night, he knew enough to survive," I say. "He had food and matches with him."

"Well, it didn't happen that way, did it?" Connor snaps. "The boy didn't make it."

"I made it," I say. "I was two years younger than Jason and nowhere near as well prepared for that experience and I made it out."

"Well, you were either luckier or stronger—or both. All kinds of bad things can happen to people in the woods," Connor says.

"I told everyone—and I mean everyone—that we were at Lone Pine, a secret place in the woods behind my house. Those are the woods I knew. It wasn't until today that I came to learn that Lone Pine is fifteen miles in the other direction."

"So you blame yourself for the fact that the searchers never found Jason?" Connor says.

"There was a map of the search area in the paper. I'm sure you remember that. There were interviews with searchers on the radio. You knew they were looking for Lone Pine, didn't you?" I ask.

"I assumed if they covered the entire woods they would find him," Connor says.

"The area they searched is five miles wide and six miles long. That's thirty square miles, a huge area. The problem is, it's the wrong area. As far as I know, you were—and are—the only one who knew the location of Lone Pine. Even so, you stayed silent. If Jason was special to you—and I believe he was—why didn't you get involved? You could have led the searchers to Lone Pine—they would have fanned out from this spot, yet you decided to do nothing."

"I did what I could," Connor says angrily.

"You did not do the one thing within your power," I say. "You kept Lone Pine a secret."

"Hack told me to stay the hell away. He said he would take care of Jason."

"When did he say that?" I ask.

"Late that night—the night Jason disappeared," Connor says.

"Hack Talbot was passed out cold the night Jason disappeared—too drunk to search for his son. That much I remember," I say. "Anyway, why would you listen to Hack?"

"Because when I angered Hack, he took it out on Martha and Valerie. I couldn't risk having him harm them," Connor says.

"So you left it to me, a ten-year-old boy, to lead a search for your grandson that was doomed to fail. You knew exactly where this place was and you refused to let anybody know about it. Was it that you didn't want anyone to find your secret hideaway? Was this place more important than Jason's life? What possible reason could you have for keeping the searchers away from Jason? You had to know that if he wasn't found, he was likely to die from exposure."

"I knew no such thing. You said it yourself—Jason was most resourceful. I thought he would make it—much as you did." Connor looks away and shakes his head. "An awful thing happened—but it was not my doing."

"It was an awful thing—to let your grandson die—to be more concerned about the secrecy of this place than the life of a family member."

"I've been playing along with your little game up to this point, but there is a limit," Connor says. "Show some respect."

"This isn't a game, Connor," I say. "If Jason died around here, I need to tell the authorities—we ought to have a funeral."

Connor looks up quickly. "A public funeral? That is out of the question. That would be a sacrilege," Connor says.

"Why would that be so?" I ask. "It's time. Tell us what happened, Connor."

"Can't you figure it out?" Connor snaps at me.

I flash back to the courtroom of Judge Miles Prentice. I can imagine him saying to me, "Well, Mr. Harper, where are we headed with all of this?"

"You won't participate in the funeral because Jason is not dead," I say.

Connor Clarke's story does not add up. Given his affection for Martha, Valerie, and Jason, there is just no credible explanation for his failure to disclose the location of Lone Pine. Lies are disclosed by patent inconsistencies—it seems inconceivable that Connor would have let Jason die, lost and alone, in these woods, just to protect this location.

I wait and watch as Connor scans the interior of the shelter he constructed. "A funeral is unnecessary," he says.

"He's alive, isn't he?" I ask.

"He's gone—forever," Connor says.

"I don't believe you," I say.

"I realized that some time ago," Connor says.

"Where is he?"

"I'll take you there, but that will be the end of this nonsense," Connor says.

Connor holds a lantern as we exit the shelter and head up the slope into which the shelter is built. At the crest of the hill there is a small mound no more than three feet across.

"Is this Jason's grave?" I say to Connor. Mickey straightens, raises his right arm, and salutes.

"It's a memorial of sorts," Connor says.

I stand and move backwards several steps until I am along side Hannah. "We should say something," Hannah says.

"I think it's okay to pray to yourself," I say. "My mother, were she here, would recite the Twenty-third Psalm from memory."

"My preference is Luke 15, Chapter 32—but it's up to you. I'm going back to the shelter," Connor says. "Take as long as you want."

We stand in silence for several minutes and finally Hannah says: "I really thought he made it out."

"So did I," I say looking at the grave. "How did he dig a grave? Do you remember how cold it was that week? The ground had to be frozen down two feet."

"Maybe he waited to bury Jason until the spring," Hannah says. "God, this is sad."

Connor has a good blaze going in the fire-pit when we return to the shelter. "Wouldn't it have been better to carry Jason out of the forest and allow him to have a proper burial?" I ask.

"Better for whom?" Connor says. "Certainly not for me."

"It would have been the humane thing to do, Connor. Martha and Valerie had a right to know that Jason was gone. You gave them hope when there was none. You let your daughter and grand-daughter mourn for years, experiencing a sorrow that I cannot begin to imagine, and you did nothing to stop it. What a senseless, brutal act."

"I took care of Martha and Valerie. Are you looking for contrition? Remorse?" Connor's voice is rising. "I've made my peace with God over Jason."

"When did you find Jason?" I ask.

Connor's eyes go from Hannah to Mickey to me. "You might as well know everything," he says. "I was here the day he disappeared."

"That's impossible," I say. "I was here—in the shelter—when Jason disappeared."

"I was a good 500 yards from Lone Pine when I saw Jason. He was up on the hillside, knocking the ice away from the vent. I didn't know you were inside," Connor says. "I did hear about you later–how you were found by a Caulfield County snow-plow."

"Why would you come to the shelter in the dead of winter?"

"This is my favorite spot, Grant. Haven't you figured that out? When I am in Caulfield County—I still have some business interests here—I usually end up here. Years ago, I would come here after a visit with Martha, Jason, and Valerie—it was my place to get away from everything."

As I think back to the police car at the Talbots'—the screaming the day before Jason vanished and Valerie moved out—Connor's escape to solitude makes sense.

"I had no idea I'd come across Jason that afternoon. I had been at Hack and Martha's the day before. I listened to a fight, to words no grandfather ever should have to hear. I saw Hack out of control. I couldn't get him to stop and called the police."

Connor walks to the wall where the traps hang. He straightens the chains on the zeros and ones and continues. "I'd seen too many fights in that house—but this one was different. Valerie was maturing and Hack had his hands all over her. That was the last straw. Martha was hysterical and begged Hack to stop—and I stepped in. I made a proposal to move Valerie to the home of one of my other daughters—her favorite aunt—and Hack finally agreed. It was a negotiation. In the end, I wrote Hack a check for $50,000 so he could pay back the money he had stolen at work—and he let go of Valerie. I tried the same with Jason but Hack wasn't interested.

"Hack needed Jason—not just for his own sick purposes ... Jason...." He stops and appears to gather himself. "Jason was special to me. Hack knew that—and he also knew that when I died, Jason would inherit a substantial share of my estate. When that happened, Hack was determined to be there, with Jason under his thumb, to cash in. This was made clear to me more than once."

"Why didn't you just take Jason with you when you left the Talbots'?" I ask. "If he was being abused...."

Connor interrupts. "That would have been impossible. Hack would have had us in court, had me in jail for kidnapping ... probably would have killed my Martha. When you crossed Hack Talbot, you paid a terrible price. Jason understood that—when he broke a rule, his father came crashing down on him."

Connor looks at Hannah, Mickey, and me, and shakes his head. "Like I said, I was about a quarter mile from Lone Pine when I saw Jason—and he saw me—and a second later he took off. He knew that if I took him home and his father learned that he had come this far into the woods without permission, he would have been beaten within an inch of his life—so he ran.

"Jason didn't know who to trust and wasn't about to take any chances. Remember, this is a child who was smacked around by his father for the slightest mistake. He may have been two years older than you, but he was still a little boy. He panicked. He was quick—he just seemed to fly across the surface of the ice."

"I would have heard you. I was right here. You must have called his name," I say.

"You were inside the shelter. When the door is closed, you can't hear much. Even when you came outside, with the wind. . . . We were probably half a mile from here before you opened the door."

"Jason would have stopped when you called him," Hannah says.

"I loved my grandson," Connor says. "There were rules about Lone Pine, however, and the first and most important one was never to come here without me. Jason knew that. This is an isolated place and if something happens, there is no easy way to get help. He was in trouble—with me—and was off like a deer.''

"Why didn't you let him go?" Hannah says.

"Because it was freezing cold and he was my grandson—and he was running away from his home, not toward it. Think about it. Would you let a small boy run off in the middle of these woods, all alone, under those circumstances?" Hannah shakes her head. "The chase continued for more than a mile, and then we hit a hillside.''

"Up or down?" I ask.

"Down—and steep," Connor says. "You know what it was like in the woods that day. The ground was ice and there was no way to stay standing on a steep hill. Jason went soaring over the top of the ridge down the hill and started to fall. He smashed into a tree at the bottom—back first—and that's where I found him. His injuries were obvious—and awful. I put my coat over him, knowing there were almost no options.

"Taking him back to civilization, walking for hours through the cold, would have been the end of him. I lifted him in my arms and started back up the icy hills. It took time—maybe half an hour—maybe more—and finally we were back at the shelter. At that point, you were long gone. Jason never regained consciousness and I never left the shelter, never left his side. He was a strong boy, but his injuries were too much.''

"Why didn't you get help?" Hannah asks.

"And leave him? In the middle of the woods? The fire goes out and he freezes to death. He wakes up from his coma, there is no one there, he panics—goes outside—and dies for sure. You can't leave someone under those circumstances."

"And after he died, you could have brought him out, let his mother bury him," I say.

"I guess I could have done just that, but I didn't. This much I knew: if I came out of the woods having failed to save Jason, having kept him for a week in this shelter, Hack and Luther Talbot—that whole damn bunch—would see me hang. They would have been on Martha and me like fire ants and they would not have stopped until we were destroyed. The Talbots would make sure I was charged with murdering my grandson and then, before the ink was dry on the indictment, they would have my businesses."

"So why tell us?" Hannah asks.

"Because you found me—you found Lone Pine. You didn't leave when I fired on you and you're probably too stubborn and curious to stay away in the future. If you let the entire world know where it is, I will lose everything." Connor pauses. "It is imperative that Jason's disappearance remain an unsolved ... event. That uncertainty protects Martha, Valerie, and me—it keeps the Talbots off-balance. That nasty bunch has been out of the picture for many years and I want it to stay that way."

"He deserves something better than an earthen mound," Hannah says.

"He does indeed, Hannah. I loved my grandson—I wanted a memorial without attracting attention. Unless you know exactly what to look for, Lone Pine, the burial mound—and everything about it—including this shelter—disappears into the forest.''

"Particularly if you're looking fifteen miles from here,'' Hannah says.

"Now you know where to look, and you know the whole story—Martha, Valerie, and I are at your mercy.'' Connor clears his throat. "I ask for your silence—in Jason's name.''

"None of this adds up,'' I say.

Hannah turns to me. "It does, Grant—it makes perfect sense—and he's right,'' she says. "I will not do anything at odds with Martha and Valerie's interest. I pledge that to you, Connor.''

He turns to Mickey. "Son, you can keep a secret, can't you?''

Mickey stands and salutes again. "Sir, I swear, sir.''

"Grant, let things stay where they are. You wanted answers—you have them.''

"I am not interested in making trouble,'' I say. "I will not repeat a word of what you told us—but we're not done.''

"You came for an explanation. Now you have it,'' Connor says.

When I say nothing further, Connor continues. "There is one other piece of information. When I put Jason to rest, the ground was frozen—I could not dig down all that deep. That spring some animals got to the grave. I came to the shelter one day and could see they'd been digging—it could have been bobcats—or coyotes. Back then, they were plentiful—even now, at dusk, I'll see them off in the distance." Connor speaks slowly, his words measured. "Of course there was no coffin ... as the ground thawed...."

"You don't need to continue," I say.

"So Jason's ... remains ... are not in the grave anymore," Hannah says.

"It's a memorial," Connor says. "And yes, if one were to dig it up, nothing would be found. They could have dragged him for miles."

I look at Mickey and wonder how much of this he has followed.

"You got any more questions?" Connor asks.

"That's enough for one day," I say.

Hannah unloads our provisions and begins dinner preparation with Mickey at her side.

—

"I'm going out to get more firewood," I say. "Connor, would you give me a hand."

We leave the shelter and walk toward Lone Pine together. I look down at the stream. "I make my living asking questions and listening to answers designed to mislead me—I know when a story doesn't add up—this one doesn't. I simply do not believe you sat around for a week and watched your grandson die. You know I'm going to get to the bottom of this."

I turn and face Connor squarely. "The police—or more precisely Caulfield County's Lieutenant

Huntington—think I know what happened to Jason. Huntington must know I didn't do anything intentionally, but I suppose he believes I am hiding information—and it plays on him. His annoying persistence and my own conscience make it inevitable—I have a duty to uncover the truth, Connor. What really happened?''

I feel Connor's hand on my back and turn to him. "I want you to be my lawyer," he says.

"Don't be ridiculous," I say.

"I can always use another good lawyer. You seem fairly sharp."

"What's this about?" I ask.

"The only way you get additional information will be as my lawyer. Nothing more in front of your two friends—only you." Connor flicks a caterpillar from the trunk of Lone Pine and inspects the bark for other invaders of his tree. "You earned this, Grant. You walked in with Jason, probably suffered his disappearance more than most, felt some responsibility for his well-being—and here you are, eighteen years later, the only one to put two and two together."

"We can't be the only ones to stumble across Lone Pine."

"You'd be surprised. This is a very remote spot. Every now and then, a hunter passes by, but they have no reason to think this is where a little boy vanished years ago. The shelter door stays covered and the tree is, well, just another big tree." Connor takes a step back and folds his arms. "So?"

"What possible reason would I have to help you?"

"Those are my conditions. I'll fill in the final pieces—but only when you are absolutely bound to keep confidential everything I tell you."

The rain stops. Connor and I stand in complete silence, listening to the stream and the sounds of nightfall.

"We ought to get some firewood," I say.

"There is plenty of wood in the shelter," Connor says. "What is it going to be?"

"What would you want me to do as your lawyer?" I ask.

"The first thing is a meeting—a very important one—I want you to join me on a trip—overseas."

"To do what?"

"Finish off some business related to my family. I hire people to help achieve my goals, both in my business and in my private life—one goal is to silence any inquiry regarding Jason. Some months ago, at the bail hearing for Mickey, he mentioned Jason. I knew Mickey was injured—heard he nearly died—but at that hearing, he said quite clearly, 'Jason Talbot.' A reporter picked up on it—one with a long memory—and found Lieutenant Huntington. Like you, Wallace Huntington had pried into the lives of my family for too many years. He paid you a visit, I understand."

"He did—several," I say. "I wasn't at the bail hearing—Mickey's father handled it."

"Years earlier, I dealt with Lieutenant Huntington—convinced him that I did not want to talk
about Jason—and he bought it. Then, Mickey's
testimony got him all fired up once again and he
reopened the investigation. I understand he managed to get a judge to sign off on a warrant to
search your place a few months ago—which didn't
bother me all that much—but then he started talking to the press."

"Not what you wanted to see, I assume."

"Not at all," Connor says. "He talked the District Attorney into convening a grand jury and was
asking for more funds to plow through the records,
search the woods again. It was time to put a stop to
it so I did a little of my own investigation and came
up with a plan to rid myself of Lieutenant Huntington." He pauses. "I knew Huntington had interests
that went beyond good police work."

"He was obsessed—pathologically—clinically,"
I say.

"That he was—but he was also an old friend of
Hack—and his brothers. At least consider this possibility: the Talbots wanted to pin down what happened to Jason because they knew Martha came
from a wealthy family—my family—and once Jason
was gone, they saw themselves one step closer to
those resources. Why wouldn't the Talbots offer
Huntington a cut—to have certainty, documented
proof, that Jason was dead and gone? Makes perfect
sense, don't you think?"

"I don't believe you," I say.

He smiles. "I assure you—Huntington was in it
for a share of the money the Talbots hoped to get

from me, from Hack, from my businesses—my money." He stops, no longer smiling. "Why on earth would a seasoned police officer pursue a ten-year-old boy under these circumstances? He saw himself as a poorly paid public servant—full of the power of the law and unable to convert that authority into money . . . until this came along."

"How do you know this?" I ask.

"Because I bought him, Grant—and you are a third-party beneficiary of the sale. Huntington sees me as a wealthy recluse on my last leg—the only one willing to pay a king's ransom to find my grandson. The Talbots made him a standing offer— they needed him to confirm Jason's death—but he never could—and they never coughed up a dime because the Lieutenant failed—again and again— and that left me. I turned over to him my "file," a set of documents we cooked up that place Jason overseas—in Denmark. I gave him highly secret but promising leads to suggest Jason was seen a few years ago in a seashore community north of Esbjerg. He will follow those leads—and then he will learn of a fishing boat capsizing in a storm in the Skagerrak—the straights north of Denmark—all hands were lost—apparently—and it will seem likely to the Lieutenant that Jason was among those who went to the bottom of the sea. He will send me a report, noting of course that no body was found— once again, no death certificate—a modest final payment will be made—and the mystery will end for Lieutenant Huntington. I guarantee you won't hear from him again."

"You spent a good deal of time and money to get Lieutenant Huntington out of the way," I say.

"Ah," Connor says. "Dawn breaks over Marble-head." Connor moves closer. "And now, Grant, my offer."

"You want to enter into an attorney-client relationship to silence me. I'm not for sale, Connor—I don't need your money."

"This isn't just about money—it's about privacy, about decent people who are entitled to some peace in their lives, people who will be hurt unless I watch out for their interests."

"And *your* interests?" I ask.

"We need no formal written agreement Grant—if I speak more, you must agree to treat further discussion as fully privileged."

Connor is right—once I agree, we will have an attorney-client relationship and all that he tells me will be confidential. "I need to think about this, Connor."

"You do that," he says. "In the meantime, give me your solemn word, Grant, not as a lawyer, but as a friend of Jason."

"That I can do."

"Thank you," he says. "Of course I was—and am—protecting my interests. I've been lucky, Grant," Connor says. "My businesses have prospered—and every member of Hack Talbot's family wanted a piece of that success. They were sure that once Jason was out of the way, they were one step closer. When Hack died, they became even more persistent."

"You must know there are many ways to protect business interests—even after your death—you could have your will written to shut out Hack, Hack's brothers—all of the Talbots—and after Hack's death...."

"You're thinking like a lawyer. You need to think like a Talbot. These grotesque people believed that if they hung on long enough, they would get their hands on a business worth many millions of dollars. It was all the motivation they needed."

I start: "This is not an insurmountable legal problem—any lawyer could have helped with this...." but Connor cuts me off.

"I have very fine lawyers, Grant. I changed my will—but I did not and will not disinherit Jason. He was—and as far as my will, all public corporate documents ... and the remaining Talbots are concerned—still is—my heir." Connor smiles broadly. "And there it is—so long as Jason's whereabouts are unknown, no body found, no formal declaration of death issued, he continues as my heir and successor ... even the Talbots came to understand that."

"So ... you explain to Hannah, Mickey, and me that Jason is dead—so we don't continue to look—and you want the Talbots to think he may be alive—on the premise that they have no shot at your business interests...."

Connor nods. "Something like that."

"You seem to have convinced Hannah and Mickey—but the Talbots? This isn't entirely in your control. After seven years, the State must have...."

"Declared Jason dead—I know, Grant," Connor says. "That is often activated by a petition from the family, and Martha wasn't about to do that. I—my lawyers—have blocked every effort to have any court make that declaration. To accomplish that objective, we have had more than our share of *in camera* meetings—I placed my trust in several very fine judges—including The Honorable Miles Prentice—to keep confidences—and they have—now the question is, can I trust you?''

"You need to give me more information," I say. "I can't make promises...."

"In good time," Connor says. "In any case, as a matter of the law of the State of New York, Jason has never been anything but lost. The Talbots check every now and then—one of them starts digging around—but I have clever lawyers—Jason's absence—not his death—is always there ... and, importantly, I didn't die." He smiles. "Don't you see, Grant? We wore them down."

"So—it's over, Connor—you won—you don't need to keep recalibrating the world around you. It's time to let everyone know what happened."

"Isn't that what you do, Grant? Isn't your career based on assessing the needs of your clients and then figuring out how to recalibrate—as you put it—the world around them using the courts and government agencies to achieve what you deem their best interests?"

"I develop a strategy with my clients, not behind their backs. I'm not interested in making them dependent on me."

"And Mickey Cabrera—you're telling me that you developed a strategy with him before putting him forward as an incompetent and having him sent away for months?"

"That was a family decision—Mickey needed...."

Connor turns as my answer stalls. He walks to the shelter stopping before he opens the door. "You have my offer—there is more to discuss."

———

Inside the shelter, Mickey and Hannah are involved in conversation and the preparation of dinner. The change in Mickey is staggering. Hannah stops her task as I approach and looks at me. I have never been one to read accurately the meanings masked in the subtle expressions of women, but somewhere from the recesses of my thick male brain, I receive a message: this is a look of deep and real affection—and more.

I walk behind Hannah and rub her shoulders. "Are you as sore as I am?" is all I can muster.

"I ache, just like you do, Grant," Hannah says. Her voice is almost a whisper and I struggle with the meaning of her words.

Hannah sautés onions and garlic in a cast-iron skillet while Mickey shreds cheese and slices oranges and apples. The scene and fragrances are narcotic. I am detailed—by Mickey—to fill a black cauldron with water from St. Clare Creek. I follow his orders and on my return hang the heavy pot on a hook above the fire. We have a pound of spaghetti to cook, homemade sauce—and the pasta is just the first course.

—

It is 3 a.m. when Hannah's soft fingers quiet my awakening gasp. Connor sleeps soundly on the cot, his face turned to the wall of the shelter. I hear Mickey's slow, deep breathing.

Hannah holds a finger to her lips and leads me to her sleeping bag in the fire-pit. We are 15 feet away from Connor and Mickey, separated by the cased opening between the pit and the main room and by a makeshift curtain hung to give Hannah privacy (fashioned from one of the blankets stored in the shelter). "Be very, very quiet," she says.

Her jersey hangs mid-thigh and as she lowers herself beside me, I realize it is the only garment she is wearing. I find her lips and feel the strength of her back and smoothness of her skin. Despite the dampness and smoke in the shelter, I inhale nothing but Hannah. It is a perfect smell, like fresh, dark vanilla.

Ours is lovemaking with whispered words, sighs and shudders. Years of longing give way to desire and the release that often limits intimacy plays no role in establishing an endpoint for us.

These sensations, tastes, this impossible closeness is not about sex and sensuality, although I am thankful for both. These hours, just before dawn at Lone Pine, mark the beginning for Hannah and me.

Sleep finds us, but not before the obvious is stated and repeated. This is love—and all at once, for both of us, it is clear as a bell.

– 43 –

I am awake before the others. I kiss Hannah just once and slide out of her sleeping bag without waking her. I stand, unforgiven by every part of my body. My muscles ache from my neck down through to the arches of my feet, pain attributable to the physical and psychological demands of yesterday. Our clothes, hung by the fire overnight, are dry and stiff and I creak as I go outside. It is a starless dawn but the dense clouds are insufficient to screen the point at which the sun is rising. More surprising than the daylight leaking through the forest is the direction of the light. Last night, had I been asked to point in an eastward direction, I would have been off by 180 degrees.

The shelter door opens and Connor emerges. "The only sane way back to civilization is due south," he says. "You hit an old logging access road in about four miles. Follow that another few miles and you'll find the highway."

"We'll take our chances in the woods. Walking along the interstate is a far more risky proposition," I say.

"Did you give my offer any more thought?"

"A bit," I say. "Tell me—the day Jason disappeared, were you wearing a brown coat?"

"No more questions."

"This is an easy one," I say.

"I probably was," he says. "I had a long brown jacket—down-filled—wore it for years. Now, what about my offer?"

"I saw you," I say. Connor gives me a quizzical look. "I saw you in the woods, off in the distance, the day Jason disappeared."

"Did you ever tell anyone about seeing me?" he asks.

"I didn't know, until now, that it was you."

"Maybe it wasn't," he says. "Now—my offer?"

"I don't think you're looking for legal representation," I say. "I have the sense you're seeking the confidentiality of the confessional. If you need to make your peace with God, Connor, find a priest, not a lawyer."

"Talk it over with your partner—Clarke Enterprises will be a very lucrative client for your firm—but be careful what you say, Grant. Confidentiality is a deadly serious matter, as far as I'm concerned."

"Jason once told me a doctor would go to jail for life if he disclosed the confidences of his patients—now I see where he got that notion."

Breakfast is far less elaborate than dinner. Connor has coffee with us but does not eat. "You have a long walk ahead of you and need your energy. I'll be here all day, doing what I always do. I don't need much fuel for that," Connor says.

"Other than firing blanks at those who come close to this spot, how do you spend your time?" Hannah asks. "There is just so much firewood you can cut."

"When you were young and went into the woods, do you ever remember being bored?" Connor asks. Hannah shakes her head. "It's no different for me."

After breakfast, we spend a few minutes at the gravesite and then return to the shelter and reload our packs. We review directions with Connor who accompanies us to the base of Cedar Dome Mountain.

We are a few steps from the crevice when I hear Connor. "I'd watch my step on the far side of these rocks if I were you. That field is full of snakes. If you're not careful, one will be crawling up your pant leg before you know it."

I turn to speak with him, but Connor is gone.

—

The hike back to DeWitt Street takes place under Mickey's command. His recollection of our journey the day before is exact and while I do not know whether this signals significant repair of his short-term memory, I do know that it is nothing but positive.

Our return hike is almost finished as night sets in. Before we emerge from the woods, fifty yards from the DeWitt Street dead end, Hannah turns to me and says quietly. "I know there is more to Connor's story."

"So why did you agree so quickly to his request for confidentiality?" I ask.

She leans over and whispers: "Because I love you. He isn't going to give a group lecture to us—and you, more than anyone, need to have this matter put to rest. I stepped aside so that there can be a real discussion—the truth."

Mickey turns abruptly. "What truth?" he says. "What do you mean?"

"We weren't talking about you, Mick," Hannah says.

"I want to meet the family of the man—who died in the bookstore—the man Arthur killed. I want to tell them I am sorry it happened." He looks at me. "I didn't do it, Grant. Arthur did."

"I know, Mick," I say. "Everyone knows that."

"Oh, Mickey," Hannah says. Mickey is coming back to us in large chunks, not just bits and pieces. She covers her mouth, breathes in deeply and says: "Grant and I will take you to them. I think they would like that."

"I tried to help him," Mickey says.

"Everyone knows that, too, Mick," I say.

Mickey nods. "Good," he says. "That is the most important thing for me."

—

The following morning, Mickey, Hannah, and I drive back to Albany. Teresa and Denise are waiting for us in the lobby.

"And the hunter home from the hills," Denise says, smiling—it is one of my mother's favorite lines from a Robert Louis Stevenson poem.

We keep the farewell brief and get in the car to return to the office for a scheduled meeting with Juan. A major decision faces us, but we do not discuss it in the car. Instead, Hannah leans over and kisses my cheek as we pull out of Mickey's apartment complex. I take her hand and we drive slowly through City Park. Hannah is the one—and I am thankful beyond words.

Once in the office, we give Juan a lengthy description of Mickey's progress. "My son has learned to organize—and keep his head down—at last," he says. "And even more impressive, he got you to lead the charge." His eyes water as he smiles. "No one knows the future—but at least this tells me Miguel has a future."

—

After coffee and finishing off a few more details about our rediscovery of Lone Pine, we give Juan an edited briefing of my interrogation in the shelter leading to one question: can and should our firm represent Connor Clarke. Within a few minutes, the answer is clear to Juan: Connor Clarke will be the wealthiest client we have ever represented. "How can you argue against revenue—I assume someone like Mr. Clarke and Clarke Enterprises will provide this firm an admirable income stream for years to come—and the resolution you have sought your entire adult life?" Juan says. "You shall become possessed of Connor Clarke's secrets and we shall profit."

"I assume the firm will be well paid," I say. "Still, he is asking me to be his counsel—personally—and that will limit the information I can share."

Hannah raises her eyebrows but says nothing.

"And so a part of this most intriguing client shall be for you alone. This presents you with some risk—considerable uncertainty." Juan looks to Hannah and then to me. "You think—both of you—I knew what would happen with our friend, Arthur Soto, when I left the office the last day of the hearing." He waits for a moment. "I had no idea. I thought he was implicated—but how? And why was it urgent for him to see me?" He shakes his head. "I took a chance—he could have killed me. I knew that. But my son needed help. In such a circumstance, there is no certainty—no clarity. Do not misunderstand—this is not bravery—it is instinct and impulse. Sometimes, when all is at stake, we must act."

Juan nods slowly. "I have no need for the secrets of Connor Clarke—but you do. I have my son. That is more than I thought possible. I am thankful for the resolution—for both Miguel and me. I meet with Judge Prentice next week to discuss the plight of foreign lawyers. We shall see. . . . Now, Grant—what about you?"

When I fail to answer Juan, Hannah jumps in. "I think it was bravery, Juan," she says. "You knew enough about Soto to understand the risk—and still you went forward—you saved your son, Juan."

"You, my sweet friend and colleague, can write my biography," Juan says with a smile.

Lawyers must guard the secrets of clients—it is among our most basic responsibilities. However, the confidences, the details, the compelling truths—and lies—belong to our clients. As I see it, Connor has the right to designate me the sole possessor of his past. With that in mind, I ask: "What if Connor reveals to me that he is criminally responsible for Jason's death?"

"Were you listening to Juan? This is no time to shy away from the chase," Hannah says.

"Connor was clear: I am to handle this aspect of his legal affairs—beginning with an overseas trip of some sort." I am not looking forward to being separated from Hannah—not for revenue—not for resolution—not even for honor.

"Make sure your passport is up-to-date, Grant. Juan is right; it's your time," Hannah says. She touches my arm. "And I promise—I will be here when you get back."

Juan looks at Hannah and then at me. "I see," he says. "You found more than Mr. Clarke at Lone Pine."

"Is it that obvious?" Hannah asks.

"It has always been that obvious—though perhaps not to our senior partner." He shakes his head. "It is risky to be in love with a colleague—but far riskier still to deny such emotions."

—

That night, I check my passport and call home to tell my parents I will be out of town with a client for at least a week. My father, the secretive doctor, and my mother, the lay clergy, understand confidentiality—and ask not a single question.

– 44 –

The final airborne leg of our trip across the Pacific takes us past the Aorangi range on the south island of New Zealand, its highest peaks well over 12,000 feet. The Māoris, the local population in this area, refuse to use the anglicized names of these mountains—in particular the impressive Mount

Cook which they simply call Aorangi. As the summit fades from view, Connor suggests I give thought to scaling the summit.

"Climb that mountain," he says. "You are looking for a moment of transition. Go up the southern ridge. That will reshuffle your interior."

I am not so sure I want my interior reshuffled but a realignment wouldn't hurt. After forty hours of flying on four different planes, my thoughts are more about a warm shower and a long sleep, rather than climbing the highest peak in New Zealand.

Our landing at the private airstrip just west of Christchurch is bumpy and we taxi for what appears to be several miles to an expansive hangar on which the words "Clarke Enterprises" are painted. The large doors open, the plane rolls inside, and the engines come to a stop. As we walk down the steps from the plane, I see our bags moving from a hand cart to the rear of a large station wagon with oversized tires. Like the hangar, the words "Clarke Enterprises" are painted neatly on the door of the wagon.

Our trip into Christchurch takes us through the magnificent countryside of New Zealand, at once both rocky and lush. I listen as the driver chats with Connor. It is the most Connor has spoken since we left New York. I asked questions for the first ten hours of our trip and he refused to answer most of them. He was not impolite, just quiet. Every now and then, he would say: "You are on this trip to observe, not to interrogate." Here, in New Zealand, he seems more relaxed.

One theory of interrogation is that a person will open up to you if you first take them into your confidence. With that in mind, I decide to fill in Connor on the one and only experience regarding Jason I have kept secret for almost two decades.

"Nine months after Jason disappeared, something happened at the Talbots' house on DeWitt Street." Connor turns to me and I continue. "It was August. I was heading home when Martha came flying by in that new black sedan."

"I gave her that car after Hack died," Connor said. "I didn't want her in a car that brought back his memory.... Sorry, go ahead—what happened after she drove by?"

"I don't think she saw me—I had to jump to keep from being hit. As I walked past the Talbots' house I noticed the front door was open. I walked in—and ended up in the garage. I remember looking at Jason's bicycle—it was hanging on the wall by hooks, kickstand in place—when somebody grabbed me, covered my eyes and mouth and dragged me into the backyard. I know this will seem hard to believe but I felt like it was Hack."

"It is just the kind of thing he might have done," Connor says.

"He had been dead for six months when this happened," I say. "Still, for all these years, I've wondered. Whoever it was mashed my face into the ground and held me down. I could hardly breathe." Connor winces as I continue. "He wanted to know where Jason was, but of course I didn't know. At some point, a delivery truck drove up the street— maybe he became concerned he would be caught—

or maybe he figured, rightly, that I just didn't know—in any case, as he got off me, he told me that if I ever disclosed this to anyone, he would kill my parents. He said he would shoot them like tin cans on a split-rail fence.''

"It had to be Luther,'' Connor says. "I'm sure you saw him at the funeral—he was the one laughing and drinking the moment they lowered the coffin into the grave. Luther wanted my business so badly he could taste it. As to his confrontation with you, my guess is he had an ugly discussion with Martha—with Jason out of the picture and Valerie safe, Martha stopped taking any guff from Luther.''

"What kind of person does that to a ten-year-old child?''

"Hack would have thought nothing of scaring you like that,'' Connor says. "People who are capable of that kind of behavior against children believe—often rightfully—that they will terrify the child into silence. That's what happened to you, Grant—and it gives you some idea of what things were like in that house. One thing I can tell you—assuming it was Luther, you have nothing to fear.''

"Given that it was eighteen years ago, I assume not,'' I say.

"Luther is good and dead,'' Connor says. "When you store up that kind of anger for too long, it will kill you—I have no doubt bitter rage did in Luther. He had a stroke about a dozen years ago.''

We stop just outside of downtown Christchurch. This is Connor's New Zealand estate. The stone complex was once a hunting lodge owned by a private club. The moment the wagon comes to a stop, the staff removes our bags and escorts us to a sunroom at the rear of the lodge where sandwiches and tea await.

From the windows of the sunroom, I can see woods. All the windows in the sunroom are wide open and the sounds and smells of this forest find me instantly.

Within the hour we are back in the station wagon and heading north from Christchurch to Pegasus Bay. As we pass through Kaiapoi, north of Christchurch, and head down a series of dirt roads that takes us out to the beachfront, Connor turns to me. "There is someone I want you to meet," he says. "It is the reason I wanted you here—with me."

"Then this would be the moment to give me some background," I say. "As your lawyer...."

"You have all the background you need, Grant."

"Everything with you is a secret," I say. "Denying information is punishing. I still don't understand how you could have kept Martha and Valerie in the dark all these years."

"Martha and Valerie knew. From the beginning," Connor says, "and they most assuredly understood secrecy. It happens in homes where there is abuse." I nod and Connor continues. "They never argued about this, Grant.

"They never said a word—never let on in any way," I say.

"When Valerie and Martha came to New Zealand the first time—after Hack died—Martha told me she was happy." He stops. "She had not used that word for twenty years."

"I understand. To be freed of Hack—to begin to feel safe—that would make anyone happy." I say. "When are you going to tell me why I am here?"

"Be patient—you'll know soon enough. Do you remember Martha saying something about a trip— maybe mentioning a passport—at the cemetery?"

"I do—but we didn't know where she was head-ed."

"She worried about that comment for years. It was her only slip-up. They visit—Martha and Valer-ie—at least once or twice a year. They never travel together—and they do not tell the good people of DeWitt Street their whereabouts." He inhales the Pacific air. "Have you ever seen more a spectacular countryside?"

"Connor—I'm not here to sightsee."

"Well, to an extent you are. I want you to see the beauty of this place. I want you to know just how idyllic open land can be."

Since Connor seems intent on controlling the discussion, I decide on a different approach. "Maybe you can help me with something: Why me? If he knew he was running away from home, why bring me along?"

"I don't think he was running away," Connor says. "Try to understand that planning, clear think-ing, is impossible when you're living the way he lived. No one, including Martha, knew what would happen next. You can't reason under those circum-stances. With Valerie gone, he would be the center of his father's attention—and that was a bad place to be."

Connor stops, his voice quite soft. "So, think about it—he was scared, roaming around the house, not sure when his father would get home, and you came along." Connor puts his hand on my shoulder. "The last thing he wanted was for you to get caught in the middle of nowhere. And when he saw me and started to run, all he could think about was getting away."

Connor clears his throat. "Taking you to Lone Pine ... that was different. That was his way of letting you in on a very good part of his life ... and on that morning, maybe more than ever in his young life, he needed a friend. Someone he could trust."

Connor pauses. "Grant, he chose you."

———

The station wagon pulls off the road. "We walk from here," Connor says. We head down a small path bordered on both sides by tall beach grasses and then walk onto the beach. The sand is fine and the water dark blue. Connor does not give me time to drink it in. He walks to the edge of the water where the surface of the sand is hard and heads up the beach. After ten minutes, he stops. "We'll be meeting in that house," he says. Several hundred yards ahead on the hillside above the beach is a gray and white home with two levels of decks and stairs leading to an elevated walkway across the dunes.

"Your beach house?" I ask.

"No," Connor says. "Not exactly."

Before I can reply, I hear a voice.

"Grandpapa!"

It is the voice of a child. Running toward us is a barefoot girl, six or seven years old, with sand-colored hair and soft gray-green eyes. She is in his arms immediately.

"Valerie," Connor growls lovingly. "You are so big I can hardly hold you." He slings the girl onto his hip and turns to me. "This is my friend, Mr. Harper."

"Hello there, Mr. Harper," Valerie says with her singing New Zealand accent. She holds out her tiny hand and I shake it gently.

"It's a pleasure meeting you, Valerie," I say.

"Where are Mum and Dad?" Connor asks.

Valerie turns and looks over Connor's shoulder. "They're coming," she says.

I turn and see a man and woman walking across the beach. The woman holds an infant in the crook of her arm. The man holds the woman's other hand. As they get closer, I have no question about their identity.

This is Jason Talbot and his family.

EPILOGUE

As the plane leaves Christchurch, I am fully aware of my responsibility to my client, Connor Clarke, and my friend, Jason Talbot.

In Juan Cabrera's view of the practice of law, there are always options and alternatives. As I contemplate my situation, however, I can think of none. I owe an explanation to my family, to all those on DeWitt Street who cared for—and mourned—Jason.

Of all of them, Hannah and Mickey have an undeniable right to hear that while there was an exhausting chase through in an unfamiliar forest, it did not end with a deadly fall down an ice-covered hill. There was no period of languishing, no missing bones from a grave at the top of the hill at Lone Pine.

I would not be surprised if they figure this out on their own. A fatal collision with the base of a large tree is not the likely fate of a boy who flies down DeWitt Street standing on his sled, who navigates on his bottom hills covered with rock-hard snowpack—even going at lightning speed—even while being chased by Connor Clarke.

It would be an enormous relief for them to learn that almost everything Connor told them was true—and even more a pleasure to hear that the worst part of the secret Connor begged them to protect—the story explaining Jason's disappearance and death—was invented by Jason and Connor.

They would understand in a heartbeat why Connor took Jason to New Zealand to start a new life—and they would be thrilled to learn of his success. Despite a nearly irresistible urge to tell Hannah and Mickey everything, by my professional and personal oath, by my conscience and sense of what is just and right, I must keep these facts to myself.

END

Discussion Guide

REDISCOVERING LONE PINE

For those who believe all stories fit within a few basic archetypes, REDISCOVERING LONE PINE provides two possibilities.[1] The first is the broad frame for the plot—the timeless "lost and then found" story. Within that narrative is the second, Grant's odyssey, a journey covering nearly two decades. About the second, there is little to say: Homer cornered the market on arduous journeys leading to a homecoming, and no one has come even close in the following millennia.

As to the first archetype, twenty-four centuries ago, long before performing the folk-hymn *Amazing Grace* required bagpipes, and hundreds of years before any mention of the return of the Prodigal

---

1. If you are inclined to read up on archetypal categorization, you might start with Carl G. Jung, *The Archetypes and the Collective Unconscious, in* 9 COLLECTED WORKS OF C.G. JUNG, PART 1 (R.F.C. Hull trans., 2d ed. 1969); David J. Burrows, MYTHS AND MOTIFS IN LITERATURE (Free Press 1973); Anthony Stevens, ARCHETYPE: A NATURAL HISTORY OF THE SELF 67–76 (1982); Joseph Campbell, MYTHIC WORLDS, MODERN WORDS: JOSEPH CAMPBELL ON THE ART OF JAMES JOYCE (New World Library 2004); Jane Garry & Hasan M. El–Shamy, ARCHETYPES AND MOTIFS IN FOLKLORE AND LITERATURE: A HANDBOOK (M.E. Sharpe 2005).

(the LONE PINE epigraph), the theme of disappearance and reunion, rediscovery of existence, identity, or purpose, was a mainstay in live performances of Euripides' ION. Disappearance stories vary considerably. In ION, for example, the main character grew up a menial worker in a Delphian temple only to discover in early adulthood that his father was the Greek deity, Apollo—who had forced himself on his birth mother—not an everyday occurrence in Haydon, New York.

There is something familiar and intriguing about both archetypes—particularly when they involve the revelation of a secret past or parentage—or the reappearance of one who vanished, presumably gone forever. Without too much difficulty, you can probably name fifty myths, novels, movies, or plays built around these storyline. Undertake that exercise and you will realize that these are not, *simpliciter,* magical stories about those who vanish and later reappear, or those who learn later in life of royal lineage. Instead, they are about the other themes and issues, the reasons, dynamics, and tensions that surround or later emerge, explaining and giving meaning to the disappearance. What follow are notes, comments, questions, and references to help explore a few of those other themes and issues of consequence to the characters in REDISCOVERING LONE PINE.

Editorial note: ***Nearly all footnotes have been omitted from the case and article excerpts below***. Citations to cases and articles are provided for

those who wish to pursue these areas more fully—
or check out the omitted footnotes.

I. Case Theory and Narrative

1. When Juan Cabrera asked Grant and Hannah
for their case theory, he was posing one of the most
important questions a lawyer—or anyone with a
story to tell—must answer. To simplify the inquiry,
Juan asks for a "slogan," a few words to sum up
Mickey's situation, words to create the appropriate
and optimal imagery and focus for a judge, jury, or
any other audience. The case theory for Mickey
must be accurate, compelling, succinct, and memo-
rable. It must stay with those who are responsible
for his fate.

a. The concept of case or client theory requires a
careful assessment of client identity, historical and
factual context, strategy (broadly defined), applica-
ble legal standards, and outcome. Further, the for-
mulation will have little or no value if it is developed without a realistic sense of how the case
should conclude. It should be crafted with a clear
sense of the just and best interests of the client.

b. One part of the development of a workable case
theory entails meaningful client communication. In
Mickey's case, of course, that is complicated. Since
he is non-communicative, Grant and Hannah cannot discuss with him the options and alternatives
that may surface. That lack of communication poses
problems of role and legal competency. (See Sections II and IV, *infra*).

c. In REDISCOVERING LONE PINE, who should decide
whether a strategy placing Mickey in extended residential care—as opposed to being "back on the

street'' without further medical care—is in his best interest? Assume that at the celebration dinner at Nuevo Leon, Mickey states unequivocally that under no circumstance does he want to be hospitalized. Should that bind Hannah and Grant?

To get a sense of the connection between case theory and client communication, there is no better starting point than Robert D. Dinerstein's, *Client-Centered Counseling: Reappraisal and Refinement*,[2] an extraordinarily effective piece.[3]

2. 32 ARIZ. L. REV. 501 (1990).

3. For additional reading, you might look at:

a. David A. Binder & Susan C. Price, LEGAL INTERVIEWING AND COUNSELING: A CLIENT-CENTERED APPROACH (1977);

b. Robert F. Cochran, Jr., *Client Counseling and Moral Responsibility*, 30 PEPP. L. REV. 591 (2003);

c. Robert D. Dinerstein, *A Mediation on the Theoretics of Practice*, 43 HASTINGS L.J. 971 (1992);

d. Robert Dinerstein, Stephen Ellmann, Isabelle Gunning & Ann Shalleck, *Legal Interviewing and Counseling: An Introduction*, 10 CLINICAL L. REV. 281 (2003);

e. Stephen Ellmann, *Client-Centeredness Multiplied: Individual Autonomy and Collective Mobilization in Public Interest Lawyers' Representation of Groups*, 78 VA. L. REV. 1103 (1992);

f. Michelle S. Jacobs, *People from the Footnotes: The Missing Element in Client–Centered Counseling*, 27 GOLDEN GATE U. L. REV. 345 (1997);

g. Katherine R. Kruse, *Fortress in the Sand: The Plural Values of Client–Centered Representation*, 12 CLINICAL L. REV. 369 (2006);

h. Eli Wald, *Taking Attorney–Client Communications (and Therefore Clients) Seriously*, 42 U.S.F. L. REV. 747 (2008);

i. Fred Z. Zacharias, *Limits on Client Autonomy in Legal Ethics Regulation*, 81 B.U. L. REV. 199 (2000);

j. Steven Zeidman, *To Plead or Not to Plead: Effective Assistance and Client–Centered Counseling*, 39 B.C. L. REV. 841 (1998).

d. Think back to the choice of case theory made at Harper & Wein. Grant and Hannah rejected the factual and historic client conceptualization—Mickey as a heroic and troubled returning veteran, yet another victim of an unpopular war. Instead, they went with a theory predicated on the impossibility of a fair trial: Mickey cannot communicate with his lawyers, understand the charges, or participate in his defense and thus cannot be tried fairly in a court of law. Is "commitment, confinement in a psychiatric institution" (the "bottom line" in Grant's opening statement), a proper objective from an advocacy perspective?

2. For the last two decades talented clinical legal scholars have been developing impressive case theory literature. Before getting to that material, consider the following recitations of case theories from the cases in the list below. Can you tell what these cases are about?

"This is not a case about a planned, premeditated or intentional crime. This is not a case about a cold heart, about benevolence or about evil. It's a case about weakness, about drug addiction, about drugs, about crazed behavior, and it's a case about tragedy."[4]

"At its heart, this is a case about two contracts, their component transactions, and their taxability."[5]

---

4. *People v. Crosby*, 185 Ill.Dec. 65, 614 N.E.2d 199, 201 (Ill. App. 1993) (reciting defense counsel's case theory, as argued in the trial court).

5. *Maurer v. Indiana Department of State Revenue*, 607 N.E.2d 985, 986 (Ind. Tax Court, 1993).

"[T]his is not a case about the meaning of an insurance policy or the interpretation of a statute; it is about a child, much loved by two families, each prepared to raise her with care and devotion, one of whom will be enriched and delighted by her presence in their home, and the other of whom will be deprived of the joy she gives."[6]

"This is a case about credibility and there are serious credibility issues."[7]

"This is a case about assumption of risk. . . . [Plaintiff] knew there were risks involved in roller skating. She knew that she could have fallen and injured herself while roller skating. She knew that there was a risk of collision with other skaters when you are at a skating rink with a bunch of people skating and that could cause her to fall and injure herself. She went anyway."[8]

"So what is this case all about? This is a case about someone who is seeking a disability, and the doctors won't give it to her."[9]

"This is a case about the road rage conduct of Kenneth DeJesus that caused a substantial permanent brain injury to Sherry Flick."[10]

3. In David F. Chavkin's thoughtful article, *Spinning Straw Into Gold: Exploring the Legacy of Bel-*

6. *Matter of Welfare D.L.*, 486 N.W.2d 375, 377 (Minn. 1992).

7. *Cincinnati Bar Ass'n v. Allen*, 702 N.E.2d 101 (Ohio 1998).

8. *St. Margaret Mercy Healthcare Centers, Inc. v. Poland*, 828 N.E.2d 396, 407 (Ind. App. 2005).

9. *Renville v. Taylor*, 7 P.3d 400, 405 (Mont. 2000).

10. *Ringle v. Bruton*, 86 P.3d 1032, 1042 (Nev. 2004).

low and Moulton,[11] he uses the term "theory of the client" to underscore the many complex strands that are essential to client representation beyond the singularity of appearing on behalf of a client in a court, agency, or other forum. Was the case theory in REDISCOVERING LONE PINE designed to address Mickey's needs beyond the time spent in the courtroom of Judge Miles Prentice?

4. Professor Binny Miller's seminal piece on case theory, *Teaching Case Theory*,[12] provides a clear way to both understand and apply the concept. Professor Miller uses the term "storyline" to describe the task at hand.

> A "storyline" is the short version of the lawyer's story ... a snapshot, a framework, the essence of the story or what the case is about. It is not the whole story ... but rather the coherent meaning that the elements create....

> A case theory ... is simply an explanation for why or how events happen in a particular way. Like applied theory, case theory considers the context of individuals and their surroundings.

> The view of case theory as storyline places law in a narrative rather than an analytic modality.... Law plays an important role in some explanations, a lesser role in other explanations, and at times, no role at all.

11. 10 CLINICAL L. REV. 245, 251 n. 28 (2003).
12. 9 CLINICAL L. REV. 293, 298 (2002).

a.   Professor Miller stresses the importance of context in conjunction with legal theory. If a matter is presented as "a case about self-defense," the decision-makers will want to know about the fight. However, if an assault is presented as a case about a year of emotional torment, bullying, and taunting, the fight is of less consequence. If a history of provocation and abuse explains an assault, a simple self-defense theory might be wholly inadequate.

b.   As Professor Miller notes: "[T]he underlying story about the client, the neighbor, their relationship, and the incident has meaning apart from doctrine. All stories told in advocacy are stories in search of a legal meaning, and often the story shapes the legal meaning as much as the legal meaning shapes the story."

5.   Another way to think through case theory comes from a piece by Professor Kimberly A. Thomas, *Sentencing Where Case Theory and the Client Meet*.[13] Thomas notes that the term "case theory" has many different meanings:

> [Case theory gives] coherence to disparate facts of the case in a way that resonates with the basic intuitions of the fact-finder.... Under this understanding, case theory should also adhere to the legal architecture of the proceeding.... [Following Professor Miller's approach, a] comprehensive definition of case theory includes four elements: the facts presented, the legal framework, the client's perspective, and co-

13.   15 CLINICAL L. REV. 187, 189 (2008).

herence with the audience's moral intu-
itions or lived experiences.

6. Professor Ann Shalleck's sophisticated and in-
sightful discussion of case theory requires conceptualization of change as a constant state—that clients
inhabit a series or sequence of stories, events flow-
ing, requiring redefinition.[14] Did the case theory
change from the moment of Mickey's arrest to the
first day of his competency hearing? Was the same
theory appropriate at the time that the criminal
case resolved? The civil case?

7. One "bottom line" in this field is stated suc-
cinctly in Professor Anthony J. Bocchino's *Ten
Touchstones for Trial Advocacy—2000*:

> Without an effective case theory no lawyer
> can win consistently. There's luck to be
> sure, but at the heart of every great trial
> lawyer performance is great case theo-
> ry.... All the technical skill in the world
> cannot make up for a bad theory of the
> case. Good skills and bad theory leads to
> bad verdicts.... [Case] theory operates on
> three levels ... legal, factual, and persua-
> sive.... Legal theory defines why it is that
> the law says your client should win....
> Factual theory explains what really hap-
> pened in the case and why.... Persuasive

14. Ann Shalleck, *Institutions and the Development of Legal
Theory: The Significance of the Feminism & Legal Theory Pro-
ject*, 13 Am. U.J. Gender, Soc. Pol'y & Law 7 (2005); Ann Shalleck,
*Pedagogical Subversion in Clinical Teaching: The Women and
the Law Clinic and the Intellectual Property Clinic as Legal
Archaeology*, 13 Tex. J. Women & L. 113, 125–126 (2003).

theory ... explains why, in equity, your client should prevail.[15]

8. In one broad-reaching piece, Ruth Anne Robbins explores case theory through story themes and archetypes, the basics of fiction, and the art of storytelling:

> [N]arrative is far more significant in law than merely one delivery method of human communication. Psychologists are also moving towards the conclusion that all of our knowledge is contained in stories and in the mechanisms to construct and retrieve them.... [A] story has a few key elements: character, point of view, conflict, resolution, organization, and description.... The more skilled lawyers understand, of course, that their client is the protagonist of the story and that the story must be told from the protagonist's point of view.

> [L]awyers must ... develop the narrative of the client's character, and to describe the lawsuit in terms of where it fits into the framework of the client's needs and goals. Here is where lawyers should consider the concept of "hero." Framing the client's narrative as heroic ... provides a possible avenue for the lawyer to develop a strategy for character development, as well as possibly a meaningful type.[16]

---

15. 74 TEMP. L. REV. 1, 9 (2001).

16. Ruth Anne Robbins, *Harry Potter, Ruby Slippers and Merlin: Telling the Client's Story Using the Characters and*

Citing the works of Joseph Campbell, James Hill-
man, and Carl Jung, Professor Robbins explores
heroic archetypes and common story themes. She
notes that there are only a limited number of
themes—and a limited collection of heroic types—
that form the basis for much of fiction and provide
a familiar and compelling setting for a client's story
to be understood and accepted. Basing her remarks
on the writings of Campbell, Robbins explains:

> We understand narrative because we join
> the story and see ourselves as part of it: We
> place ourselves into the story and walk
> with the characters.... If we can marry
> the concepts of storytelling to the "collec-
> tive conscious" in our statements of the
> case, we will potentially create powerfully
> persuasive undercurrents in the case that
> should help persuade in a more subtle way.

How did the themes—and heroes—in REDISCOVERING
LONE PINE affect your understanding or appreciation
of the story?

9. Case theory falls under the category "easier
said than done."[17] For a challenging exercise, take a

Paradigms of the Archetypal Hero's Journey, 29 SEATTLE U. L.
REV. 767, 772 (2006).

17. There are many fine articles in this field. Here is a
sampling:

a. Anthony J. Bocchino & Samuel H. Solomon, *What Juries
Want to Hear: Methods for Developing Persuasive Case Theory*,
67 TENN. L. REV. 543 (2000);

b. David F. Chavkin, *Fuzzy Thinking: A Borrowed Paradigm for Crisper Lawyering*, 4 CLINICAL L. REV. 163 (1997);

c. David F. Chavkin, *Spinning Straw Into Gold: Exploring
the Legacy of Bellow and Moulton*, 10 CLINICAL L. REV. 245 (2003);

d. David F. Chavkin, CLINICAL LEGAL EDUCATION: A TEXTBOOK FOR LAW SCHOOL CLINICAL PROGRAMS (2004);

e. Robert D. Dinerstein, *A Meditation on the Theories of Practice*, 43 HASTINGS L.J. 971 (1992);

f. Robert D. Dinerstein, *Client-Centered Counseling: Reappraisal and Refinement*, 32 ARIZ. L. Rev. 501 (1990);

g. Brian J. Foley & Ruth Anne Robbins, *Fiction 101: A Primer for Lawyers On How To Use Fiction Writing Techniques To Write Persuasive Facts Sections*, 32 RUTGERS L.J. 459, 465–72 (2001);

h. Carolyn Grose, *A Field Trip to Benetton . . . and Beyond: Some Thoughts on "Outsider Narrative" in a Law School Clinic*, 4 CLINICAL L. REV. 109, 122 (1997);

i. Carolyn Grose, *A Persistent Critique: Constructing Clients' Stories*, 12 CLINICAL L. REV. 329 (2006);

j. Margaret Moore Jackson, *Confronting "Unwelcomeness" From the Outside: Using Case Theory to Tell the Stories of Sexually–Harassed Women*, 4 CARDOZO J.L. & GENDER 61 (2007);

k. Binny Miller, *Give Them Back Their Lives: Recognizing Client Narrative in Case Theory*, 93 MICH. L. REV. 485, 487 (1994);

l. Binny Miller, *Telling Stories About Cases and Clients: The Ethics of Narrative*, 14 GEO. J. LEGAL ETHICS 1 (2000);

m. Binny Miller, *Teaching Case Theory*, 9 CLINICAL L. REV. 293 (2002);

n. Bernard P. Perlmutter, *George's Story: Voice and Transformation Through the Teaching and Practice of Therapeutic Jurisprudence in a Law School Child Advocacy Clinic*, 17 ST. THOMAS L. REV. 561 (2005);

o. John Pray & Byron Lichstein, *The Evolution Through Experience of Criminal Clinics: The Criminal Appeals Project at the University of Wisconsin Law School's Remington Center*, 75 MISS. L. J. 795 (2006);

p. Ruth Anne Robbins, *Harry Potter, Ruby Slippers and Merlin: Telling the Client's Story Using the Characters and Paradigms of the Archetypal Hero's Journey*, 29 SEATTLE U. L. REV. 767, 768–69 (2006);

q. Ann Shalleck, *Institutions and the Development of Legal Theory: The Significance of the Feminism & Legal Theory Project*, 13 AM. U. J. GENDER SOC. POL'Y & L. 7 (2005);

r. Ann Shalleck, *Pedagogical Subversion in Clinical Teaching: The Women and the Law Clinic and the Intellectual Property*

look at *Romanksi v. Detroit Entertainment.*[18] Ms. Romanski entered a casino with the intention of playing slot machines. While walking through the area where the machines were located, and before she began playing the slots, Ms. Romasnki found a nickel slot in the bin of a machine. She picked up the slot and, moments later, was approached by security employees who accused her of "slot-walking." She was detained against her will for several hours and ultimately ejected from the casino. Believing she was unfairly accused, she sued the casino and its employees for false imprisonment and deprivation of her civil rights, the latter claim based on her contention that the security employees were acting "under color of law." The casino defended on the grounds that Ms. Romanski broke the rules regarding "slot-walking," that as a private business they had the right to determine who could be on their premises, and that they did not violate any of Ms. Romanski's rights.

If you have a chance to read the full case, using the main parties, try to answer the question that undoubtedly would have been posed by Judge Miles Prentice: "Counsel, what's this case about?" How would the case theory be framed by Ms. Romanski? How would it be framed by the casino employee? By the casino? Try articulating a case theory for each party using only one or two sentences.

Clinic as Legal Archaeology, 13 Tex. J. Women & L. 113, 125–26 (2003);

s. Ann Shalleck, *Symposium on Civic and Legal Education, Panel Three, Clinical Education: Constructions of the Client Within Legal Education*, 45 Stan. L. Rev. 1731 (1993).

18. 428 F.3d 629 (6th Cir. 2005).

10. Finally, consider the narrative choices made in REDISCOVERING LONE PINE. For the most part, the story is told in the first person and proceeds in chronological order. By design, flashbacks are used sparingly.

There are many other options in voice and chronology that have a profound effect on a narrative. In presenting a case—or, for that matter, in any presentation—these choices are of consequence. A first-person present narrative is intimate—but intimacy with a client, cause, or political perspective is not always optimal. Sometimes seeing the world through the eyes of a client may be counterproductive. For example, in a case involving a violent crime (whether one is in a prosecutorial or defense role), it may be more important for a judge or jury to understand the events looking "backward," starting with the present and slowly moving back in time to the alleged criminal act. In such a presentation, a first-person narrative is not the likely choice for either side.

Factual content of a narrative is also a matter of choice. Grant's opening statement had almost nothing to do with the crime—it had to do with his professional relationship with Mickey. Would you have used a different approach? Order of presentation? Likewise, Owen Hollister's response was devoid of a storyline narrative and focused on Grant's statement. From the State's perspective, was that a proper presentation? After all, a violent crime had taken place, an innocent person was dead, the defendant—a known drug addict—was identified by the clerk just prior to his demise. Do these facts belong in Mr. Hollister's narrative?

Do not underestimate the seemingly simple task of telling a client's story. Before uttering a word—whether to a judge, jury, or any other audience—decisions need to made regarding focus, strategy, probable outcome, and, importantly, central themes and issues. What are the fundamental questions—legally, theoretically, and pragmatically—that need to be answered? Will the story you are about to tell provide the foundation needed to give those answers? Once your presentation has begun, as you add facts and information to your narrative, are you clarifying or clouding the issues that need to be resolved?

Beyond rethinking and critiquing the narrative choices in REDISCOVERING LONE PINE, consider any recent political election. With that political event in mind, (a) consider how you would articulate a case theory for the election, and (b) retell the story—as in: "This was an election about ... and here is what you need to know to understand what happened."

II. Conflating Personal and Professional Roles

1.   Grant and Hannah have a complex relationship with Mickey—deeply personal and also professional. Any time a lawyer represents a family member or friend, the ability to exercise independent professional judgment on behalf of the client is in play. While there is no clear rule covering this situation, as the two excerpts below suggest, there are strongly held beliefs:

> It is a delusion of young, inexperienced lawyers to think that they can separate

their personal from their professional lives and their personal from their professional morality. The current jargon refers to this dichotomy as "role-defined" ethics. It is true intellectual rubbish.[19]

—

[A] central component of the conventional lawyering framework is the dissociation of personal and professional ethics. Lawyers operate in the realm of "role-differentiated morality" . . . [and] are expected to subordinate their personal ethics to the professional obligations they owe to their clients. Moral or political apprehension or affinity toward clients could compromise lawyers' ability to advocate their clients' interests objectively and rationally.[20]

2. Rules regarding ethics and professional responsibility are drafted and adopted in each state and while there is some variation, the basic position is fairly clear. For example, based on the Texas Disciplinary Rules of Professional Conduct, one commentator noted:

[T]he representation of family members by an attorney does not generally trigger ethical problems. Problems may arise, however, depending on the specific circumstances of the representation, and [the rules and

19. Daniel R. Coquillette, *Professionalism: The Deep Theory*, 72 N.C. L. Rev. 1271, 1272 (1994).

20. Patrick J. Bumatay, *Causes, Commitments, and Counsels: A Study of Political and Professional Obligations Among Bush Administration Lawyers*, 31 J. Legal Prof. 1, 4 (2007).

> commentary in the field] provide surprisingly little information regarding how to handle specific situations that could create ethical problems when representing a family member. [A]ttorneys ... wade ... unassisted, into the often confusing mire of professional conduct to identify and avoid hazardous ethical situations involving family members. ...
>
> The fact that a familial relationship [is] involved [has] little apparent bearing on the conclusions. The underlying message seems clear: representation of a family member does not create any additional requirements in analyzing ethical problems.[21]

3. The American Bar Association produces model rules of professional responsibility states can adopt. The Model Rule most often in play in cases where there is a personal or familial relationship between a lawyer and a client is Rule 2.1: "In representing a client, a lawyer shall exercise independent professional judgment and render candid advice." Can Hannah and Grant exercise independent professional judgment and render candid advice?

In a highly publicized divorce case some years ago, commenting on a personal relationship of one of the lawyers, a reporter noted:

> When an attorney's judgment becomes clouded ... by his or her personal feelings toward a client, the attorney has the ethi-

---

21. Jason W. Whitney, Comment, *Brother's Keeper: The Legal Ethics of Representing Family Members*, 38 St. Mary's L. J. 1101, 1103–04, 1123–24 (2007).

cal obligation to step back and ensure that the client has the opportunity to seek the advice of independent counsel. . . .[22]

4. In a recent issue of the ILLINOIS BAR JOURNAL, Helen W. Gunnarsson provides straightforward advice on the matter of representing friends and family.[23]

a. Gunnarsson notes that when family or friends seek legal advice, there is an impulse to help—and difficulty saying "no"—but often "no" is the best answer for both lawyer and client.

She posed the question to a number of experienced lawyers, one of whom noted that it is "almost always a bad idea to represent a close friend or family member." Gunnarsson notes there can be problems when lawyers seek to

> communicate objective advice—and also questions about whether your friend or loved one can "hear that advice from you. Are they able to hear advice from you, the lawyer, simply as sound legal advice, without discounting it as the result of baggage from your personal relationship with them. . . ."

Gunnarsson also raises legitimate other issues: competence (does the lawyer possess the specialization required?), malpractice (what if the case has a cata-

---

22. H. Joseph Gitlin, *'Gifts' From Client Spell Trouble for Divorce Lawyer,* CHICAGO DAILY LAW BULLETIN, May 8, 2001, at 6.

23. *My Mother, My Client,* ILLINOIS BAR JOURNAL, July, 2008, available at http://findarticles.com/p/articles/mi_6997/is_7_96/ai_n28541130/pg_1?tag=artBody;col1

strophic outcome?), and legal fees (an issue that Mickey's sister, Teresa, raised in LONE PINE).[24]

b.   In *Love, Hate, and Other Emotional Interference in the Lawyer/Client Relationship*,[25] Marjorie A. Silver discusses "the emotional dimension in lawyering and the need for attorneys to accept and endeavor to understand their own emotional lives." Silver notes that among other complex and powerful phenomena in client representation is countertransference—a significant hazard in representing friends and family with whom the lawyer identifies and sympathizes.

5.   Of the many sources available to think through the problem of representing friends and family, one of the most up-to-date and comprehensive is Professor Sande L. Buhai's *Emotional Conflicts: Impaired Dispassionate Representation of Family Members*:

> [L]awyers should be required to take potential emotional conflicts into account both before undertaking to represent and while representing any person with whom they have family or emotional ties, whether spouse, lover, cousin, sibling, or parent. . . . [T]he lawyer's role as counselor and problem solver exacerbates the conflicts that can arise when clients and lawyers have emotional ties outside their lawyer-client relationship. . . . When the lawyer is herself emotionally involved, her ability to provide

24.   For a further source raising some of these issues, see, Stacey Smith, *Friends, Family, and Favors—Or No Good Deed Goes Unpunished*, http://www.wvbar.org/barinfo/lawyer/2001/july/friends.htm

25.   6 CLINICAL L. REV. 259 (1999).

such dispassionate counsel may be impaired.[26]

Professor Buhai's encyclopedic article urges the ABA to amend the Model Rules of Professional Conduct to address the dangers posed by familial and other personal conflicts:

> A lawyer shall not represent a client with whom the lawyer has a familial or other significant emotional relationship unless: (1) the lawyer reasonably believes that the relationship will not substantially affect the competent and diligent representation of the client; (2) the client gives informed consent in writing after full disclosure of the possible conflicts inherent in the representation; and (3) there is no interference with the lawyer's independence of professional judgment or with the client-lawyer relationship.

Based on Professor Buhai's proposal, should Harper & Wein represent Mickey?

6. On the matter of defining "family," not all families are quite like the Harpers, the Weiners, or even the Talbots. For a thorough discussion of the problems related to representing family members and friends in a most unusual family setting, take a look at *In re Complaint as to the Conduct of Charles O. Porter*.[27] *Porter* involved a group of fourteen women and several men who formed what they characterized as a family. After the murder of a local law enforcement official, several female mem-

26. 21 Geo. J. Legal Ethics 1159, 1160, 1193 (2008).

27. 584 P.2d 744 (Ore. 1978).

bers of the family were charged—and one of the male members, an attorney, served as their lawyer. The case explores conflict of interest, independent professional judgment, representation of multiple clients, and related ethical matters.

a. The *Porter* case (cited above) deals with the always thorny problem of representing multiple parties with conflicting interests. Assume the lawyer was representing only one "family member" with whom the lawyer was involved romantically. Under those circumstances, was a different outcome likely?

b. In light of the discussion in *Porter* pertaining to disclosure, was there more Hannah and Grant should have said or done before taking on Mickey as a client? Parenthetically, did the ethical challenge of representing a close friend cross your mind as you read the story?

c. Was Grant's judgment truly independent and professional, or was it clouded by his affection for Mickey—or Hannah? Assuming Grant was fairly sure Mickey was not involved in planning or executing the robbery at the bookstore, was the resolution crafted by Grant requiring months of institutional confinement appropriate?

d. Mickey's parents appeared to agree with the decision to have him institutionalized. How does that affect the efficacy of the counseling decisions made by Grant? Did you have a sense that everyone was participating in the essential dialogue between the lawyers and the client—except Mickey?

III. Returning Veterans

1. Drug dependence incident to military service. Returning veterans of the Vietnam War, Operation

Desert Storm, Operation Iraqi Freedom, and the war in Afghanistan present significant public health challenges, whether they sustained life-changing physical injuries, suffered from post-traumatic stress disorder, or experienced other debilitating effects. Mickey, like all too many returning veterans, is not the same person who left his quiet upstate New York town a few years earlier.

In particular, the phenomenon of drug addiction is common, understandable, and, in many instances, treated as a criminal justice problem rather than as a national health care matter.

The issue of drug addiction was considered recently by the House Committee on Veterans Affairs. Dr. Patricia Greer, President of the National Association for Addiction Professionals, set out the dimensions of the problem:

> In 2004, Dr. Richard Suchinsky, Department of Veterans Affairs Associate Chief for Addictive Disorders, ranked substance use disorders among the three most common diagnoses made by the Veterans Health Administration (VHA). Nevertheless, they remain under-diagnosed and under-treated in the VHA. . . .

> Young veterans (under age 25) suffer from substance use disorder rates as high as 25 percent, and veterans are more likely than their civilian peers to engage in heavy alcohol use and to take part in risky behavior like drunk driving. In total, it is estimated that 1.8 million veterans suffered from a

diagnosable substance use disorder in 2002 and 2003. . . .

Some experts estimate that about 40 percent of veterans who have served in Iraq or Afghanistan will experience a mental health problem, and of those, approximately 60 percent will have a substance use disorder. . . .

In 2002 and 2003, the National Survey on Drug Use and Health estimated that 340,- 000 male veterans suffered from co-occurring substance use disorders and "serious mental illness," defined as a diagnosable mental condition that substantially interfered with a normal life activity. Post-traumatic stress disorder—one of the most commonly diagnosed combat-related mental disorders—is frequently co-morbid with substance use disorders. During the Vietnam War, for example, 60–80 percent of veterans with PTSD also suffered from addiction disorders.[28]

2. Untreated drug addiction in returning veterans is particularly tragic since there is some reason to think that this phenomenon can be more readily addressed than addiction in the non-veteran population. Alan Leshner notes the following:

28. *Substance Abuse/Co–Morbid Disorders: Comprehensive Solutions to a Complex Problem: Hearing Before the H. Comm. on Veterans Affairs, Subcomm. on Health*, 110th Cong. (2008) (statement of Dr. Patricia Greer, President, NAADAC, The Association for Addiction Professionals), *available at* http://veterans. house.gov/hearings/Testimony.aspx?TID=33502 & Newsid=187 & Name=PatriciaM.Greer.

> Addiction is not just a brain disease. It is a brain disease for which the social contexts in which it has both developed and is expressed are critically important. The case of the many thousands of returning Vietnam War veterans who were addicted to heroin illustrates this point. In contrast to addicts on the streets of the United States, it was relatively easy to treat the returning veterans' addictions.[29]

In some states, the criminal justice system has at least recognized the nature of the problem of addiction with Vietnam veterans. California Penal Code, Section 1170.9 provides:

> In the case of any person convicted of a felony who would otherwise be sentenced to state prison the court shall consider whether the defendant was a member of the military forces of the United States who served in combat in Vietnam and who suffers from substance abuse or psychological problems resulting from that service. If the court concludes that the defendant is such a person, the court may order the defendant committed to the custody of federal correctional officials for incarceration for a term equivalent to that which the defendant would have served in state prison. The court may make such a commitment only if the defendant agrees to such a commitment, the court has determined that appropriate federal programs exist,

29. Alan Leshner, *Addiction Is a Brain Disease, and it Matters*, SCIENCE, Oct. 3, 1997, at 45.

and federal law authorizes the receipt of the defendant under such conditions.[30]

3.   Would Mickey have benefitted from the above provision in the California Penal Code (assuming it was adopted in New York)?[31]

4.   <u>Head injuries</u>. While Mickey's traumatic brain injury (TBI) was not sustained in combat, there is a troubling TBI incident rate evident with Operation Iraqi Freedom (OIF) returning veterans.[32]

5.   More than a quarter-century after the Vietnam War ended, the problem of traumatic head injuries was finally front and center in the veterans affairs community.

> One of the most well known studies is the Vietnam Veterans Head Injury study. It examined aggressive behavior in 279 veterans with frontal lobe lesions as compared to a matched control group of 57 non-

30.   CAL. PENAL CODE § 1170.9 (Deering 2006 & Supp. 2007).

31.   For application of the provision, see, *People v. Ruby*, 204 Cal.App.3d 462, 251 Cal.Rptr. 339; 251 Cal.Rptr. 339 (1988).

32.   The following may be of use to those seeking further information in the field: Helen D. O'Conor, *Federal Tort Claims Act is Available for OIF TBI Veterans, Despite Feres*, 11 DEPAUL J. HEALTH CARE L. 273, n.28–32 (2008); Department of Veterans Affairs, VHA Directive 2007–013, April 13, 2007, *Screening And Evaluation Of Possible Traumatic Brain Injury In Operation Enduring Freedom (OEF) And Operation Iraqi Freedom (OIF)*, http://www1.va.gov/optometry/docs/VHA_Directive_2007–013.pdf; *VA Health Care: Mild Traumatic Brain Injury Screening and Evaluation Implemented for OEF/OIF Veterans, but Challenges Remain*, GAO–08–276 Report, Feb. 8, 2008; Brain Injury Association of America (www.biausa.org); Defense and Veterans Head Injury Program (DVHIP) (www.dvbic.org); Veterans Health Initiative on Traumatic Brain Injury, http://www1.va.gov/vhi/docs/TBI.pdf; Defense and Veterans Brain Injury Center, http://www.dvbic.org/.

injured veterans. The brain-injured veterans were reported by family and friends to be significantly more aggressive; twenty percent became aggressive after their injury and fourteen percent were violent. [33]

a. Grant was taken aback by the abruptness and apparent insensitivity of the neurosurgeon who operated on Mickey. Yet Grant, like anyone who has seen the miracle of modern neurosurgery, understands the astonishing challenges faced by these physicians. The tiniest misstep in the course of Mickey's operation could have produced devastating—or deadly—consequences. After all, neurosurgeons hold in their hands all that we are. These are the doctors trusted to manipulate and repair a damaged brain or spinal cord. Given the pressures involved, it is no wonder the physician was a bit short in his discussion with Grant and Hannah regarding Mickey's addiction.

b. Representation of adult clients with TBI presents unique challenges for attorneys, not the least of which is that client communication skills or perceptual capacity may be temporarily or permanently compromised. While a parent or guardian may speak for and make decisions on behalf of clients who have not reached majority, it is not clear who should speak for a client with TBI who is "not himself"—and yet not declared legally incompetent. Mickey was in that exact condition. Should Grant have secured a court order declaring Mickey legally incompetent before making decisions on his

33. Richard E. Redding, *The Brain Disordered Defendant: Neuroscience and Legal Insanity in the Twenty–First Century*, 56 Am. U. L. Rev. 51, 62 (2006).

behalf? Had he gone to court for that purpose, it is likely that Juan would have been designated the guardian of his adult son, not Grant.

6.   Take a look at *Discovery House v. Metropolitan Bd. of Zoning Appeals*[34] on dispensation of methadone when there is something other than the traditional doctor-patient relationship. Hannah supplied Mickey with methadone for an extended period of time. Had her role come to light, can you envision Owen Hollister prosecuting Hannah for unauthorized practice or a drug-related offense?

7.   Veterans face many challenges beyond those raised in REDISCOVERING LONE PINE. As was the case with Mickey, military service can disrupt one's education, transform personal and family relationships, and lead to many and varied economic problems.

This is in no way to denigrate or impugn the honor, dignity, courage, intelligence, and patriotism of those who serve. There is no greater sacrifice—and no gesture, parade, program, regulation, or benefit can ever come close to expressing the deep respect and appreciation due to every veteran.

These few notes do suggest that there was a time—not that long ago—when respect, appreciation, and programs were sorely lacking. For too many of Mickey's generation, the programs and parades, statements of appreciation and admiration, medals and commendations came far, far too late.

IV. Legal Competency and Client Representation

1.   REDISCOVERING LONE PINE raises the following client-counseling question: What happens when a

---

   34.   698 N.E.2d 343 (Ind. App. 1998).

client is arguably not "legally competent" to participate in his or her defense? This matter is separate
from an insanity defense in that competency issues
do not go (necessarily) to the alleged commission of
a crime or otherwise unlawful or actionable behavior but rather to the subsequent trial or hearing.

a.   Mickey's head injury, sustained in the course of
the robbery, rendered him unable to communicate
with his lawyers. Can one represent a client who
cannot communicate with counsel or with the court,
who cannot understand or appreciate the nature of
the charges or claims that have been levied, the
nature of the process, or the possible sanctions?
These questions are usually not answerable in abso-
lutes but rather with comparative or relativistic
responses. What level of comprehension is sufficient? What level of cognitive capacity, perceptual
capacity, or general understanding is required?
When does the lack of cognitive or perceptual capacity render a trial unfair from a Sixth Amendment
perspective?

b.   The general standard is not hard to articulate—
a defendant must understand "the nature of the
proceedings as well as the charges against him, and
[be] able to assist his counsel in his own defense."[35]

In *Dusky v. United States*,[36] the Supreme Court
stated the question as follows:

> [W]hether [the defendant] has sufficient
> present ability to consult with his lawyer

35.   *Mack v. State*, 891 A.2d 369, 376 (Md. Ct. Spec. App.
2006).

36.   362 U.S. 402, 80 S.Ct. 788 (1960).

> with a reasonable degree of rational under-
> standing—and whether he has a rational as
> well as factual understanding of the pro-
> ceedings. . . .

The most recent Supreme Court case in the field
reiterates that standard and holds as follows:

> The two cases that set forth the Constitu-
> tion's "mental competence" standard,
> *Dusky v. United States*, 362 U.S. 402, 80
> S.Ct. 788 (1960) and *Drope v. Missouri*, 420
> U.S. 162, 95 S.Ct. 896 (1975), specify that
> the Constitution does not permit trial of an
> individual who lacks "mental competency."
> *Dusky* defines the competency standard as
> including both (1) "whether" the defen-
> dant has "a rational as well as factual
> understanding of the proceedings against
> him" and (2) whether the defendant "has
> sufficient present ability to consult with his
> lawyer with a reasonable degree of rational
> understanding." 362 U.S. at 402. . . . *Drope*
> repeats that standard, stating that it "has
> long been accepted that a person whose
> mental condition is such that he lacks the
> capacity to understand the nature and ob-
> ject of the proceedings against him, to con-
> sult with counsel, and to assist in prepar-
> ing his defense may not be subjected to a
> trial." 420 U.S. at 171. . . .[37]

Another statement regarding factors to be assessed
in competency cases comes from the Tenth Circuit:

37. *Indiana v. Edwards*, 128 S.Ct. 2379, 2383; 171 L.Ed.2d
345, 352 (2008).

The well-settled legal standard for assessing competency is that the defendant must have "sufficient present ability to consult with his lawyer with a reasonable degree of rational understanding [and have] a rational as well as factual understanding of the proceedings against him." *Dusky*, 362 U.S. at 402. In determining whether "bona fide doubt" of competence exists, courts may look to the defendant's "irrational behavior," "demeanor at trial," "any prior medical opinion[,]" "evidence of mental illness[,]" and "any representations of defense counsel[.]" *McGregor v. Gibson*, 248 F.3d 946, 954–5 (10th Cir. 2001). "We examine the totality of the circumstances. . . . The question is . . . whether the trial court 'failed to give proper weight to the information suggesting incompetence which came to light during trial.' " (quoting *Drope*, 420 U.S. at 179–180).[38]

Based on the above, can you formulate a definition for "rational understanding"? Do you think, based on the information in LONE PINE, that Mickey was legally incompetent?

2. Competency cases may presuppose a medical recovery, permitting a trial or hearing after the defendant recovers from the event (often an accident or illness). That presupposition was in play in Mickey's case in LONE PINE. However, in some cases, the court is faced with a situation of a person who is

38. *United States v. Herrera*, 481 F.3d 1266, 1272 (10th Cir. 2007).

incompetent to stand trial *and* cannot be "treated to competency."

In *In re Daniel H.*,[39] the defendant was a sixteen-year-old boy who sexually assaulted a two-year-old girl. Due to a traumatic brain injury, however, the court was constrained to find that it was unlikely the defendant would ever be able to participate in his own defense and thus dismissed the charges completely. Such determinations raise profound questions:

> We ... acknowledge the implicit tension between the public's right to be protected from dangerous juveniles and an incompetent child's right to be free from indefinite subjugation to the criminal process.

Keep in mind that competency hearings are a matter of constitutional right.[40]

3.   Competency determinations are separate from a finding of insanity. To get a sense of how these assessments can be linked, you might take a look at cases involving filicide and postpartum mental illness. Professor Michelle Oberman discusses the problem in *Lady Madonna, Children at Your Feet*:

> ... American mothers who kill their children are charged with a wide variety of offenses, including murder.... To the extent that the criminal law recognizes postpartum mental illness, it recognizes it as a form of insanity as it pertains either to the

39.   68 P.3d 176, 182 (N.M. Ct. App. 2003).

40.   *See Tate v. State*, 864 So.2d 44; Fla. Dist. Ct. App. 2003), discussed in, Joseph Yalon, *Constitutional Right to a Competency Hearing*, 26 J. Juv. L. 127 (2006).

woman's competence to stand trial or to her culpability for the crime.

The issue of competence to stand trial refers to the ability of a defendant to understand the charges against her and to assist her counsel at trial. A woman with extremely severe postpartum mental illness may be incompetent to stand trial, but generally speaking, most women who were suffering from postpartum mental illness when they killed their children have recovered enough to be found competent by the time of trial.[41]

4. What if the defendant is deaf, a problem discussed in Michele LaVigne and McCay Vernon's *An Interpreter Isn't Enough: Deafness, Language, and Due Process*?[42] What if the defendant does not speak English or speaks a language for which an interpreter cannot be found? These cases raise both fairness and resource questions. LaVigne and Vernon suggest that in some instances, an interpreter alone may not be enough.

5. Competency requires the capacity to comprehend the nature of the charges and participate in one's defense—a challenging problem for most, particularly juveniles.

Competency requires that citizens accused of criminal misconduct understand the charges against them, have rudimentary understanding of the court process, be able to understand and answer questions posed

41. 10 WM. & MARY J. WOMEN & L. 33 (2003).

42. 2003 WIS. L. REV. 843, 849.

to them by their counsel, and be able to make decisions about their trial such as whether to testify, and whether to accept or reject plea bargains.[43]

6. In all of the above problem areas, there is one constant: the difficulties inherent in *proof* of competency. One way to confront the problem is to utilize a more precise scientific determination of brain function.[44]

7. While a finding of competency is a Sixth Amendment entitlement, the consequence of an incompetency finding may be indeterminate incarceration—with fewer rights available than for those incarcerated in the criminal justice system. In *Health Law in the Criminal Justice System Symposium: Competency to Stand Trial on Trial*,[45] Grant H. Morris, Ansar M. Haroun, and David Naimark set out the issues faced by those found incompetent—where the charges are not dismissed.

> [A]n adjudication that the defendant is incompetent deprives the defendant of any trial—[they] will remain in limbo as "accused" until ... restored to competency. For some ... that day will never come....

43. David R. Katner, *The Mental Health Paradigm and the MacArthur Study: Emerging Issues Challenging the Competence of Juveniles in Delinquency Systems*, 32 Am. J. L. & Med. 503–04 (2006).

44. Richard E. Redding, *The Brain Disordered Defendant: Neuroscience and Legal Insanity in the Twenty–First Century*, 56 Am. U. L. Rev. 51 (2006).

45. 4 Hous. J. Health L. & Pol'y 193, 198, 200 (2004).

A finding of incompetence produces unanticipated consequences. While criminal defendants and

> civilly committed patients have a right to refuse psychotropic medication unless they lack the capacity to understand the risks and benefits of the medication ... incompetent criminal defendants may be forcibly medicated to restore their trial competence even if they [lack] that capacity.... One would anticipate that the severe consequences of an incompetency adjudication would lead lawyers to fiercely dispute the issue whenever it is raised in court. Such a contest, however, rarely occurs....

The authors note that there are also a series of issues lawyers face in these cases.

While the lawyer of the accused may have "the best-informed view of the defendant's ability to participate in his defense," lawyers often elect not to testify due to "an ethical responsibility not to disclose confidential communications or [matters] protected by the attorney-client privilege."

The authors also discuss questions raised by the powerful—and perhaps disproportionate—role played by expert witnesses. In REDISCOVERING LONE PINE, Mickey's case-in-chief consisted entirely of Dr. Starling's testimony—the State's consisted entirely of Dr. Merton's testimony—until Arthur Soto surfaced. As Morris et al., note:

> [C]ompetency determinations by and large turn on the testimony of psychiatric experts, not lawyers. One recent study reported that courts agreed with the forensic

> evaluator's judgment in 327 out of the 328
> cases studied—a 99.7% rate of agree-
> ment. . . .

Finally, the authors note that only "eight states . . .
use a standard of competency that includes a re-
quirement that the defendant be able to either
assist in or to conduct his or her defense in a
'rational manner.' " The remainder follow the plain
language of *Dusky* and *Drope* discussed in note two,
above.

8. Every state must have a process to address
competency issues—and every state must deal with
the challenge of determining if the asserted lack of
competency is real or feigned. For a compelling
discussion of the problem of determining if a defendant is "acting" or is genuinely incompetent, take a
look at *Pickles v. Florida.*[46]

9. There is no ironclad formula to determine legal
competency. Should the matter be resolved exclu-
sively by experts—by psychologists and psychia-
trists? If your answer is yes (in which case, you
would be in agreement with the process and practices that unfold in the vast majority of states),
what should happen in those cases where defense
experts testify the defendant is incompetent—and
prosecution experts testify that the defendant is
competent to stand trial? Should such cases be
presented to a panel of experts for resolution instead of a judge? How are due process interests
protected in such a proceeding? Would you trust
medical experts to rule on complex evidentiary matters—particularly where life or liberty is at stake

46. 976 So.2d 690 (Fla. Dist. Ct. App. 2008).

for the accused? The risks in this model have been evident—and discussed—for the last half-century.[47]

V. A Conspiracy of Silence

1. While neighbors heard yelling—and saw signs (the imprint of Hack Talbot's hand on Jason's face)—there was little discussion on DeWitt Street about the awful events in the Talbot home. The story is set in a time when discussions of domestic violence occurred only rarely. Of course the hope is that the "conspiracy of silence" that covered abuse for generations is no more—that there are safe venues to file complaints and seek assistance. However, family violence continues—and is still shrouded in whispers or, worse yet, silence. The magnitude of the abuse problem is staggering:

> In 1993, over 2.8 million children in America were the victims of abuse at the hands of their parents, caregiver, or another person whom they knew. Furthermore, child abuse and, in particular, sexual assault, result in the death of nearly two thousand children each year, and occur in every strata of society, without regard to socioeconomic, racial, or cultural background.[48]

47. Bernard L. Diamond, *The Fallacy of the Impartial Expert*, 3 ARCHIVES CRIM. PSYCHODYNAMICS, 221, 223 (1959); Howard K. Berry, *Impartial Medical Testimony*, 32 F.R.D. 539 (1962); Elwood S. Levy, *Impartial Medical Testimony—Revisited*, 34 TEMP. L.Q. 416, 419–29 (1961); Sander Greenland, *The Need for Critical Appraisal of Expert Witnesses in Epidemiology and Statistics*, 39 WAKE FOREST L. REV. 291, 297–301 (2004).

48. Debra Todd, *Sentencing of Adult Offenders in Cases Involving Sexual Abuse of Children: Too Little, Too Late? A View from the Pennsylvania Bench*, 109 PENN ST. L. REV. 487, 496 (2004).

This staggering number from 1993, 2.8 million, appears to be for *reported* cases. Fifteen years later, the number of reported child abuse cases was up to 3 million.[49] The number of actual findings of abuse in 2006, (the last year for which complete statistics are available from the U.S. Department of Health and Human Services) is approximately one million.[50] No matter how one reads these reports, the findings made by the U.S. Advisory Board on Child Abuse nearly twenty years ago are still accurate: "[C]hild abuse and neglect in the United States ... represents a national emergency.... Protection of children from harm is not just an ethical duty; it is a matter of national survival."[51]

2. No work has been more powerful in setting out the phenomenon of abuse—coupled with a refusal to discuss, much less testify about domestic violence—than Sandra Butler's CONSPIRACY OF SILENCE: THE TRAUMA OF INCEST (Volcano Press 1996).[52]

49. Childhelp, National Child Abuse Statistics, http://www.childhelp.org/resources/learning-center/statistics.

50. *See* U.S. Dep't of Health and Human Services, Administration for Children and Families, Summary, Child Maltreatment 2006, http://www.acf.hhs.gov/programs/cb/pubs/cm06/summary.htm, and http://www.childhelp.org/uploads/h1/x6/h1x6ds5xBH2q_RPlWvyUzw/The–Department-of-Health-and-Human–Services—2006–Child-Abuse–STATS.pdf and http://www.acf.hhs.gov/programs/cb/pubs/cm06/summary.htm.

51. U.S. Department of Health and Human Services, Advisory Board on Child Abuse and Neglect, *Child Abuse and Neglect: Critical First Steps in Response to a National Emergency* 2, 4 (1990).

52. For an application of Butler's work, see *Jones v. Jones*, 242 N.J.Super. 195, 576 A.2d 316; 576 A.2d 316 (1990).

3. To get a sense of the history of child abuse, take a look at *Nicholson v. Williams*.[53] *Nicholson* provides valuable background information and insights into the dimension of the problem and the issues of proof these cases present.

4. Was Connor taking the easy way out by moving Jason halfway around the world? Jason was separated from his mother, his friends, his school—all losses of consequence. In retrospect, it would have been preferable to remove Hack Talbot from the home—but given the time in which the story is set, that was a most unlikely outcome.

5. How likely was it that Hack would have been removed permanently? Can you imagine Martha and Valerie testifying against Hack? Given the friendship between Lieutenant Huntington and Hack Talbot, what were the chances of a successful criminal prosecution in 1959?[54]

6. Resistance to "abuse profiling." Jason's silence—as well as the silence of the Talbot family—may reflect the child sexual abuse accommodation syndrome (CSAAS). The syndrome includes feelings of helplessness and entrapment and efforts—by the

53. 203 F. Supp. 2d 153 (E.D.N.Y. 2002).

54. See *Pennsylvania v. Ritchie*, 480 U.S. 39, 60, 107 S.Ct. 989 (1987) ("Child abuse is one of the most difficult crimes to detect and prosecute, in large part because there often are no witnesses except the victim. A child's feelings of vulnerability and guilt and his or her unwillingness to come forward are particularly acute when the abuser is a parent."); *Morgan v. Foretich*, 846 F.2d 941, 943 (4th Cir. 1988) ("[In] two-thirds of child abuse cases, the incident is never even reported...."); M. Straus, R. Gelles & S. Steinmetz, BEHIND CLOSED DOORS (1980); Manvinder Gill, *Protecting the Abused Child: It is Time to Reevaluate Judicial Preference for Preserving Parental Custody Rights Over the Rights of the Child to be Free from Physical Abuse and Sexual Exploitation*, 18 J. JUV. L. 67, 70 (1997).

abused—at accommodation, delay, secrecy, refusals to disclose, and finally, even if the child does testify, retraction, and feelings of guilt and responsibility.[55] Getting a court to accept CSAAS is no small task—there is powerful judicial resistance to profiling.[56]

7. Notwithstanding the cruel, brutal realities of child abuse and domestic violence, it is not hard to see why there is judicial resistance to "abuse profiling" even by those who try hard to consider the best interests of children, who comprehend their unique vulnerability. The consequences of an allegation of child abuse are devastating—and in some instances irreversible, regardless of the outcome of a trial.

8. A finding of culpability in a child abuse case will destroy reputation, standing in the community, and may result in incarceration—and those found guilty of child abuse do not fare well in jails and prisons.[57]

55. For a web presentation on the fundamentals of CSAAS prepared by the Office of Juvenile Justice and Delinquency Prevention at the United States Department of Justice, take a look at http://www.ndaa.org/pdf/slides_archive.pdf. [Web cast funded through DOJ Grant Number 95–MU-FX–0017].

56. For a judicial perspective on the problems with "abuse profiling," see *Utah v. Rimmasch*, 775 P.2d 388; 108 Utah Adv. Rep. 20 (Utah 1989).

57. Mary Sigler, *Sentencing and Punishment: Just Deserts, Prison Rape, and the Pleasing Fiction of Guideline Sentencing*, 38 ARIZ. ST. L.J. 561, 567 (2006) ("Certain categories of offenders are known to be more vulnerable, including sex offenders, especially those who have victimized children."); James E. Robertson, *A Clean Heart and an Empty Head: The Supreme Court and Sexual Terrorism in Prison*, 81 N.C. L. REV. 433, 462 (2003) ("Sex offenders ... convicted of victimizing children ... represent an anathema in the inmate subculture."); Reginald Fields, *Jailed Mother of Three is Called a 'Victim'*, THE BALTIMORE SUN, Jan. 30, 2003, at 3B ("[Defendant] was moved to protective

9. Abuse cases require more than speculation and presumption—and profiling is both speculative and presumptive. Of course this does not mean courts should craft special and preferential rules in abuse cases. It does mean that the presumption of innocence is no less important in these cases than in other proceedings where such fundamental interests are at stake. Abuse investigations can take on the characteristics of an angry mob—and understandably so. Angry mobs form when they catch wind of unfathomably reprehensible acts perpetrated on those least able to defend themselves. Angry mobs and due process do not mix—hence the hesitancy to shortcut proof by profiling.

10. <u>Grandparental Custody</u>. The notion that the home of a grandparent (though few would be able to match the resources of Connor Clarke) might be a better solution for an abused child is not that unusual. However, grandparents do not enjoy the same entitlements to visitation or custody that parents enjoy.[58] Further, grants of custody to grandparents are usually temporary and subject to review and change. Finally, grandparental custody requires "extraordinary circumstances." The circumstances in the Talbot home were, on a good day, extraordinary—but had Martha Talbot wanted to retain custody of Jason, there is little question she could have done so.

custody ... because the charges against her involve crimes against children, and that sometimes incites violence by other inmates, a jail official said.")

58. *Troxel v. Granville*, 530 U.S. 57, 120 S.Ct. 2054 (2000); *L.F.M. v. Dep't of Social Servs.*, 507 A.2d 1151, 1154–55 (Md. App. 1986).

11. Was Connor Clarke correct when he asserted that the Talbot brothers could have urged Lieutenant Huntington to bring kidnapping charges against Clarke? Had Hack lived—and had Jason come back to the United States—would Clarke have lost custody? Assuming the answer is yes, was Connor Clarke right to "take the law into his own hands"?

> The resolution of cases must not provide incentives for those likely to take the law into their own hands. Thus, those who obtain custody of children unlawfully ... must be deterred. Society may not reward, except at its peril, the lawless because the passage of time has made correction inexpedient. Yet, even then, circumstances may require that, in the best interest of the child, the unlawful acts be blinked.[59]

While "blinked" is not a formal legal term, its meaning is clear—close your eyes or look away—and quite consistent with the storyline in REDISCOVERING LONE PINE. Think through fully the likely outcome had a judge (use Judge Miles Prentice as your model) been presented the option of returning Jason to his mother and father—or "blinking"—ignoring the traditional rules for custody—permitting Connor to find a safe and supportive new home for Jason on the other side of the world. Assume the judge has strong suspicions, but a paucity of direct evidence, regarding the toxic setting in the Talbot home. Suspicion of abuse is not a basis to take

59. *Bennett v. Jeffreys*, 40 N.Y.2d 543, 550; 387 N.Y.S.2d 821, 827; 356 N.E.2d 277, 284 (1976).

permanent custody from a parent—and in any case, Connor Clark was not willing to take the risk inherent in our system of justice.

—

I hope you have enjoyed REDISCOVERING LONE PINE and this GUIDE.

I want to thank Diane, Jeff, Meaghan, Brian, Niki, and Katie for listening to me (at length) and providing endless support and insight. I am blessed to have a wonderful family—and in case you are wondering, they are nothing like the characters inhabiting this book.

Thanks are also due to Dean Claudio Grossman for his generous support of my writing, and to the many students, staff, and faculty at the American University Washington College of Law who helped with this work. Special thanks are due Erik Garcia of our law school professional staff for his creative and innovative work on the cover design. Particular thanks are due faculty administrator Frankie Winchester and my senior research assistant, Kim Nguyen, for their unflinching and professional assistance with the preparation of this material.

AFP

Washington, DC

February 2009

—

About the Author

For nearly three decades, Andrew F. Popper has been on the faculty of American University, Washington College of Law, teaching Torts, Administrative Law, and seminars in Government Litigation and Advanced Administrative Law. He is the author of more than one-hundred published books, articles, papers, and public documents.

Professor Popper is the lead author of ADMINISTRATIVE LAW: A CONTEMPORARY APPROACH (West Publishing, 2009, with Gwendolyn M. McKee, available in hard cover with an interactive/on-line version). He is also the author of the novel BORDERING ON MADNESS: AN AMERICAN LAND USE TALE and the lead author on the recently published casebook companion for that novel (Carolina Academic Press, 2008, with David Avitabile and Professor Patricia E. Salkin).

Professor Popper has served as a consumer rights advocate and pro bono counsel for the Consumers Union, testified as an expert witness before Congressional committees more than 30 times, and authored number of amicus curiae briefs before the United States Supreme Court. Prior to his career in legal education, he practiced law in the Washington DC.

†

Errata Sheet

This is the first edition of REDISCOVERING LONE PINE. There are no substantive changes scheduled for the second edition, due out from Thomson/West/Reuters in late spring 2010. However, the technical errors will be addressed. A list of those errors follows:

p. II, below "Printed in the United States of America" add: Cover photograph by Michael S. Quinton

p. 92, 7 lines from bottom: "his" should be "this"

p. 107, line 2: "awhile" should be "a while"

p. 125, 6 lines from bottom: "clerical" should be "a clerical"

p. 205, 3rd paragraph from the bottom, 1st line: "walk passed" should be "walk past"

p. 244, 13 lines from bottom: "there" should be "there's"

p. 244, the last line on the page currently reads "We're a good very team, Grant." It should read: "We're a very good team, Grant . . . you and me."

p. 248, 3rd paragraph from bottom: "as well as annuity" should be "as well as an annuity"

p. 309, 16 lines from the top: "more a" should be "a more"

p. 312, paragraph 3, line 3: delete "in"

p. 321, there is a colon after "Sentencing" in the title of the Thomas article: "Sentencing:"

p. 356, paragraph 2 line 4: "hard cover" should be "hardcover"

p. 356, paragraph 2 line 7: "on" should be "of"

p. 356, paragraph 3 line 5: "number" should be "a number"

p. 356, paragraph 3 line 7: "in the" should be "in"